METAPHYSICS

Fundamentals of Philosophy

Series Editor: A. P. Martinich, University of Texas at Austin

Each volume in the Fundamentals of Philosophy series covers a key area of study in philosophy. Written with verve and clarity by leading philosophers, these authoritative volumes look to reveal the fundamental issues and core problems that drive interest in the field.

1. Julia Driver, *Ethics: The Fundamentals*
2. Mark C. Murphy, *Philosophy of Law: The Fundamentals*
3. Linda Trinkaus Zagzebski, *Philosophy of Religion: An Historical Introduction*
4. Robert C. Koons and Timothy H. Pickavance, *Metaphysics: The Fundamentals*

Forthcoming
Thom Brooks, *Political Philosophy: The Fundamentals*
Randall Curren, *Philosophy of Education: The Fundamentals*
Thomas Kelly and James Pryor, *What Should We Believe? The Fundamentals of Epistemology*
Ned Hall, *Philosophy of Science: The Fundamentals*

METAPHYSICS
THE FUNDAMENTALS

Robert C. Koons and Timothy H. Pickavance

WILEY Blackwell

Library of Congress Cataloging-in-Publication Data

Koons, Robert C.
  Metaphysics: the fundamentals / Robert C. Koons and Timothy H. Pickavance.
    pages cm
  Includes bibliographical references and index.
  ISBN 978-1-4051-9574-4 (hardback) – ISBN 978-1-4051-9573-7 (paper)
1. Metaphysics. I. Pickavance, Timothy H. II. Title.
  BD111.K665 2015
  110–dc23
                                                    2014030070

A catalogue record for this book is available from the British Library.

Cover image: © atribut/Shutterstock

Set in 10/12pt Sabon by SPi Publisher Services, Pondicherry, India

To Bruce and Margaret Koons
and
To Ann Lawson and Tom and Sue Pickavance

Contents

Acknowledgments

We would like to thank our series editor, Al Martinich, for his invitation to undertake this project and for his encouragement and patience in seeing it through. We would also like to thank our editors at Wiley Blackwell, Nick Bellorini, Jeff Dean, Liam Cooper, and Deirdre Ilkson, and editorial assistants Tiffany Mok, Nicole Benevenia, and Allison Kostka.

Thanks also to Al Plantinga, Laurie Paul, Graham Priest, Peter Forrest, Dan Korman, Trenton Merricks, and Josh Parsons for the helpful feedback on earlier drafts of the book. Thanks to Robert Garcia, from whom we've learned most of what we know about tropes, and to Alex Pruss for his many insights into material composition.

We both have taught this material in metaphysics seminars at our respective institutions, and a number of our students supplied helpful feedback, with respect to both content and presentation. Especially notable contributions came from Daniel Eaton, Patrick Grafton-Cardwell, Nicole Garcia, Tim Houk, Sarah Nicholson, and Jarod Sickler. Thanks to Richard Lawton Davis for insight into composition as identity, and to Bryan Pickel and Nick Mantegani for their contributions to our understanding of ostrich nominalism and Quinean ontology.

We want to acknowledge the living titans of contemporary metaphysics on whose shoulders we are sitting, including Saul Kripke, Alvin Plantinga, Peter van Inwagen, and Robert M. Adams, as well as those who have died, especially David K. Lewis and David M. Armstrong. In addition to those we've already mentioned, our debt to the work of John Hawthorne, Dean Zimmerman, Ted Sider, Jonathan Schaffer, José Benardete, Kit Fine, Michael Loux, Sydney Shoemaker, Michael Tooley, and David Chalmers is obvious and substantial.

Finally, our gratitude to our patient and longsuffering wives, Debbie and Jamie, without whom we could have done nothing.

THP adds: Thanks to Biola University for a Faculty Research and Development Grant in 2010, as well as to Dennis Dirks, Mike Wilkins, and Scott Rae, each current or former administrators at Biola, for a semester-long research leave in fall 2011. These provided helpful breaks from teaching that greatly spurred this project along. Another round of thanks to my dear friend, Robert Garcia, who has been a source not only of philosophical stimulation, but of faithful encouragement and support. Finally, I've somehow stumbled into the privilege of writing philosophy with my first metaphysics teacher, J. P. Moreland, as well as with my last metaphysics teacher, my dissertation supervisor, Rob Koons. Both are incredible philosophers who are even more incredible human beings. I owe not only my knowledge of metaphysics, but also my philosophical career to the pair of them. My deepest gratitude to them both.

1

What Is Metaphysics?

The great Greek philosopher Plato wrote (in the dialogue *Theaetetus*) that philosophy "begins in wonder," a phrase repeated by his student Aristotle in his *Metaphysics*. This is especially true of that branch of philosophy that we, echoing the title of Aristotle's book, call "metaphysics." In metaphysics we puzzle and wonder about what exists and what existing things are like, in their most fundamental features and interrelationships.

1.1   The Subject of Metaphysics

The first part of metaphysics is known as "ontology," the study of what there is. In ontology we attempt to give, in broad outlines, an inventory of reality. Are there particular things, such as cabbages, kings, quarks, and galaxies? How many such things are there? One? Many? Infinitely many?

Are there properties, ways things are? For example, is there, in addition to all the individual horses, the *property* of being a horse (equinity)? If so, how many such properties are there? Is there a property for every common noun and every adjective? A property of being red, of being ugly, of sleeping? Do some of these properties exist as separate *universals*? That is, is one and the same property somehow *shared* by everything that has that property? If so, do each of these universals inhere *within* many particular things, or do they in some other way explain the similarities and common characteristics of those many particular things? And are there *relations*, like that of being more massive than or being the same color as, that hold between or among two or more things?

Metaphysics: The Fundamentals, First Edition. Robert C. Koons and Timothy H. Pickavance.
© 2015 Robert C. Koons and Timothy H. Pickavance.
Published 2015 by John Wiley & Sons, Ltd.

Are there things that could be called "facts" or "states of affairs," such as the fact that water molecules contain hydrogen or the state of affairs of all native mammals in Australia's being marsupials? Are there negative facts, such as the fact that there is no plant life on the sun? If there are facts, are they the things that, by simply existing, are responsible for *making* certain beliefs and statements true? Is truth itself a property, and if so, of what things? Do facts contain both particular things and universal properties? Are there merely possible facts, and if so, what are they like? What is the fundamental difference between merely possible facts and the actual ones?

Other parts of metaphysics constitute the study of the fundamental structure of reality as a whole. How do things fit together to make a world? Plato describes this task of philosophy "carving nature at the joints," comparing the metaphysics to a skillful and knowledgeable act of dissection. Here are four relations that seem to be among the fundamental relations of this worldly structure: the relation between things and their properties, between wholes and their parts, between causes and effects, and between things related to each other in space and in time. We will examine all of these foundational relations in some detail.

1.2   The Methods of Metaphysics

Since metaphysicians study reality in its most fundamental and general aspects, in doing it we must marshal as much evidence about the world as we possibly can. All of our knowledge of the world, whether innate or acquired through ordinary life or through specialized sciences, contributes data to the metaphysical theorist. So, too, do hunches and intuitions of the truth, when more secure knowledge is unavailable. The method of the metaphysician is a mixture of the testimony of pure reason, that which is prior to and independent of experience (the *a priori*), and the testimony of experience itself (the *a posteriori*), in all its breadth and variety. Metaphysics is in this way like most other sciences. (We use the word "science" here in a broad sense, as a label of any systematic field of knowledge.)

What exactly the methods of metaphysics should be is one of the most hotly disputed topics among metaphysicians. In addition, some critics have disputed the very right of metaphysics to exist as a separate science. They argue that we best study the fundamental nature of reality through some more specialized discipline, such as physics, history, psychology, or linguistics. However, such thinkers do not thereby avoid doing metaphysics – instead, they do metaphysics in a particular way, with an especially truncated set of data and methods. In this book, we will attempt to be relatively broad and inclusive in our survey of metaphysical methods, including input from all of the natural and human sciences, as well as from that source of knowledge that we call "common sense," anchored in the common experience of humanity.

Another methodological issue that divides metaphysicians is the question of the role that speculation or invention should play. Some metaphysicians seek simple, elegant, and unifying theories, including the postulation of novel entities and properties, while others seek metaphysics as a kind of grammar of ordinary human thought and experience, as merely making explicit what every adult human being knows. On either view, metaphysics can reach results that are surprising, even revolutionary, as the example of mathematics demonstrates: geometry and number theory are able to derive many new and useful results, starting from nothing but a few commonplaces about numbers or space.

1.3   The Waxing and Waning of Metaphysics

Metaphysics is the oldest branch of philosophy, already underway in the speculations of ancient Greek-speaking thinkers, including Thales, Heraclitus, and Parmenides, in Greece, Turkey, and southern Italy in the 600s and 500s BC. Metaphysics continued to be central to the work of Plato and Aristotle, as well as to the "materialism" of Democritus and Empedocles, who sought to answer all of the metaphysical questions in terms of the fundamental material components of things. During the Hellenistic period (between the conquests of Alexander the Great and the rise of Rome), the central focus of philosophy shifted from metaphysics to the theory and critique of knowledge (the branch of philosophy known as "epistemology"), although both the new philosophical schools of the Stoics and Epicureans and the successors of Plato and Aristotle continued in substantial metaphysical investigations.

Metaphysics regained its predominance in late antiquity and throughout the medieval periods, thanks to the pre-eminence within Western philosophy of Platonists and Aristotelians. A synthesis of the two traditions, known as "Scholastic" philosophy, provided a common framework of terminology, questions, and methods among Christians, Jews, and Moslems for over a thousand years. In the later Middle Ages (after 1300 AD), there was a gradual turn toward the study of language and toward epistemological concerns. During the Renaissance, scholars sought to return to ancient sources, including Plato. At the same time, these scholars recovered writings of some of the ancient materialists and Atomists, such as Democritus and Lucretius, which then began to influence the course of Western philosophy.

The scientific revolution of the sixteenth century brought with it a revolt against Aristotle and Scholasticism. Metaphysical thought fragmented into several distinct streams. Some, including the German seventeenth-century philosopher Gottfried Leibniz, continued important features of the Scholastic tradition. Others turned instead to a form of Atomism about the created world, reviving Democritus's idea that the material world is ultimately composed of indivisible "corpuscles." (We say "created" world because these thinkers believed in the existence of God.) Such Atomism had been rejected by Aristotle and his Scholastic followers in favor of a view in which all of matter is infinitely divisible. The French philosopher René Descartes introduced a new form of dualism, which divided reality into two domains, one purely quantitative and material (the physical), and the other qualitative and subjective (the mental). Still others moved all the way to Idealism, the view that all of reality, including the natural world, is fundamentally mental or spiritual. In fact, Idealism of one kind or another dominated European and American philosophy in the nineteenth century.

Descartes altered the course of Western philosophy for 200 years by introducing an overriding concern, amounting almost to an obsession, with attaining certainty. Descartes held that it was the responsibility of philosophers to provide a watertight answer to the challenge of the skeptic, who insists upon doubting every belief that can possibly be doubted. The Cartesian philosopher seeks to build an absolutely secure and indubitable set of foundations for all of our scientific and common sense beliefs. This quest for certainty necessitated a turn inward, relying on Descartes' famous *cogito* argument: I think, therefore I am ("*cogito ergo sum*" in Latin). The guiding idea was that introspection of one's own subjective thoughts and feelings was immune to skeptical challenge. One might be wrong about the past or about the physical facts, but one cannot be wrong about the present contents of one's own thoughts and experiences. It was this broad agreement about the subjective or "phenomenological" method that gave the advantage to various forms of Idealism in the mid- to late nineteenth centuries.

1.4 Modern Challenges to Metaphysics

With the loss of the Scholastic framework, the rise of the success and prestige of experimental science, and the premium placed on certainty, metaphysics faced a series of challenges. A number of significant thinkers began to sound a new note in the late eighteenth century, raising doubts about the right of metaphysics to stand as a science among other fields of knowledge. David Hume, the great philosopher of Scotland, stands out as pre-eminent among these new anti-metaphysicians. Near the end of his *Enquiry Concerning Human Understanding*, Hume issues his famous challenge to the value of metaphysics:

> If we take in our hand any volume; of divinity or school metaphysics, for instance; let us ask, Does it contain any abstract reasoning concerning quantity or number? No. Does it contain any experimental reasoning concerning matter of fact and existence? No. Commit it then to the flames: for it can contain nothing but sophistry and illusion. (Hume 1777: Section XII, Part III, 165)

Hume's assault had a deep effect on a younger German metaphysician, Immanuel Kant. Kant described Hume as having "awakened" him from his "dogmatic slumber." In response, Kant engineered what he called "a Copernican revolution" in philosophy. Henceforth, those following Kant would not seek to understand things as they are *in themselves* but only as they are *for us*. Post-Kantian philosophers examine how things appear to us, and how the structure of our own sensibility and understanding shape those appearances. Kant believed that a new, more sober and restrained metaphysics could result from following this subject-focused and phenomenological method.

If Kant's response to Hume constituted some sort of victory for metaphysics, it proved to be a Pyrrhic one. If we assume that human thought and meaning cannot reach beyond the range of sensory appearances (the empirical domain), then the usual empirical sciences (physics, chemistry, biology, and so on) would seem to exhaust the possibilities for novel discoveries or systematic theorizing, leaving nothing for metaphysicians to do. The effort to limit science to what can be empirically verified came to be known as "positivism." In addition, historical and anthropological research indicated that human experience is more variegated and fluid than Kant had supposed, suggesting that traditional metaphysics be replaced by cultural or historical studies.

The positivists of the nineteenth century were succeeded by the *logical* positivists of the Vienna Circle in the early twentieth century, who insisted that metaphysics (along with other non-empirical fields like ethics, theology, or aesthetics) were nonsensical, since their propositions could not be empirically verified. The Vienna Circle, in turn, influenced Anglo-American philosophy through the early work of Ludwig Wittgenstein and through the Cambridge philosophers Bertrand Russell and Frank Ramsey.

The complementary movement toward historicism and cultural relativity culminated in the work of Georg Hegel in Germany. Hegel described a process by which the *true* metaphysical theory evolves over time, in response to cultural and political factors. Karl Marx, Friedrich Nietzsche, Michel Foucault, and others in the late nineteenth and twentieth century drew the conclusion that any attempt to escape the limitations of one's time or one's own personal biases, as would be required by the pursuit of metaphysical truth, is futile and should be abandoned.

In America, the pragmatists offered a new source of opposition to metaphysics. William James proposed that "truth" should be identified with "whatever works." Pragmatism thus renders many traditional metaphysical theories and disputes irrelevant, since metaphysical truth can often seem to have no immediate "cash value." Thus, pragmatic impulses in philosophy further undermined any interest in metaphysical questions.

Some philosophers who had been part of the logical positivist movement came to be dissatisfied with the positivists' focus on individual and subjective sense experience. They came to see that science, in order to reach results that are publicly verifiable, must primarily pertain to the natural world, the world beyond the individual human mind. At the same time, the Cartesian epistemological foundation was crumbling. Otto Neurath rejected Descartes' fixation on certainty, arguing that our theory of the world is like a raft in the middle of the ocean: we can try to make incremental improvements from within the raft, but we can never hope to find solid ground outside it on which to build for it a new foundation. Further, post-positivist philosophers wanted to maintain the unity of the natural sciences, and they saw fundamental physics as the unifying framework within which all other scientific disciplines could be constructed. These "physicalists," including Neurath, Alfred Tarski, and Willard van Orman Quine, looked to modern mathematics and physics for answers to traditional metaphysical questions, rejecting the legitimacy of any metaphysical question that could not be subjected to investigation through the *scientific method* as exemplified by mathematical physics.

In summary, metaphysics faced opposition from five sources in the early twentieth century:

1. The subjectivist and phenomenological turn (in response to Cartesian skepticism)
2. The positivist challenge
3. The relativist and historicist challenges
4. The pragmatist challenge
5. The physicalist challenge

1.5   The Renaissance of Metaphysics in the Later "Analytic" Era

Given the breadth and depth of this opposition to metaphysics, the late twentieth century has been the occasion of one of the most remarkable reversals in the history of thought: the renaissance of metaphysics in Anglo-American philosophy. The need to overcome such intense resistance has forced modern metaphysicians to rise to a level of sophistication that is almost unprecedented, as well as to draw on all of the best of the 2000-year tradition of metaphysical reflection from the past.

The dominant school of thought of philosophy in the English-speaking world (and in the Netherlands and Scandinavia) has been the so-called "analytic" school. Analytic philosophy has its origins in the work of the British philosophers G. E. Moore, Bertrand Russell, and John Cook Wilson in the early 1900s, who led a revolt against the British Idealism of the late nineteenth century. Russell saw Kant's "Copernican revolution" as a great step backwards, as a kind of "Ptolemaic revolution" back to a geocentric view of the world, since Kant placed the human mind and not its objects at the center of philosophical inquiry.

Russell and his colleague Alfred North Whitehead were among the first Anglophone philosophers to recognize the importance of the work of the German logician Gottlob Frege, who revolutionized logic by, for the first time, precisely analyzing the idea of mathematical proof. (The American philosopher Charles Saunders Peirce made the same discovery independently in America.) Russell and Whitehead believed that careful attention to questions of the *logical form*, the precise grammatical structure, of our thoughts would make possible substantial progress toward solving many traditional metaphysical problems. For analytic philosophers, logic and mathematics replace phenomenology or history as the central method of discovery.

Analytic developments in logic contributed to the revival of metaphysics. Harvard's Clarence I. Lewis and Rudolf Carnap, a leading logical positivist who ended his career at the University of California in Los Angeles, resurrected the study of the logic of possibility and necessity, a sub-field that had been neglected since medieval times.

Further developments in this *modal* logic by Arthur Prior, Ruth Barcan Marcus, David Kaplan, and Saul Kripke led inevitably to renewed interest in the nature of possible things and their relation to the actual world in the 1970s.

The physicalists that we mentioned in the last section also opened the door wider to the revival of metaphysics. Work on the philosophy of science in the twentieth century raised serious doubts about the unity of science and about the competency of physics to answer all meaningful questions. The American W. V. O. Quine revived the field of ontology – the investigation of what exists – arguing that we should accept all and only the things and kinds of things required by our best scientific theories.

Physicalism eventually evolved into a new materialist school of metaphysical thought, with its principal representatives in England and Australia. Both Quine and the Australian metaphysicians helped to shape the thinking of the most wide-ranging and influential metaphysician of the twentieth century, Princeton's David K. Lewis. You may notice that Lewis's work is mentioned in every chapter of this book.

In one of history's ironies, David K. Lewis built his impressive metaphysical system on the empiricist tradition of David Hume, the arch-skeptic and opponent of metaphysics. Lewis replaced Hume's Idealism with a materialist theory of mind and a realism about physical phenomena, but he sustained the spirit of Hume's empiricism by seeking to minimize the commitments of his theory to contentious metaphysical notions (such as powers, causation, and properties), except where these can be reduced to or defined in terms of more basic elements, such as physical qualities and quantities and the framework of space and time. Lewis's students, including Laurie Paul and Cian Dorr, as well as students of his students, like Theodore Sider, have continued work on this Neo-Humeist project.

Questions about causation provided analytic philosophers with a final avenue back to metaphysical investigations. Logical positivists, following Hume, had tried to build philosophical systems without any reference to cause and effect. Bertrand Russell wrote an essay in 1908 declaring causation to be a scientifically obsolete notion. Since then, causation has reclaimed its status as a central notion in philosophical theory. Edmund Gettier, in a famous article in 1963, challenged the traditional definition of knowledge as *justified true belief*, leading to new theories of knowledge that relied upon some kind of causal connection between states of knowledge and the world. Modern theories of sensory perception and memory, in particular, require reference to appropriate causal mechanisms. Work in the philosophy of language by Keith Donnellan, Saul Kripke, and Gareth Evans, among others, introduced causal theories of the meanings of words and the content of thought. Finally, the philosopher of science Nancy Cartwright demonstrated that causation is far from obsolete in the experimental sciences.

Metaphysical work on causation has followed three tracks among analytic philosophers: a Neo-Humeist approach, that seeks to reduce causation to patterns of succession, the approach of the Australian Realists, who look to the laws of nature as the ultimate ground of all causal relations, and a Neo-Aristotelian approach, that takes causal powers to be a fundamental and irreducible feature of the world. The Aristotelian "powers ontology" movement has drawn support from England (Stephen Mumford, Alexander Bird), America (John Heil, Peter Unger), and Australia (George Molnar, Brian Ellis) in recent years.

Well, so what? Why does this list of questions and views and philosophers matter? The point of the forgoing is that metaphysics is far from dead, despite repeated attempts to kill it off. Metaphysics, it turns out, is a resilient discipline. Indeed, it appears that metaphysical questions are virtually impossible to escape. This brings us to a final point about what metaphysics is.

1.6   Metaphysics as First Philosophy

Aristotle describes metaphysics as "first philosophy," indicating that all other branches of philosophy depend in some way on it. The subsequent history of philosophy confirms Aristotle's judgment. We have already discussed some of the connections between epistemology (the theory of knowledge) and causation, as well as the role of causation in the philosophy of language. The field of ethics, the study of moral value and obligation, presupposes certain facts about human nature and human actions. Moral obligations can apply to us only if we are, in some sense, capable of acting in different ways, which naturally raises questions about the nature of possibility and contingency. In addition, we bear moral responsibilities for some of the consequences of our actions, which fact brings questions about the nature of causation to our attention.

Analytic philosophers have worked intensively on the theory of mind and the mind-body problem in the last 100 years, and this research has also moved inevitably toward deeper metaphysical issues. Once again, causation plays a crucial role in understanding sensation, memory, and action. In addition, our experience of time raises fundamental questions about the nature of time itself, and the nature of change and the persistence through change, both of perceived objects and of persons. Human sensation and thought involve a relation, not just to particular things, but also to general properties and kinds, which demands attention to the metaphysical theory of properties and the relation between properties and their instances.

Recent experience has also dashed hopes that one of the special sciences, such as physics or biology, could supplant metaphysics. Contemporary scientific theory raises far more metaphysical questions than it answers. For example, there are many questions about the fundamental nature of space and time that contemporary physics renders meaningful without being able to answer them. Is space or spacetime a real thing, in addition to the things that are spatially located? Are regions of space composed of dimensionless points? What gives time its direction (from earlier to later)?

The inevitability of metaphysics is demonstrated by the fact that even the would-be critics of metaphysics rely on tacit metaphysical assumptions. For example, Hume's claim that all knowledge is either logical or sensory in nature presupposes that there is a relation of knowledge or acquaintance, which holds only between the mind and the sensations and ideas that it "contains." These presuppositions raise unavoidable metaphysical questions: what sort of things are these ideas, and how does the mind "contain" them?

Consider also those post-Kantian or post-modern thinkers who insist that all of reality is a *construction* of one's social community. Such a theory presupposes that communities or social practices exist and are able to construct theories or models of the world. In the end, these apparently anti-metaphysical schools of thought are nothing but alternative ways of doing metaphysics. The only way to avoid metaphysics is to avoid thinking.

1.7   Overview of the Book

We begin in Chapter 2 with a discussion of truth and the grounds of truth. We address the question of whether truth is a genuine property of thoughts and statements, as opposed to a mere device for making certain assertions in a more convenient form (as the so-called "deflationists" about truth have it). If truth is a property, then we have to consider whether every truth is grounded in reality, that is, in things that exist. If so, these can be called the "truthmakers." We examine and evaluate several competing theories about what (if anything) makes truths to be true. Philosophers' positions on the existence and character of truthmakers have a direct influence on metaphysical method, as later chapters illustrate.

In Chapter 3 we take up the problem of what makes a thing act the way it does – a thing's dispositions and powers. These dispositions and powers have to do with not only how something is actually observed to behave but also with what it *would* do under a variety of wholly hypothetical situations. We discuss four theories about the truthmakers for dispositional and hypothetical truths, focusing primarily on two of these: Neo-Humeism and Powerism. Neo-Humeists seek to ground truths about dispositions entirely in the pattern of qualities as they are instantiated across space and time (a qualitative mosaic), while Powerists hold that facts about powers and dispositions must be admitted to be among the fundamental and irreducible facts of the world, over and above the facts about their actual manifestations. The Neo-Humeist program promises a simple and uncluttered picture of the world, but the Powerists have wielded some weighty objections against its adequacy.

Powers and dispositions are a kind of property, and it is to properties in general that we turn in Chapter 4, considering the ancient *problem of universals*. Those who affirm the existence of special things (the *universals*) that exist over and above the world of particular things are traditionally known (in this context) as "Realists" (after the Latin word for "thing"). Their opponents are called "Nominalists" (after the Latin word for "name"). Realists believe that universals, such as the property of being a horse or the property of being a water molecule, are real things needed to ground or explain in an ultimate way the obvious similarity of particular horses or particular water molecules to one another. The universals are somehow shared by or present in those particular things. Nominalists, in contrast, deny that we need any such metaphysical explanation of similarity: the particular things themselves suffice to explain why we use common names (like "horse" or "water molecule") as we do.

Both sides claim that they can provide the simplest account of the phenomena, so the debate turns on the question of which theory is really simpler, and what sort of simplicity is desirable, and why. There are several versions of Nominalism, from the Ostrich Nominalists (so-called because their opponents accuse them of sticking their heads in the sand) who simply deny that there are any phenomena about similarity that need to be accounted for in our metaphysics, to various kinds of Reductive Nominalists, who try to account for similarity without invoking universals, either by supposing there to be a single relation of resemblance between particular things or in terms of their common membership in a special kind of class. According to Reductive Nominalists, we don't have to introduce universals to make sense of such basic facts of resemblance or class-membership.

We look next (in Chapter 5) to competing theories about the internal structure or constitution of ordinary particular things and the possible relations between those things and properties. According to *Extreme* Nominalists, such things have no internal structure (except for the internal structure attributed to them by physics and chemistry), and similarity is simply a relation between two such things, taken as a whole. Other Nominalists believe in individualized or particular properties, known as "tropes." A trope is a property that, unlike a universal, can pertain to only one particular. The roundness of the earth, for example, would be a trope, while the universal of roundness would be shared by all round things. Moderate or Trope Nominalists suppose ordinary things to be nothing more than *bundles* of such tropes. So, for example, a particular rock might be nothing more than an aggregate made up of the rock's hardness, shape, volume, mass, color, and so on.

Realists (believers in universals) also come in two varieties, Relational and Constituent, depending on whether they think that universals relate to their instances from the outside or that universals are actual internal parts of those instances. There are, therefore, two kinds of constituent ontologies: Trope Nominalists and Constituent Realists, both of whom think that ordinary particular things contain their properties as parts. Constituent Ontologists think of ordinary things as either bundles of nothing but properties or as bundles that combine properties with some additional element of particularity (a "bare" particular or "substrate"). We evaluate the pros and cons of each option.

Of course, some things are *parts* of others in a much more everyday, common-sense understanding of the word, and this ordinary part–whole relation is the subject of Chapter 6. At this point we confront what Peter van Inwagen has called "the Special Composition Question": when do some things compose a whole? If we pile some books on a table, do the books now compose a new thing, the *pile*? Or do we still have nothing more than what we started with – the books – now merely in a new relationship? Of course, we can ask the same question about the pages of one of the books – is the book a new thing, or merely an arrangement of pages? Indeed, do the fundamental particles of the page really compose a further entity (the page), or are they the only things that really exist, in the strictest sense of the word?

Universalists claim that corresponding to every set of things, no matter how scattered or disparate, there is a whole composed of just those things (and their parts). Universalists would suppose, then, that the Eiffel Tower and the Moon together compose a single thing, despite the quarter of a million miles separating them. Compositional Nihilists, at the other extreme, maintain the paradoxical position that there are no composite things at all! There are many intermediate theories, according to which some but not all sets of things correspond to real wholes. We can also ask about the relative priority of parts and wholes: are wholes really nothing "over and above" their parts, or are parts nothing but aspects or manifestations of certain wholes? Putting the issue this way gives rise to three plausible answers: Atomism (according to which the fundamental things are all simple, without parts), Monism (according to which there is only one fundamental thing, which contains everything else as a part), and Pluralism (according to which there are composite things other than the universe as a whole that are fundamental).

In Chapter 7 we return to the issues of possibility and necessity (or *modality*) that first made an appearance in Chapter 3. At this stage we investigate the nature of the merely possible – things that could have been but are not actual facts. Since the time of Gottfried Leibniz, metaphysicians have found it convenient to talk in terms of "possible worlds": ways that the world as a whole could have been. We consider here two competing theories about possible worlds: Concretism and Abstractionism. On the Concretist picture, another possible world is something like a parallel universe, composed of material objects and living organisms just like us and the things around us. Abstractionists, in contrast, suppose possible worlds to be more like huge, complex stories or diagrams, representing alternative ways for things to be. David Lewis was the great champion of Concretism, and we consider his thought-provoking objections to Abstractionism, as well as the most important objections to his Concretism.

In Chapters 8 and 9, we begin to consider the world in its temporal dimension. In Chapter 8 we survey the debate over whether time really flows. In this chapter, we rely on a distinction first introduced by J. M. E. McTaggart between the A and the B series. In the A series, we relate times to the present, as either past, present, or future. The B series looks only at the positions of times in relation to each other, as earlier than, simultaneous with, or later than. B Theorists hold that a complete description of the metaphysical structure of the world requires only the facts about the B series, while A Theorists insist that A-relational facts are also metaphysically real and objective. Defenders of the B Theory rely primarily on its greater simplicity and its concordance with modern physics, especially relativity theory, while A Theorists rely on our common-sense understanding of what is involved in real change and in our experience of the fleetingness of the present and the passage of time.

In Chapter 9, on continuity and persistence, many of the threads we have built up throughout the book converge for the development of theories about the nature of change and of those things that persist through change. The pursuit of the understanding of persistence and change has been at the core of metaphysics from the very beginning, with the earliest theories of the Greek philosophers. We focus here on a single issue: is all change grounded in a temporal succession of essentially unchanging states, or are temporally extended processes of change among the fundamental facts of the world? The first is sometimes called the "at-at theory" of motion and change: for a thing to move is simply for it to be *at* different locations *at* different instants of time. The alternative, Neo-Aristotelian view sees instantaneous states as mere boundaries of more fundamental *processes*. On the Aristotelian view, the states of things at each moment of time are based in the nature of the ongoing processes they participate in, and not vice versa. At the end of Chapter 9, we survey the variety of metaphysical theories that we have considered throughout the book, grouping them into two packages: the Neo-Humeist and Neo-Aristotelian frameworks.

Finally, we return in Chapter 10, our "Concluding Unmetaphysical Postscript," to the challenges to metaphysics that we introduced in Section 1.4 above. We look at questions of the language of metaphysics: are metaphysical questions nonsensical, and are all metaphysical disputes merely verbal? We then consider the question of knowledge: can we ever know that any metaphysical claim is true, and, if so, how? Finally, we consider and reject the possibility that metaphysics should be thought of as the development of a kind of fiction. We postpone these issues until the end, because the best answer to the challenge of whether metaphysics is possible is the actual doing of metaphysics, something we have undertaken in chapters 2 through 9.

Two final comments that should color the reader's approach to our text. First, there are very rarely knock-down arguments in philosophy generally and metaphysics in particular, and so there is almost always a number of views that might be true. But further, the question is not just whether a philosophical view explains what it's meant to explain, but whether it explains what it's meant to explain better than the other views on offer. Therefore, one cannot judge the truth of a metaphysical view in isolation from its competitors. What philosophers must do is weigh the costs and benefits of the various views on offer, and then judge which one is *best*. It is the best view – not the only possible view, and not just some view that does the relevant work – that we hunt for. Insofar as we are doing this well, we will be more likely to arrive at the truth. Still further, the view one adopts in one area of metaphysics will, in many cases, impact the plausibility of views in other areas. We hope to chart many of these connections throughout the text. The reader would do well to bear these facts in mind, and to delay delivering a final verdict about a view or collection of views, insofar as he or she is able, until we have completed our survey.

Second, because we will canvass a variety of positions in a number of areas –metaphysics is a huge area of philosophy! – we have been forced to truncate the discussion of each. No doubt this will leave some readers dissatisfied, especially when resources available to one's own views are not fully articulated or brought to bear on objections. We hope, however, that this book will not only provide a useful overview of the most important issues, views, and arguments discussed in contemporary metaphysics, but will also invite the reader to continue the discussion. So we have made no effort to be comprehensive, only an effort to set the reader up for the comprehensive consideration she carries out on her own and in discussion with others. We suggest readers inclined in this direction consult the bibliography of this book for further conversation partners, as well as our more thorough (and much longer!) *Surveying the World: A Compendium of Metaphysics*.

2

Truthmakers

Metaphysics is, at bottom, an attempt to develop a true theory of the world's most fundamental things, a theory that describes the features of those fundamental things and the relations that they stand in to one another and to less fundamental things. The categories that metaphysicians are interested to analyze are, therefore, abstract and general. It's not easy to say exactly where one ought to start such an endeavor, and metaphysicians disagree about the appropriate starting points. As will emerge throughout the course of this book, however, the views one adopts in one area of metaphysics will impact the views available to one in other areas. In this way, it's not clear that there is just *one* way one ought to begin one's first foray into metaphysics. What is clear, though, is that one must continually return to areas over which one has already tread in order to reevaluate one's conclusions in light of what one has learned in other areas. In this way, the question of where to begin shouldn't detain us for too long; one simply isn't finished with an area once one has traveled through it the first time.

So we choose to begin our study of metaphysics by making a simple observation, one that we believe will bear fruit. The observation is just this: there are sentences that are true, and sentences that are false.[1] Suppose, for example, that THP said, out loud, as this is being written, "I had yogurt with granola and strawberries for breakfast this morning." That sentence, uttered by THP at that time, would be true. Had he instead uttered at that time, "I had oatmeal with cinnamon, brown sugar, and walnuts for breakfast this morning," what he said would have been false. And there seems to be a straightforward explanation for *why* these sentences are true and false, respectively. In particular, THP *did in fact* have yogurt with granola and strawberries for breakfast

Metaphysics: The Fundamentals, First Edition. Robert C. Koons and Timothy H. Pickavance.
© 2015 Robert C. Koons and Timothy H. Pickavance.
Published 2015 by John Wiley & Sons, Ltd.

on the morning of April 22, 2013 (the day of this writing). There's nothing special about these sentences. Many (maybe all!) grammatically well-formed sentences are either true or false, from "Snow is white," "Three plus three is seven," and "There are many mountains over 14,000 feet tall," to "Three plus three is and must be six," "Intentionally teaching small children falsehoods is morally objectionable," and "Either Jesus of Nazareth is the Incarnation of the Second Person of the Triune God of Israel or he isn't."

What fruit can be grown from this simple observation? As it happens, the nature of truth (and falsehood) is a historically contentious subject among metaphysicians. The Greek philosopher Aristotle, for example, said the following:

> [Thus] we define what the true and the false are. To say of what is that it is not, or of what is not that it is, is false, while to say of what is that it is, and of what is not that it is not, is true. (*Metaphysics* 1011b25–8 (Aristotle 1984: 1597))

The natural way to understand Aristotle's suggestion is, initially anyway, quite plausible: a sentence is true if the world is the way the sentence says the world is and false if the world is not the way the sentence says the world is. As will emerge below, there is not universal agreement that Aristotle's insight here is correct. But we think it serves as, at the very least, a useful starting point and foil.

So we will call any view of truth that commits to Aristotle's suggestion a Correspondence Theory of Truth. Correspondence Theories, more precisely, share the following commitment: the truth of a sentence is grounded in a *match* – a *correspondence* – between what the sentence says and the way the world is. Sentences are false, according to Correspondence Theories, when no such match is present. Various Correspondence Theories can then be distinguished by reference to their particular views about what it takes for the meaning of a sentence to match or *correspond to* the world.

Correspondence is, therefore, meant to be a relation between two things. On the one hand, there are the things, if such there be, that we have talked about as "what a sentence says" and "the meaning of a sentence." On the other hand, there is what we have been calling "the world," what is *in fact* the case. We might picture the situation as in Figure 2.1:

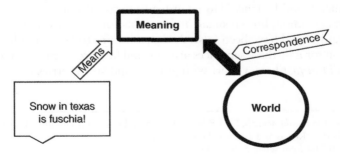

Figure 2.1

Presumably, we all have some inchoate idea about what *meanings* and *the world* are like. But that's not good enough for a metaphysician; we want to dig deeper, to understand more clearly what these things are and how they go together to make sentences true. Indeed, how different Correspondence Theories understand the nature of correspondence is settled in large part by considering the nature of the things that are meant to stand in this relation of correspondence, especially on the world side.

The remainder of this chapter will undertake to do some of the aforementioned digging; we will proceed as follows. Before moving on to the world side of the correspondence relation (Sections 2–4), we will briefly consider the nature of propositions (Section 1), as they are the most common answer to the question, "What are the meanings of sentences?" We will then articulate and evaluate a certain variety of Correspondence Theory, namely Classical Truthmaker Theory (Section 2). To contrast with Classical Truthmaker Theory, we will consider a view, Deflationism, that rejects the Correspondence Theory of Truth altogether (Section 3). Finally, we will consider a Correspondence Theory that is opposed to Classical Truthmaker Theory, namely Truth Supervenes on Being (Section 4).

2.1   Propositions

A traditional and plausible view of the meanings of assertional sentences has it that the meanings of such sentences are *propositions*. The idea is that when one utters a sentence, one thereby *expresses* a proposition; this is the sense in which propositions count as the meanings of uttered sentences. The proposition in turn *represents* the world somehow (more below). We might picture the situation as in Figure 2.2:

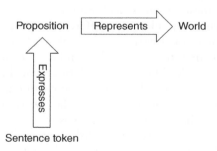

Figure 2.2

If the proposition expressed by the sentence is true (or false), then the sentence that expressed it is true (or false) as well. Standardly, then, the truth of sentences is taken to be derivative. In the first instance, it is

propositions that are true, and sentences get to be true in virtue of expressing a true proposition.

It is worth emphasizing that *propositions must be representational*. It is
in virtue of being representational that objects may be accurate or inac-
curate, true or false. Take a picture, for example, of THP's house, as
viewed from the street, in the fall of 2009. (There is such a picture.) Such
a picture was accurate to the state of the house at that time; in that sense
it was true to the world then. For example, in virtue of features of the
picture, it represented that there was no landscaping in the garden beds
around the base of the house. But there are now a great many plants
growing in those garden beds. That picture, then, is no longer an accurate
representation of THP's house. Similarly, the proposition that there is no
landscaping in the garden beds around the base of THP's house used to
represent the world accurately, but now fails to do so. This is why that
proposition was true, but is now false. So, to repeat, propositions must be
representational, for that is how, in conjunction with the world, they get
to be true or false.

The reader would be right to wonder why we've added these propositions
in between the sentences and the world. Could we not just stick with the
sentence itself, and say that it has these representational features and is able,
thereby, to stand in a direct relation of correspondence (or not) to the world?
Why not cut out the middleman, as it were?

Probably the most important reasons why philosophers have thought it
necessary to go in for propositions, rather than sticking just to sentences, are
these two. First, there is the rather mundane fact that we seem to be able to
express exactly the same truth in different languages. Propositions can help
us understand this possibility. Second, and relatedly, native speakers of different languages can presumably have the same thought, and propositions
are generally thought to be the immediate objects of certain *mental attitudes*. Let's dwell on these two reasons for a bit.

First, then, we turn to the idea that different languages can express the
same truth. For example, an utterance of the sentence "snow is white" means
in English just what an utterance of the sentence "la neige est blanche"
means in French.[2] Examples like this would, of course, be easy to multiply.
Given that these two utterances have the same meaning, though, it cannot
be that meanings are just sentences. For if they were, then the meaning
expressed in English by the utterance of "snow is white" would be an English
meaning, since that sentence is an English sentence. And the meaning
expressed in French by an utterance "la neige est blanche" would be a French
meaning. Since English and French are different languages, these meanings
could not be *the same*, any more than the sentences that express them are
the same. But the meanings are the same! So if all we have are sentences, we
have a problem.

So far, all we have is that sentences won't do the trick; we have yet to see how propositions are meant to do better. However, the structure of this need for something beyond sentences points to a constraint on the nature of the meanings of sentences, namely that they be *non-linguistic*. If sentence meanings need to be something that can be associated with different sentences in different languages, then they ought not have features that are necessarily connected to a particular language. Propositions are meant to lack such ties to particular languages; they are meant to be non-linguistic. In this way, they are better situated to be the meanings of sentences than are sentences themselves.

The second reason to believe in propositions, rather than just in sentences, is that native speakers of different languages can have the same thought. The idea here is very similar to that related to the first reason. Consider the thought (or belief) that a monolingual English speaker would express using the sentence "snow is white" and the thought that a monolingual French speaker would express using the sentence "la neige est blanche." These thoughts have a certain *content*, where the content of a thought is, roughly, that in virtue of which it is right to report that it is a thought *that such-and-so*. It would seem, therefore, that the content had by the English-speaker's thought is *the same* as that had by the French-speaker's thought: both are thoughts that snow is white. For the sort of reasons articulated above, we cannot say that the sentences that one would use to express a thought function also as the thought's content. For, in that case, contents would be language-bound things, and it would not be possible for these two thoughts to have the same content. Here again, philosophers have thought that propositions can be of help, by serving as the contents of thoughts, beliefs, desires, and other such mental attitudes. We might picture the situation as in Figure 2.3:

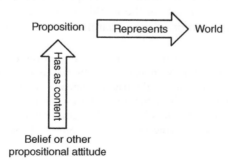

Figure 2.3

As with sentences that are uttered, we say that thoughts and beliefs are true and false in virtue of their contents, that is, in virtue of propositions. A thought is true (or false) in virtue of having a true (or false) proposition as its content.

By way of summary, propositions are standardly taken to be the meanings of assertional sentences and the immediate objects of certain mental attitudes like belief and desire. These characterize the theoretical role of propositions. Further, propositions have two characteristic features: first, they are *representational*, and second, they are *non-linguistic*. The need to have objects with these features gives us reasons to think that there really are propositions, and together these features constrain the type of entity that can rightly be said to play the role that propositions are meant to play. However, we don't yet have much insight into the *nature* of propositions. In particular, we have no sense for *how it is* that propositions represent the world. We will have a bit more to say about the question of the nature of propositions and how they represent in Chapter 7, during the discussion of so-called *possible worlds*. For now, we will have to rest content at the mention that there are a number of views about the nature of propositions. Some philosophers maintain that they are fundamental *abstract* objects. Some philosophers maintain that they are sets of possible worlds. Some maintain that they are certain sorts of facts (see Chapter 5 for a discussion of facts).

2.2   Classical Truthmaker Theory

We turn now to the *world* side of the Correspondence Theory of Truth. The question that will occupy us is this: What, exactly, must a proposition correspond *to* in order to be true? For it is clear that the talk of corresponding to the world should not be taken to mean that true propositions must correspond to the *whole* world. Consider, for example, the proposition that snow is white. It's not the overall state of the world that matters to the truth of this proposition; it is just *the color of snow* that matters. Here again, is Aristotle:

> [I]f there is a man, the statement whereby we say that there is a man is true, and reciprocally – since if the statement whereby we say that there is a man is true, there is a man. And whereas the true statement is in no way the cause of the actual thing's existence, the actual thing does seem in some way the cause of the statement's being true: it is because the actual thing exists or does not that the statement is called true or false. (*Categories* 14b15–22; (Aristotle 1984: 22))

Picking up on this idea, philosophers like Bertrand Russell, Ludwig Wittgenstein, and G. E. Moore defended the idea that there are *truthmakers*, that is, parts of the world in virtue of which propositions are true. More carefully, we define truthmakers in this way: x is a truthmaker for the proposition p if and only if (i) p must be true if x exists, and (ii) if x exists and p is true, the p must be true at least in part because x exists (or in virtue of the existence of *x*). The truthmaker for a proposition is that bit of the world which *makes* that proposition *true*.

One might, for example, say that the fact that snow is white is the truth-maker for the proposition that snow is white, or that the fact that a man exists is the truthmaker for the proposition that a man exists.[3] For the fact that snow is white seems to satisfy the definition of a truthmaker. Take the first clause of the definition of a truthmaker: given that the fact that snow is white exists, the proposition that snow is white must be true. And the second clause: given that the fact that snow is white exists and the truth of the proposition that snow is white, it is plausible to think that the proposition that snow is white is true (at least in part) in virtue of the fact that snow is white. Examples like this are easy to multiply. The fact that THP's oldest son is named "Lyle" is the truthmaker for the proposition that THP's oldest son is named "Lyle." When the former exists, the latter must be true, and given that the former exists and the latter is true, the truth of the latter ought to be explained in terms of the existence of the former. The fact that Austin is the capital of Texas is the truthmaker for the proposition that Austin is the capital of Texas. When the former exists, the latter must be true, and given that the former exists and the latter is true, the truth of the latter ought to be explained in terms of the existence of the former. And so on.

We are interested here to dig more deeply into the merits of Classical Truthmaker Theory, which is just the view that there are truthmakers (in the sense just articulated). This truthmaking story has a lot going for it. It is both natural and plausible, at least here at the outset of our inquiry. The question is whether there actually are good arguments for it, and whether it can withstand scrutiny. First, we will turn to some reasons for believing in truthmakers, which are of course reasons to believe in Classical Truthmaker Theory. Then, we will develop two more specific varieties of Classical Truthmaker Theory, which will allow us to consider some troubles for Classical Truthmaker Theory.

2.2.1   Three Arguments for Truthmakers

Classical Truthmaker Theory, you will recall, is just the view that there are truthmakers, bits of the world in virtue of which propositions are true. But does it have more going for it than it's being natural and plausible? Are there good arguments in its favor? In this subsection, we present three arguments that have been offered on behalf of truthmakers and, thereby, Classical Truthmaker Theory.

Argument 1: From the Correspondence Theory to Truthmakers   The Correspondence Theory of Truth seems to lead rather naturally to the exist-ence of truthmakers. Indeed, we motivated truthmakers on the basis of the

Correspondence Theory. But it will be useful to return to that motivation, and develop more explicitly an argument that truthmakers are the best way to develop a Correspondence Theory of Truth. The argument has three stages.

Stage 1. The Correspondence Theory of Truth is very plausible. For if it is true, it explains why we turn to an investigation of the way the world is when we're interested to determine whether a given sentence is true or false. That is, when the truth of a sentence is in question, we seem to begin with our knowledge of the meaning of the sentence, and then we undertake to determine whether the world is the sort of place that is a match for that meaning. When there is the right sort of match, we count the sentence true; when there isn't the right sort of match, we count the sentence false. For example, suppose we were wondering about the truth of the following sentence: "Fewer than 90% of the (single-family, detached) homes inside the Austin city limits are owner-occupied." If we were unable to get testimonial evidence about whether this sentence is true or false (maybe Googling failed us in this case), what would we do? The answer is almost too obvious to state: we would have to go about producing an inventory of the occupiers and owners of all the homes inside the Austin city limits, and then we'd do some simple calculations. (No doubt this would be time-consuming and tedious, but the strategy isn't complicated!) The Correspondence Theory can explain this quite readily. We know what the relevant sentence means, and so we know what the world would have to be like in order for the sentence to be true. The meaning of the sentence has to match the state of the world. That's just the Correspondence Theory. This is our inchoate way of understanding truth. Let's suppose, at least provisionally, that it's *true*.

Stage 2. Recall the first clause of the definition of a truthmaker given above: "*p* must be true if *x* exists," where "*p*" denotes the proposition expressed by the relevant sentence. The chunk of the world that we would go about investigating to determine whether the sentence, "Fewer than 90% of the homes inside the Austin city limits are owner-occupied," is true is an "*x*" which satisfies that first clause. Suppose, for example, that there are 185,622 detached, single-family homes in Austin, and that 164,060 are owner-occupied. Consider, then, the fact that 88.4% (164,060/185,622) of the homes in Austin are owner-occupied. This is the fact we discover when we go about our investigation. Given the existence of that fact, the proposition expressed by the sentence, "Fewer than 90% of the homes inside the Austin city limits are owner-occupied," *must* be true. Given that fact, the proposition expressed by that sentence couldn't fail to be true.

Stage 3. Not only is it the case that the sentence, "Fewer than 90% of the homes inside the Austin city limits are owner-occupied," must be true if there exists the fact that 88.4% of the homes in Austin are owner-occupied, but it also seems that there is an asymmetric sort of dependence here. The sentence is true *in virtue of* or *because of* the existence of the fact. Again, this is a natural thing to think, that there is this sort of dependence. But to sense the asymmetry here, consider a dependency in the other direction: consider the claim that the fact exists because the sentence is true. This seems not only false but borderline *crazy*. No one, at least without some very good argument, would think that is true. But thinking that the reason why the sentence is true has to do with the way the world is not crazy at all; it almost seems *obvious*. If there is such a dependency, then the fact that 88.4% of the homes in Austin are owner-occupied also satisfies the second clause of the definition of a truthmaker: "If *x* exists and *p* is true, the *p* must be true at least in part because *x* exists (or in virtue of the existence of *x*)."

So we have a three-step argument for the existence of truthmakers, that is, for Classical Truthmaker Theory, from the Correspondence Theory of Truth. The chunk of the world to which sentences correspond when they are true satisfies both clauses of the definition of truthmakers.

Argument 2: Distinguishing Theories   As it happens, however, there are arguments that truthmakers exist which do not depend at all on the Correspondence Theory. Indeed, some philosophers have argued for truthmakers without relying on any theory of truth at all! (Horwich 1998 and Lewis 2001, for example.) It is to one such argument that we turn presently.

A theory is a view of at least part of the world; it describes the world a certain way. After all, a theory is true if and only if the world is as the theory says it is. That is, a theory is true if and only if the world has certain things with certain features in certain arrangements. It is obvious that different theories can – indeed, often do – describe the world differently. One theory may say that the world is fundamentally made of bits of physical stuff, say, while another may say that in addition to the fundamental bits of physical stuff, there are also bits of fundamental spiritual stuff.

What may not be so obvious, however, is that different theories may describe the world in exactly the same way by using different terminology. One obvious way this can happen is if the theories are formulated using different languages. The differences can be subtler, though. Different theories in the same language can differ with respect to the propositions or concepts they use to express the theory. For example, consider one theory formulated using the concept "bachelor" and a second theory formulated without that concept but with the concepts "unmarried," "adult," and "male." The first theory, but not the second, could imply the sentence "There are bachelors," though the second could imply the sentence "There are unmarried adult males." While these theories use different terminology, there doesn't seem to be any substantive difference in the way that they describe the world.

Truthmakers can help us make sense of why this is so. First, however, we need a bit of terminology. Let us call pairs of theories that describe the world differently, that say the world contains different things or things with different features or in different arrangements, "ontologically distinct." On the other hand, let us call pairs of theories that similarly describe the world but using different terminology "ideologically distinct." Truthmakers can help us differentiate between theories that are merely ideologically distinct and theories that are ontologically distinct, and can do so quite simply. If it is the case that any (possible) set of truthmakers that makes one theory in a pair true also makes the other theory true, then the pair of theories are at most ideologically distinct; they cannot be ontologically distinct. If, on the other hand, there is a (possible) set of truthmakers that makes one of the theories true but does not make the other theory true, then the two theories are ontologically distinct.

We can apply this to our two theories above, the one with "bachelor" and the other with only "unmarried adult male." These two theories will be merely ideologically distinct, since there is no set of truthmakers that could make "There are bachelors" true without also making "There are unmarried adult males" true, and vice versa. Thus, there can be no ontological difference between the two theories. More substantively, we might consider two theories, one that talks of crowds and another that only talks of persons and their spatial arrangements. Whether these two theories are ontologically or merely ideologically distinct would turn on whether there could be, for example, a truthmaker for the sentence "There are over 4000 people in close proximity to one another downtown" without also making true "There is a crowd downtown" (or vice versa). In a more ontological vein, we can put the point like this: do the truthmakers for sentences involving asserting the existence of a crowd have to involve a single thing, a *crowd*, over and above the plurality of people in close proximity one to another?

So, we can see that truthmakers allow us to distinguish cleanly between ontological and mere ideological differences, and making this sort of distinction without truthmakers is rather difficult. Given that we *are* able to make this distinction between ontological and mere ideological difference, we have some reason to believe in truthmakers.

Argument 3: Catching Metaphysical "Cheaters"   Metaphysical "cheaters" are metaphysicians who claim that sentences about certain bits of the world are true according to their preferred metaphysical theory, but who are unwilling to identify or say anything metaphysically serious about those bits of the world. They are "cheating" because they refuse to answer metaphysical questions about the grounds for the truths in question. Truthmakers, according to some philosophers, can help us catch metaphysical cheaters of this sort; indeed, some philosophers seem to think that truthmakers are the best way, maybe even the only way, to catch metaphysical cheaters.[4]

An example from the philosophy of time (see Chapter 8 for more) may help. One important dispute about time is whether Presentism or Eternalism accurately describes the world. Very roughly, a Presentist is someone who believes that the only things that exist are those things that exist at the present moment. Put differently, Presentism is just the view that only the present exists. Eternalism, on the other hand, is (again roughly) the view that things that exist in the past and future are just as real as things that exist in the present. The past and future are no less real than the present; there is nothing special, from an ontological point of view, about the present. Presentists and Eternalists agree that there are *now* no dinosaurs or human outposts on Mars, but disagree about whether there are dinosaurs and Martian outposts. Presentists think there are none of these things, while Eternalists think there are (though they would hasten to emphasize that they don't *now* exist).

Presentists have a problem making sense of the truth of ordinary sentences like, "There used to be dinosaurs." They cannot say, and Eternalists can say, that there are these things, dinosaurs, that only exist at times temporally prior to the present. For that is to commit to the existence of dinosaurs, which is just what they don't want to do! If there are dinosaurs, then dinosaurs exist, even if only in the past. This problem is notorious for Presentists, and when faced with it, some Presentists have made the following sort of speech:

> "Here's the deal. These past tense statements ought to be understood as involving an 'irreducible tense operator'. By that, I mean that the true form of 'There used to be dinosaurs' is this: WAS(Dinosaurs exist), where WAS(p) is true just in case p *was* the case. (We can say something similar for future tense, involving a WILL-BE operator.) However, propositions involving irreducible tense operators don't commit you to believing in the things that you would be committed to if you asserted the proposition without that tense operator. One can believe that WAS(Dinosaurs exist) is true without believing in the existence of dinosaurs. After all, everyone has to believe that there are operators like this: Folks can *believe* there's a Fountain of Youth without there being this thing, the Fountain of Youth, that they believe in. Like WAS, BELIEVES is a *non-factive* or *opaque* operator: one that does not permit the exporting to reality of things that exist only within its scope."

Let's say, though, that the Correspondence Theory of Truth is true. This Presentist speech leaves us completely in the dark about the way in which "There used to be dinosaurs" corresponds to the world. Further, it is difficult to see how they *could* do such a thing, given that there is no past, and there are no dinosaurs, for the sentence to correspond to. The philosopher who is charging the Presentist with metaphysical cheating will say, then, that unless the Presentist can identify a truthmaker for the claim that there used to be dinosaurs – something that really does exists and that grounds the sentence's truth – the Presentist is trying to have her metaphysical cake and eat it too. She is trying to commit to the Correspondence Theory without saying how certain sentences are able to correspond. She's a metaphysical cheater. And truthmakers can make the charge of cheating, and what it takes to meet the charge, clear: identify the truthmaker.[5]

No doubt there is more to say about all three of these arguments for truthmakers. At the very least, you should now have some sense for why some philosophers have thought Classical Truthmaker Theory attractive.

2.2.2   Two Varieties of Classical Truthmaker Theory

One thing we have not done, however, is answer the question: which truths have truthmakers? We will now canvass two views that can be distinguished via their answers to that question. In particular, Truthmaker Maximalism is the view that every truth has a truthmaker, whereas Atomic Truthmaker Theory, to which some subscribe in light of certain problems for Truthmaker Maximalism, is the view that only truths in a special subclass, the *atomic* truths, do. We will tackle these varieties of Classical Truthmaker Theory in turn.

Variety 1: Truthmaker Maximalism   Truthmaker Maximalism is, quite simply, the view that every truth has a truthmaker. Given the sorts of motivations we've seen for believing in truthmakers at all, the most natural thing to think is that *all* truths have truthmakers. Truthmaker Maximalism is, then, a plausible starting point when one is considering specific varieties of Classical Truthmaker Theory. Further, it is a simple theory with significant explanatory power, two hallmarks of a good theory. For given Truthmaker Maximalism, one has no trouble accounting for how it is that each truth is true, and the view uniformly and straightforwardly accounts for various truths. In every case, the question about why a given proposition is true is just: it has its own truthmaker.

On the other hand, Truthmaker Maximalism faces some serious challenges. We will consider two. The first has to do with negative existential sentences, like, "There is no Fountain of Youth," and universal generalizations, like, "All dogs are mammals." The second has to do with sentences that are conjunctions of other sentences, like, "The dog is wagging its tail, and THP is standing," and other logically complex sentence forms.

Problem 1: Negative Existentials, Universal Generalizations, and Totality Facts. Negative existentials are sentences like, "There is no Fountain of Youth," "Pegasus doesn't exist," and "There are no dinosaurs." Uniqueness claims are closely related to negative existentials as well, since "THP is the only husband of JKP" can be paraphrased as "There is no husband of JKP other than THP." Other types of sentences can be treated similarly, but we will here focus on negative existentials.

Truthmaker Maximalism has trouble with negative existentials. The truthmaker for "There are no golden mountains" must be something that, by its very existence and nature, makes that sentence true. So it must be something whose existence guarantees the truth of "There are no golden mountains." Thus, it must be something whose existence excludes the possibility of adding a golden mountain to the world. But truthmakers such as this would require numerous necessary connections (both entailments and mutual exclusions) between and among separate possible things. For example, the truthmaker for "There are no golden mountains" would require that there be *no* truthmakers for the existence of any particular golden mountain. Further, the lack of truthmakers for the existence of any particular golden mountain would require the existence of the truthmaker for "There are no golden mountains." But since there are literally an infinite number of possible golden mountains, the truthmaker for "There are no golden mountains" excludes an infinite number of other possible truthmakers.

If negative existentials require truthmakers, then the non-existence of some truthmakers entails the existence of others, and vice versa, despite the fact that all such truthmakers are separate and distinct beings. After all, the truthmaker for the absence of a golden mountain could hardly contain a truthmaker for the existence of a golden mountain as one of its parts, or vice versa, since wholes include and don't exclude their parts.

Philosophers, however, tend to frown upon these sorts of brute, unexplained necessary connections. One reason for this is a philosophical principle called "Ockham's Razor," which says that we should prefer the simplest theory when faced with otherwise comparable alternatives. And one corollary of Ockham's Razor, one dimension along which theories might be more or less simple, concerns the number of brute, unexplained necessities and impossibilities. What we have seen is a reason to think that Truthmaker Maximalism has a great many brute, unexplained necessities and impossibilities, and that this is a strike against the simplicity of the theory. Therefore, Truthmaker Maximalism is, if there is a theory that is its equal along other dimensions, problematic.

There may be a more serious worry in this neighborhood, however, having to do with negative existentials for possible but non-actual things. As an example, consider a possible dinosaur. It will help if he has a name: Steggy Stegosaurus.[6] "Steggy does not exist" is true, since Steggy doesn't exist. (Trust us on that one.) If Truthmaker Maximalism is true, then "Steggy does not exist" needs a truthmaker; call the truthmaker for this sentence "NoSteggy." NoSteggy exists, but might not have, which is to say, NoSteggy is a contingent thing. For if Steggy had existed, NoSteggy would not have existed. After all, NoSteggy is a truthmaker for "Steggy does not exist," so NoSteggy guarantees the truth of "Steggy does not exist"; but if Steggy exists, then "Steggy does not exist" *can't* be true, and so NoSteggy could not exist. In all those cases in which Steggy exists, NoSteggy does not, and in all the cases where NoSteggy exists, Steggy does not.

This points to a strange consequence, or maybe cluster of consequences, of Truthmaker Maximalism: whenever some contingent thing fails to exist, there is a distinct contingent thing that is guaranteed to exist. The contingent thing that is guaranteed to exist is the truthmaker for the proposition that the non-existent contingent thing in question fails to exist. For example, since Steggy fails to exist, there exists a truthmaker for the proposition that Steggy fails to exist. Since Pegasus fails to exist, there exists a truthmaker for the proposition that Pegasus fails to exist. And so on. These truthmakers for negative existentials, just like Steggy and Pegasus, are contingent.

This, first of all, implies that there must be at least one contingent thing. God himself is unable to create a world without contingent things, since by deciding not to create Steggy, he would thereby be committed to creating NoSteggy.

Second, consider two possibilities that differ only with respect to whether or not Steggy exists. These possibilities would not differ with respect to the number of contingent things that exist, since the non-existence of Steggy, as we have seen, guarantees the existence of NoSteggy. Likewise, the existence of Steggy precludes the existence of a different contingent thing, NoSteggy. This means that one cannot *thin out* the world's population of contingent beings, despite that this seems perfectly possible.

Generalizing, and third, there is some number n of contingent things such that the proposition expressed by "There are n contingent things" is necessarily true. Take all the possible contingent things. You can divide them between the ordinary contingent things, like Steggy and so on, and the truthmakers for the negative existentials having to do with those ordinary contingent things.[7] Further, we can pair the ordinary contingent things with the truthmakers for the negative existentials having to with them: Steggy gets paired with NoSteggy, Pegasus with NoPegasus, and so on. But one and only one member of each of these pairs *must* exist, either the ordinary thing or the truthmaker for the relevant negative existential. Thus, exactly half of the possible contingent things are guaranteed to exist. These consequences are, shall we say, unpalatable; Truthmaker Maximalism is less attractive by virtue of implying them.

We can push still further, by considering universal generalizations. Universal generalizations are sentences like, "All dogs are mammals," "All metals are malleable," and "No trees are sentient." These sentences are all related to negative existentials ("There are no non-mammalian dogs,"

"There are no non-malleable metals," and "There are no sentient trees"), but they point to a slightly different problem for Truthmaker Maximalism. We'll have to work our way to the problem.

If Truthmaker Maximalism is true, then each of these universal generalizations has a truthmaker. Let's focus on the sentence, "All dogs are mammals." What would the truthmaker for this sentence have to be like? Notice first that whatever it is, it will have to make true every instance of this kind of sentence: "Either x is not a dog or x is a mammal." Which is to say, the truthmaker for "All dogs are mammals" would guarantee that, for every actually existing thing t, either t fails to be a dog or t is in fact a mammal. Let's suppose there is such a truthmaker, and let's call it, "Biggie." Pick some existent thing, Lyle, for example. Biggie's existence guarantees that Lyle fails to be a dog or is in fact a mammal. Similarly for any other thing.

Surprisingly, though, Biggie does *not* guarantee that all dogs are mammals! The existence of Biggie is compatible with there being something that is a non-mammalian dog. Biggie only demands that actually existing things are either non-dogs or mammals, but does not preclude the existence of other things that are non-mammalian dogs. Biggie guarantees nothing about such *new* entities, and so Biggie could exist in a world with non-mammalian dogs. Thus, Biggie does not guarantee the truth of "All dogs are mammals."

This means the Truthmaker Maximalist needs what David M. Armstrong (1997) has called Totality Facts. Totality Facts are truthmakers that guarantee that nothing exists except the things in a certain class. So, for example, the Totality Fact for the actual world guarantees that nothing exists except the things that actually exist. More generally, consider a class of possible things, T. There is a possible Totality Fact that guarantees that only the things in T exist. It *says*, as it were, "Nothing to see here but members of T! That's all there is!" Just as with the truthmakers for negative existentials, Totality Facts require numerous brute necessary connections. The Totality Fact having to do with the things in T, for example, is brutely incompatible with the existence of things not in T. As we noted above, however, this is a cost for the theory, since Ockham's Razor demands that we minimize brute necessary connections.

There is a further complication, for Totality Facts have to do with knowledge. Given the complexity of the Totality Fact (it speaks to the existence of everything that exists, and the non-existence of everything that doesn't!), it's difficult to see how we could know it in any detail. But if our knowledge of truths is importantly related to our knowledge of their truthmakers, then it is difficult to see how we could have knowledge of any universal generalization, even very mundane ones like "All dogs are mammals." Still further, as Trenton Merricks (2007) has argued, "All dogs are mammals" doesn't seem to concern the character of the whole world, like how many supernovas there are or which grains of sand exist. But

Totality Facts do concern that total character. So the Truthmaker Maximalist seems committed to a truthmaking story for universal generalizations that is problematic.

Problem 2: Conjunctions and Fundamentality. A second problem, one that will point us toward a restriction on Truthmaker Maximalism, concerns conjunctive sentences like, "The dog is wagging its tail, and THP is standing." This sentence is a conjunction (in virtue of the "and") of two conjuncts, namely the sentences, "The dog is wagging its tail" and "THP is standing." Supposing that the conjunctive sentence is true, "The dog is wagging its tail" and "THP is standing" each has its own truthmaker. But if Truthmaker Maximalism is true, the conjunction, "The dog is wagging its tail, and THP is standing," must also have its own truthmaker, in addition to those two. That is, if Truthmaker Maximalism is true, not only are there truthmakers for the two conjuncts, but there is a further truthmaker for the conjunction. This point, quite clearly, can be generalized to any conjunction. However, this seems like overkill. The existence of the truthmakers for the individual conjuncts seems, together anyway, to be sufficient for the truth of the conjunction. We have no need of the extra truthmaker for the conjunction. Here again, Ockham's Razor suggests that this unnecessary additional entity is problematic for Truthmaker Maximalism.

The deeper point here is that the conjuncts seem to be more fundamental than the conjunction. We can see this by reflecting on the fact that the truth of the conjunction seems to depend on the truth of the conjuncts in an asymmetrical way. Even though the truth of the conjunction is sufficient for the truth of the conjuncts, it is in virtue of the truth of the conjuncts that the conjunction is true, but it is not in virtue of the truth of the conjunction that the conjuncts are true. Truthmaker maximalism, however, seems to not have space to accommodate this asymmetry.

A Truthmaker Maximalist might suppose that it is the aggregate or *sum* of the truthmakers for the conjuncts that is the truthmaker for the conjunction. We can still get the result that the truth of the individual conjuncts is more fundamental, if the aggregate of the individual truthmakers depends on the individual truthmakers in a way that they do not depend on the aggregate. However, it seems far from obvious that such an aggregate will always exist, while it seems quite obvious that the conjunction must be true whenever all its conjuncts are.

The natural thing to say, of course, is that the *joint existence* of the truthmakers for the conjuncts is what makes true the conjunction. This can allow us to keep Classical Truthmaker Theory (there are still truthmakers!), but constitutes an abandonment of Truthmaker Maximalism. In its place, we have a view according to which, for each true proposition, either there is a truthmaker for that proposition, or there are some truthmakers that jointly make true that proposition. One wonders, though, how far we can extend this sort of restriction. What, exactly, are the sorts of facts that get their own, unique, fundamental truthmaker? What, put differently, are the fundamental truths? Atomic Truthmaker Theory promises to answer these questions, and to avoid certain troubles for Truthmaker Maximalism.

Variety 2: Atomic Truthmaker Theory In light of these problems for Truthmaker Maximalism, some philosophers have thought that the only truths that have unique truthmakers are a special subclass of truths, the *atomic* truths. What are atomic truths? Atomic truths are simple and positive. They concern the existence of a single thing ("Lyle exists"), or the having of a single feature by a single thing ("Lyle is 45 inches tall"), or a plurality of things' standing in a single relation ("Lyle is older than Gretchen"). Simplicity, in this context, can be contrasted with logical complexity. So non-simple, or logically complex, truths include conjunctions like those discussed above, but also disjunctions ("The dog is wagging its tail, or THP is standing"), sentences with logically complex predicates ("Lyle is 45 inches tall and has blonde hair"), and so on. Positive truths contrast with negative ones, where the latter class includes negative existentials, sentences that deny a feature of a thing ("Lyle is not 50 inches tall") or that a relation obtains among some objects ("Gretchen is not taller than Lyle"), and so on. Atomic truthmaker theory is the view that only atomic truths have a truthmaker.

Atomic truthmaker theory accounts for the truth of non-atomic sentences in ways one might expect. A conjunction "*a* and *b*" (where "*a*" and "*b*" are atomic truths) is true just in case the sentence "*a*" has a truthmaker and the sentence "*b*" has a truthmaker. A disjunction "*a* or *b*" is true just in case either the sentence "*a*" has a truthmaker or the sentence "*b*" has a truthmaker. (Matters aren't so clear in the case of conditionals "if *a* then *b*"; see Chapter 3 for discussion, though one not structured around the issue of truthmaking *per se*.) Negative sentences, like negative existentials and ordinary negations ("It's not the case that *a*" or "*o* is not-*F*") are a bit trickier. Consider a negation "Not-*a*," where "*a*" is atomic. The ground of the truth of "Not-*a*" is that "*a*" *fails* to have a truthmaker. It is the *lack* of a truthmaker for "*a*" that grounds the truth of "Not-*a*." Put another way, any truthmaker for "*a*" is going to make "Not-*a*" false, and so "Not-*a*" is true not because it has a truthmaker but because it *lacks* a *falsity*maker (that is, there is no existing thing that makes it false).

Interestingly, if Atomic Truthmaker Theory is true, all truths must "weakly supervene" on facts about which atomic propositions are true and false. Weak supervenience can be defined as follows: A class of propositions A weakly supervenes on a class of propositions B if and only if you cannot change the truth-value (truth or falsity) of a proposition in A without changing the truth-value of at least one proposition in B.[8] The idea is that the *B*-truths *fix* the *A*-truths: you couldn't get different *A*-truths without changing the *B*-truths. For example, facts about clouds (*A*-truths) are fixed by facts about water molecules in the sky (*B*-truths), and facts about beaches (*A*-truths) are fixed by facts about grains of sand (*B*-truths), and some argue that facts about mental states (*A*-truths) are fixed by facts about brain states (*B*-truths). In each case, the former set of facts weakly supervenes on the latter. (See Section 9.4 for more details about supervenience.)

Atomic truthmaker theory maintains that the atomic truths fix all the truths, and so in that sense all truths supervene on the atomic ones. Once one settles the truthmaker facts, one has thereby settled which atomic propositions are true and false. But thereby, one will have fixed *all* the truths. One will not be able to get a difference in overall truth without a difference in atomic truth. For example, the conjunctive truths, in the manner articulated above, supervene on the atomic truths. Once one settles the atomic truths, the conjunctive truths fall into place. One cannot change the latter without changing the former.

Atomic truthmaker theory constitutes a significant weakening of Classical Truthmaker Theory, relative to Truthmaker Maximalism. It is worth asking whether the three arguments for truthmakers survive that weakening. It seems that the spirit of those arguments can be retained.

From Correspondence to Truthmakers. It seems that the Atomic Truthmaker Theorist must circumscribe their commitment to the Correspondence Theory of Truth, for not every truth will correspond directly to the world, that is, to a truthmaker. We have seen, though, that this expectation might have been well motivated in certain cases while being problematic in others. Indeed, it is in part this fact that motivates Atomic Truthmaker Theory. The Atomic Truthmaker Theorist can still say that every atomic truth corresponds to reality, and might suggest that this was the core of the correspondence intuition in the first place. She could then hasten to add that all other truths weakly supervene on the atomic truths. Arguably, this maintains the spirit of the Correspondence Theory, and can still be motivated by it.

Distinguishing Theories. Atomic truthmaker theory does allow one to distinguish between ontological and mere ideological differences: two theories differ ontologically if and only if there is a combination of the existence of truthmakers of various sorts and the absence or non-existence of truthmakers of other kinds that makes one theory true while failing to make the other theory true.

Catching Cheaters. Atomic truthmaker theory allows for truths without truthmakers. Thus, it might seem that Atomic Truthmaker Theorists cannot use their view to catch metaphysical cheaters, since they themselves must cheat about, for example, negative existentials. Since there is no truthmaker for some true negative existential, the Atomic Truthmaker Theorist seems to be refusing to supply a metaphysical ground for it. They cannot then go on to complain about, for example, Presentists who fail to supply a metaphysical ground for the truth of claims about the past and future.[9]

However, Atomic Truthmaker Theorists maintain that all truths weakly supervene on the atomic truths, which are in turn grounded in truthmakers. Presentists, by contrast, do not (or anyway should not!) insist that truths about the past and future supervene in any sense on truths wholly about the present. Thus, it seems that there is a difference between the kind of grounding that negative truths get if Atomic Truthmaker Theory is true and the kind of grounding that past and future claims get if Presentism is true. The failure of supervenience makes the Presentist commitment more problematic from a "cheating" standpoint than that of the Atomic Truthmaker Theorist.

On the other hand, the Atomic Truthmaker Theory has built in to the notion of supervenience the truth of negative existentials by insisting that the set of all truths weakly supervenes on the set of atomic propositions that are *and are not* true. Presentists, it seems, could simply insist that truths about the past and future supervene on the set of truths that are, *were, and will be* true. There is no substantive difference here. In light of this, the Atomic Truthmaker Theorist would be wise to avoid deploying the "catching cheaters" argument.

Fundamentality. There is an additional argument for Atomic Truthmaker Theory not shared by all varieties of Classical Truthmaker Theory. Atomic truthmaker theory can identify the fundamental truths. If a truth corresponds to a single possible truthmaker, then the truth is fundamental. That is to say: for any fundamental truth t, that truth has only one truthmaker m, and moreover, necessarily, if t is true then m is t's truthmaker. Suppose, for example, that quark q has spin s, and that there is nothing in virtue of which this is true. In that case, the proposition expressed by "q has s" is both true and fundamental because q's having s is and must be the truthmaker for "q has s," and nothing else is a truthmaker for "q has s." We can, more generally, define the fundamental propositions as those propositions that could only be made true by one possible truthmaker. Indeed, these fundamental truths are just the atomic truths the Atomic Truthmaker Theorist was concerned to identify.

Further, we can extend this idea to account for all truths in a way that displays the supervenience of all truths on the fundamental truths, in the way you would expect were Atomic Truthmaker Theory true. Negations of fundamental propositions are true in virtue of the absence of truthmakers for the relevant fundamental propositions. Suppose, for example, that q did not have s; in that case, "q does not have s" is true, and it is true in virtue of the non-existence of the truthmaker for "*q* has *s*." Conjunctions of fundamental propositions are true in virtue of the existence of the truthmaker of both conjuncts; disjunctions of fundamental propositions are true in virtue of the existence of the truthmaker for at least one of the disjuncts. Similarly, if a predicate *P* is definable in terms of fundamental predicates *F* and *G*, then true predications of *P* are true in virtue of the truth of fundamental propositions having to do with *F* and *G*. (Consider, for example, the predicate "red and round," which is definable in terms of the predicates "red" and "round.") And so on.

It seems that Atomic Truthmaker Theory has quite a bit going for it. Are there other views that fare better?

2.3   Deflationism

As we have seen, one of the fundamental motivations for Classical Truthmaker Theory is the Correspondence Theory of Truth. A number of philosophers, however, have argued that the Correspondence Theory is false, and that we should instead opt for Deflationism about truth.[10] According to the Correspondence Theory, and implicit in our discussion so far, is the idea that the predicate "is true" expresses a property had by certain things, like sentences, propositions, and beliefs. Truth is, on this understanding, like colors, shapes, sizes, natural kinds (like human, dog, and gold), and other features. There really is a property of *being true*. According to Deflationism, on the other hand, the predicate "is true" does not express a property.[11] To say that something is true is just a roundabout way of saying the something itself. To say, "'Snow is white' is true," is just to say, "Snow is white," and to say, "'Eight numbers the planets' is true," is just to say, "Eight numbers the planets." In this way, predications of truth and falsity aren't about correspondence at all. They are simply a different way to endorse an ordinary claim.

Importantly, though Deflationists are *anti-realists* about the property of *being true*, they can be as *realist* as they like about any other things, from attributes like color and shape, to natural kinds, to the past and future, to moral facts, to non-actual possibilities, and on and on. Deflationism simply doesn't speak to the reality or otherwise of these things; it is only a view about the predicate "is true" and the property of *being true*. An interesting consequence of Deflationism is that true propositions do not, in virtue of being true, have anything in common with one another. Because of this, truth cannot play a part in metaphysical or causal explanations. And truth cannot be a part of causal laws or other laws of nature.

A number of philosophers have objected to Deflationism. We will canvass three such objections.

1   *Truth as constitutive of belief.* When we believe something, or assert something, or undertake certain actions (consider the decision to try to learn something in metaphysics by reading a book!), truth seems to be an overriding *aim* or *goal*. Because of this, some philosophers have argued that truth is a *constitutive norm* of these types of activities. What that means is that *what it is* to be an activity of these types is in part to be aimed at truth. Try to consider, for example, a belief that isn't aimed at truth; it's difficult to make sense of what this could mean. The property of *being true* is, therefore, a fundamental component of what it is to believe. This is a problem for Deflationism, of course, since this part of the nature of belief, assertion, and so on cannot be easily explicated if Deflationism is true.

2   *Truth as essential to the methodology of science.* Relatedly, scientific practice seems to require that truth is a property. Our scientific practices – indeed, all forms of intellectual inquiry – depend crucially on our ability to identify sources of information that are *reliable*. Reliability, in this context, just means *tending to deliver the truth*. Further, we take our past experience to be a guide to what we ought to expect in the future. So the reliability of various methods in the past is evidence that those same methods will be reliable in the future. These notions are, again, difficult to analyze without the property of *being true*, and so Deflationists have a difficult time accounting for this fact about scientific methodology.

3   *Truth as necessary for epistemology.* Finally, there are a number of logical principles that most philosophers take to be necessarily true, even self-evident. For example, the law of non-contradiction states that no proposition can be both true and false. Gottlob Frege referred to these sorts of laws as "laws of truth." The reason is that our knowledge of these truths seems to depend on our ability to know something about the property of *being true*. In particular, we are able to grasp facts about the property of *being true*, and it is in virtue of this grasping that we are able to know that the law of non-contradiction holds, even before we consider various instances of it. Deflationists, however, cannot tell this story about the epistemology of these laws of truth, because according to them there is no property of *being true*. They must instead say that these laws are just constitutive of rationality, but that is a strike against the simplicity of their theory. Another corollary of Ockham's Razor is that better theories, other things being equal, require fewer primitive postulates of reason or rationality.

Panning out, Deflationism faces some serious challenges. It might be, though, that there are other views that are more in keeping with the spirit of Classical Truthmaker Theory, but that are more plausible than Classical Truthmaker Theory and Deflationism. Non-Classical Truthmaker Theory promises to be just such a view. We will presently turn our attention to one variety of non-Classical Truthmaker Theory, namely, Truth Supervenes on Being.

2.4   Truth Supervenes on Being

We will start this section by unearthing an assumption of the foregoing discussion of truthmakers that deserves to be called into question. We have been assuming that there are *facts* like snow's being white, and that these facts are the bits of the world to which propositions correspond. But we have given no reason to think that this is true. Maybe, for example, there's just *the snow*. Maybe it's the snow to which the proposition that snow is white corresponds, in virtue of the snow's having certain features. If that is right, though, then the sheer existence of the snow is not enough to guarantee the truth of the proposition that snow is white. Snow, after all, might have been some other color! If one embraces this sort of picture, according to which propositions correspond not to facts but just to objects in the world (where those objects of course have certain features), then the things that make propositions true are not truthmakers, for they fail to satisfy the first clause of the definition. That first clause says that *t* can be a truthmaker for *p* only if *p* must be true given the existence of *t*. But on the sort of view we are now entertaining, it's not just the existence of, for example, the snow that is required to make a proposition true; it must also be the case that the snow has certain features.

Non-Classical Truthmaker Theory embraces this sort of picture. It asserts that propositions are made true by the way things in the world are, but that there are no truthmakers. There is truthmaking, but no truthmakers! (That is, there are no truthmakers in the sense we defined above.) What unifies non-Classical Truthmaker Theories is a commitment to truthmaking coupled with a denial of the Classical Truthmaker Theorist's claim that it is the sheer existence or non-existence of certain things that do the truthmaking work. Rather, non-Classical Truthmaker Theorists insist that things must exist *and* be certain ways in order to make propositions true. Various non-Classical Truthmaker Theories are then distinguished by their various takes on what it is for things to *be certain ways*.

We will consider only one variety of non-Classical Truthmaker Theory here, namely, the thesis that Truth Supervenes on Being (Lewis 2001). According to Truth Supervenes on Being, truthmaking is sometimes a relation between a proposition and many things in the world, together with their features and their relations to one another. More precisely, Truth Supervenes on Being is the view that the set of all truths weakly supervenes on which things (do and don't) exist and what *fundamental* properties they have (and don't have) and what *fundamental* relations they stand in (and don't stand in).

One advantage that Truth Supervenes on Being (and indeed, any non-Classical Truthmaker Theory) has over Classical Truthmaker Theory concerns *determinables* and *determinates*. Determinable properties are those that come in different varieties, where the determinates are those varieties. For example, the property of *being blue* is a determinable with properties like the property of *being navy*, the property of *being royal blue*, and the property of *being sky blue* as determinates. Similarly, the property of *being blue*, the property of *being red*, and the property of *being yellow* are all determinates of the determinable, the property of *being colored*.[12] On Classical Truthmaker Theory, the truthmaker for "*o* is navy" is the fact that *o* exemplifies the property of *being navy*. But that view would also predict that "*o* is not sky blue" is true in virtue of the fact that the truthmaker for "*o* is sky blue" fails to exist, *not* that "*o* is not sky blue" is true in virtue of the existence of the truthmaker for "*o* is navy," namely the fact that *o* exemplifies the property of *being navy*. This is a bit weird, for it means that the truthmaker for "*o* is navy" is *unrelated* to the truth of "*o* is not sky blue." The fact that one thing cannot exemplify two determinates of the same determinable is, therefore, a brute necessity, if Classical Truthmaker Theory is true. If Truth Supervenes on Being is true, however, one can ground these incompatibilities. This is because Truth Supervenes on Being does not require separate truthmakers for each determinate property. And since nothing can have the kind of internal state that would make true predications of two different determinates of the same determinable property, we should expect that whenever "*o* is navy" is true, "*o* is not sky blue" will be true as well.

However, we must again return to the arguments for truthmakers in order to discern whether Truth Supervenes on Being is able to be similarly motivated. It should be clear that, given the definition of Truth Supervenes on Being, the unique advantage of Atomic Truthmaker Theory, the ability to identify the fundamental truths, does not apply. The notion of fundamentality is built into the definition of Truth Supervenes on Being, and so one cannot then go on to use the theory to identify the fundamental truths. That would be a problematic kind of circularity.

Truth Supervenes on Being does seem to sit favorably with the spirit of the Correspondence Theory of Truth. One can understand correspondence in terms of supervenience, that is, in terms of difference-making. True propositions cannot be false, nor false propositions true, without a change in what exists, or what properties things have or relations they stand in.[13] In addition, Truth Supervenes on Being can be used to distinguish merely ideological from genuinely ontological differences between theories. If two theories agree on what things exist and agree on what natural properties and relations they instantiate, then there can be only an ideological or terminological difference between them (like "bachelor" vs. "unmarried male adult"). However, as with Atomic Truthmaker Theory, Truth Supervenes on Being cannot obviously be used to catch cheaters, and for the same reasons.

Truth Supervenes on Being must, therefore, be motivated by arguing that it is the best theory that can salvage the Correspondence Theory of Truth. Its ability to ground the incompatibility of different determinates of the same determinable might function as an important component of that argument.

2.5   Conclusion

The Correspondence Theory of Truth, which is plausible in its own right, leads quite naturally to truthmaking, and even to truthmakers. Of course, neither the Correspondence Theory nor Truthmaker Theories are free of troubles or detractors, and Deflationism stands as a serious challenger to the former and, thereby, the latter. Though we have not here settled the question, What is the One True View of truth? we have supplied an initial inventory of issues and options. Ignoring Deflationism, the results of our discussion are summarized in Table 2.1:

Table 2.1   Theories of Truthmaking

	Truthmaker Maximalism	Atomic Truthmaker Theory	Truth Supervenes on Being
Correspondence Theory of Truth	Yes	Yes, but only for atomic truths	Yes, but in terms of difference-making
Distinguishing Theories	Yes	Yes	Yes
Catching Cheaters	Yes	Arguably, by supervenience	Arguably, by supervenience
Identifying Fundamental Truths	No	Yes	No

We will continually be returning to issues having to do with truthmaking. In the next chapter, for example, we turn to questions regarding conditionals, powers, and laws, and the issue of truthmaking will play a crucial role.

Notes

1   We ignore non-assertive sentences – questions and commands, for example – for simplicity.

2   There is a related phenomenon that occurs *within* a *single* language: different sentences of, say, English can have the same meaning. For example, if THP were

to utter on April 22, 2013, the sentence "It is cloudy today," he would express the same thing that he would express on April 23, 2013, with an utterance of the sentence "It was cloudy yesterday." (Or anyway, there is one precisification of the notion of *meaning* on which this is true. Believers in propositions tend to be targeting that notion of *meaning* when they suggest that propositions are the meanings of sentences.)

3   As a reminder, we take up the nature of facts in Chapter 5.

4   Armstrong (1968: 85) and Sider (2001: 35–41) use truthmakers to catch metaphysical cheaters. Merricks (2007) discusses metaphysical cheating without conceding that it is problematic.

5   Importantly, we do not mean to be settling here whether the charge of metaphysical cheating that some level against the Presentist is, all things considered, insurmountable. We are merely illustrating how truthmakers might help one catch cheaters. Other examples of putative cheating involve brute dispositions and primitively true counterfactuals (see Chapter 3).

6   When are in debt to Lyle Pickavance for this suggestion.

7   This isn't quite true, but repairing it would introduce unhelpful complications without upsetting the conclusion.

8   The modifier weakly is necessary because there are many varieties of supervenience relations. Jaegwon Kim (1993) initially classified them into "strong" and "weak" varieties. See McLaughlin (1997).

9   See Merricks (2007).

10   Prominent deflationary accounts can be found in Ramsey (1927), Grover (1992), and Horwich (1998).

11   Or anyway, "is true" does not express a "natural" property, in David Lewis's (1983) sense. We will, in the sequel, collapse this distinction. The arguments we present against Deflationism are actually much more plausible when construed in terms of Deflationism's denial that truth is a natural property.

12   A property is not a determinate or determinable *simpliciter*. Rather, properties are determinates and determinables *in relation to* other properties.

13   There is a complication here, as Bennett (2011) points out: the thesis that Truth Supervenes on Being does not, by itself, capture the idea that truths depend on being, since supervenience does not entail that the supervening things depend on what they supervene on. The TSB thesis points to a relation of dependency of derived things and properties on fundamental things and properties, not of truths on the world.

3

Causation and Powers

As the great Greek philosopher Aristotle observed, philosophy begins with a sense of wonder. The metaphysician, in particular, begins by observing certain basic and pervasive facts and then asks, what is going on here? How are we to understand this? In this chapter, we begin with two such basic and pervasive facts: the fact that things have changed, and the fact that there exists the potentiality for a variety of changes in the future. These phenomena seem connected: if we can explain why change has happened in the past, we may be able to understand what sorts of changes are possible in the future, and why.

When we think about explaining change, we look for what we call "causes." Consequently, we will begin this chapter with a section on the existence of causes. We will then turn, in Section 3.2, to the question of investigating the nature of the potentiality or disposition for future change. This will involve close attention to the meaning of certain conditionals, or statements with an "if ..., then ..." structure: if some particular thing were to happen, then some other thing would also happen. This will lead to the consideration four different theories about the basis for causal dispositions or potentialities (3.3), followed by a detailed consideration of two of those theories: Neo-Humeism (3.4) and Powerism (3.5).

We return to the problem of causation in the last section of the chapter. We will look briefly at the relation between causation and time, asking whether there is such a thing as discrete causation (with each cause linked to its effect by a finite number of indivisible steps), and whether there is such a thing as continuous causation (with causation occurring continuously

Metaphysics: The Fundamentals, First Edition. Robert C. Koons and Timothy H. Pickavance.
© 2015 Robert C. Koons and Timothy H. Pickavance.
Published 2015 by John Wiley & Sons, Ltd.

throughout an interval of time). This last section (3.6) will help to lay the foundations for a later chapter (8) on the metaphysics of time itself.

3.1   Do Causes Exist?

It seems to be a matter of common sense, or even more than common sense, that whenever change happens, there must be a *cause* of that change. Philosophers of a rationalist bent (including Aristotle, Thomas Aquinas, or René Descartes) sometimes go so far as to say that the principle of causation is a first principle of reason, something beyond the pale of tenable doubt. However, this has been challenged, most famously by the eighteenth-century Scottish philosopher David Hume. In this section, we'll weigh the arguments for and against the existence of causes.

3.1.1   Objections to Causes

There have been two challenges to the existence of causes: an argument (by the twentieth-century English philosopher Bertrand Russell) that causation is a scientifically obsolete notion, and David Hume's argument, based on the impossibility of "necessary connections" between "separate existences."

Challenge 1: Causation Is Obsolete   In an essay in 1913, Bertrand Russell (Russell 1913) argued that modern science has moved irreversibly beyond the use of the concept of *causation*. According to Russell, speaking of "causes" and "effects" characterized an earlier stage in the development of science. Nowadays, the role of causation has been replaced by mathematical laws of nature, which enable us to describe abstract or *functional* relationships between the states of physical systems at different points in time. Instead of saying that the pitcher causes the forward motion of the ball, we should simply describe the state of the ball at each moment in time as a function of its earlier trajectory, together with a description of the fields of force through which it is moving. We don't find the words "cause" or "effect" (or any causative verbs, like "push" or "pull") in the formulation of modern laws of nature. Instead, all we find are arrangements of physical quantities in space and time.

Challenge 2: Causation Requires Necessary Connections between Separate Existences   David Hume argued that the notion of *cause* is inseparably connected to a kind of necessity: causal or nomological (law-governed) necessity. Whenever we suppose that one event A has caused an event B, we must suppose that B followed A with some sort of necessity. If we believe in a causal connection, we cannot also believe that B *just happened* to follow A. Effects are the sort of thing that in some sense *must* follow their causes.

Some philosophers, including Elizabeth Anscombe (Anscombe 1975), have argued that Hume is somewhat overstating the strength of the connection that must hold between cause and effect. It does seem possible for *A* to have caused *B*, even given the supposition that it was not *impossible* for *A* to occur without being followed by *B*. A provocative remark by a speaker, for example, might cause the listener to respond in anger, even if it had been possible for the listener to have repressed the emotional reaction. Nonetheless, Hume is certainly right that a causal connection implies some kind of non-accidental connection between the cause and effect. The occurrence of the cause ordinarily increases the probability of the occurrence of the event. In addition, in normal cases, the cause supplies a necessary condition for the effect, in the sense that the effect couldn't have occurred in those same circumstances in the absence of the cause. A world utterly devoid of such non-accidental connections altogether would be a world without causation.

Hume urged us to reject the very possibility of any such non-accidental connection between logically distinct events. He offered two reasons for this rejection. First, Hume relied upon imagination or conception as an infallible guide to possibility. It is always possible to imagine the cause without the effect, or the effect without the cause. We can imagine an egg that fails to fry, despite the application of heat, or one that does fry despite the absence of heat. In fact, we could imagine eggs never frying when heated, or always frying when cold. Therefore, we have conclusive reason to reject any sort of non-accidental connection between separate events, and so any instances of cause or effect.

Second, Hume pointed out that we can never directly observe the supposed causal connection between the cause and the effect. All we ever see is the repetition of a certain pattern, the "constant conjunction" of one event's being regularly followed by another. We can observe heat being applied to eggs, and we can observe eggs' taking on the color and consistency of fried eggs, but we can never see the connection between the two events. Hence, we are not justified in believing that there is any such connection. We should believe only in the constant conjunction, not in the invisible linkage supposed to accompany each case.

3.1.2   Arguments for Causes

Argument 1: Appeals to Common Sense, Human Agency   As we've said, common sense seems to endorse the reality of causes. If Hume's theory of rationality or knowledge rules out belief in causation in ordinary cases, so much the worse for his theories! We know that rocks break windows, that heat melts ice, and that pushing causes motion.

Elizabeth Anscombe (1975) argued that, contrary to Hume's claim, we can in fact observe causal connections. According to Anscombe, we do so all the time. I can observe the guard's tackling of the quarterback: I see the one player knock the other to the ground. These causal facts are as much a matter of *direct* observation as are the purely qualitative facts that Hume admits that we observe (e.g., the color of the quarterback's jersey).

In addition, as George Berkeley pointed out in the eighteenth century, anticipating Hume (Berkeley 2009; orig. pub. 1710), we have first-hand knowledge of causation, from *the inside*. We are each agents, who intentionally bring about certain changes in our bodies and our environments. We can even produce changes within our own minds, through acts of imagination or through the inner voice of conscious thought. To deny this is to undermine the very possibility of reasoning, and so of philosophy itself.

Argument 2: Practice of the Special Sciences   Bertrand Russell pointed out that the fundamental laws of physics do not mention causes or effects. The philosopher of science Nancy Cartwright (Cartwright 1983, 1994) has argued that, taken in this pure form, the fundamental laws of physics lie to us. In practice, physicists combine these statements with a host of auxiliary principles that do make explicit use of causal language. What the fundamental laws of nature in their pure form tell us is how basic particles would behave when under the influence of certain forces only, that is, when not otherwise interfered with. In practice, working scientists make use of various *phenomenological* laws, laws adjusted with a variety of "fudge" factors, designed to take into account the causal influence of factors like friction that we cannot entirely isolate our experimental subjects from.

In addition, in all of the special sciences, including chemistry, geology, astronomy, medicine, and economics, the laws of nature do invoke explicitly causal notions. Medical researchers, for example, search for the causes of cancer or the effects of red meat consumption. Astronomers seek the cause of the formation of stars or galaxies, and economists investigate the effects of changes in tax or trade policy.

Argument 3: Needed for an Adequate Account of Knowledge and Semantics   In 1963, Edmund Gettier wrote a very influential little article entitled "Is Justified True Belief Knowledge?" (Gettier 1963). Gettier provided several thought-experiments which seem to demonstrate that an adequate analysis of knowledge must take into account the causal connections between justified true beliefs and the things and conditions to which they refer. Suppose, for example, that I believe accurately that Jones owns either a Toyota or a Honda. Suppose, further, that I have excellent reasons for thinking that I have often seen Jones drive a Toyota, and I know that, if he owns a Toyota, then it follows logically that he owns either a Toyota or a Honda. Now, suppose that Jones owns a Honda and not a Toyota (having just traded in his Toyota Camry). Did I know that he owned either a Toyota or a Honda? I had true and reasonable belief in this proposition, but it seems clear that I didn't know it. Gettier offered no positive account of knowledge, and he didn't mention causation at all. However, many later epistemologists have concluded that knowledge in such a case as Gettier described requires a cause-and-effect connection between my justified true belief and the relevant fact: I should first gain the knowledge (through sense perception or testimony) that Jones owns a Honda, and then infer from that he owns a Toyota or a Honda.

In the subsequent 50 years, epistemologists have developed causal accounts of perceptual knowledge, of testimony, and of memory. In perception, there must be a causal connection between the qualities of the objects being perceived and the sensory state of the perceiver, if there is to be a real difference between perceiving and merely having a veridical hallucination. Consider the difference between seeing a rose and seeing the projected image of a rose on a screen that is interposed between oneself and a real rose. The difference remains even if, in the second case, the image produces sensory experiences that perfectly match the occluded rose. Causation plays a similarly indispensable role in making the difference between real memories and pseudo-memories. If there were no such thing as causation, much (if not all) empirical knowledge would be impossible.

In addition, philosophers of language have found causation an indispensable tool in accounting for the meaning of human language. Referring expressions, like names, demonstratives ("this" and "that"), and some definite descriptions ("the man drinking champagne" or "the beer in the fridge") refer to things in the world through a chain of causal connections that link the use of the expression with its referent. (See Donnellan 1966; Kripke 1980; Evans 1982; Kaplan 1989.)

For example, in Saul Kripke's theory of proper names, a proper name like "Moses" or "Kurt Gödel" refers to one person rather than another because of a causally connected historical practice of using that proper name, with the name linked to the bearer by an original user through sensory perception, and passed on to subsequent users through the acts of linguistic communication between speaker and listener (or author and reader). Kripke demonstrates that the true bearer of a name is not typically determined by finding someone or something that uniquely satisfies some associated description (or that best satisfies some bundle of descriptions). It could easily turn out, for example, that the real Moses or the real Homer satisfies few of the descriptions we typically associate with the name, or that someone else actually satisfies those descriptions. Suppose, for example, that all I know about the person named "Kurt Gödel" is that he is the one who discovered the incompleteness of arithmetic. It is conceivable that we could discover that, in fact, it was someone else, with an entirely different name, who was the true discoverer of that fact. The reference of the proper name follows a causal track back to its original uses, not the satisfaction of this or that description associated now with the name.

3.2   Causal Dispositions and Conditionals

How is change possible? Parmenides, a very early Greek philosopher who lived in Elea in Italy, issued some famous challenges against the possibility of change. One of his challenges was causal in nature, based on the following dilemma. Change involves the appearance of some new thing. Does this new thing come into being from the realm of being, or from the realm of non-being? It cannot come into being from being, since if it were already in the realm of being it would already have existed and so could not be new. But it cannot come into being from non-being, since nothing comes from nothing.

Aristotle responded to this challenge by introducing (in his *Physics* and *Metaphysics*) the distinction between *actuality* and *potentiality*. Change involves something new becoming actual, but this new actuality comes into being from the realm of potentiality, not from sheer nothingness. In other words, when something changes, there always exists something before the change with the potentiality of undergoing that specific kind of change. Change doesn't come from nowhere.

Change is always preceded by causal *powers and dispositions*. For example, the breaking of a window by a stone is preceded both by the window's fragility and by the stone's causal power, its power to break glass of this kind.

It is somewhat misleading to speak (as we just did) of potentiality and actuality as representing separate realms of being, as though nothing could be both a potentiality and an actuality. In fact, all potentialities are themselves actual, as potentialities. The fragile glass is actually fragile, but to be actually fragile is to be potentially broken. Everything is actually something, and some things also have the potentiality for being something different from what they actually are. A fragile window is potentially but not actually broken. There is also such a thing as being potentially fragile: for example, a form of plastic might be durable at room temperature but fragile at extremely low temperatures. But to be potentially fragile is to have some actual disposition that is two steps removed from being actually broken.

Potentiality is always defined in relation to actuality. All potentialities are potentialities to be actually something or other. It wouldn't make sense to talk of a potentiality that couldn't be actualized, but there might be such a thing as an actuality that couldn't become merely potential. (Aristotle thought that God was such a necessary being.) Actuality is at least conceptually fundamental; that is, there are no other concepts that we use to *build* the concept of actuality. The concept of actuality is like the concept of blueness, not like the concept of blue-or-red-ness.

There is a dichotomy between two kinds of properties: those properties that have to do only with how a thing is actually, and those properties that also have to do with the ways a thing could potentially be. The first class of properties are called *categorical*, and the second class *dispositional*. Being square, for example, seems a plausible case of a categorical property, since to describe a surface as square is to describe how it is actually, without saying anything about what it might do or become. Fragility or flammability, in contrast, are clearly dispositional, carrying implications about what its bearer might do or become.

Dispositional properties are associated with conditionals, with statements of an "if ..., then ..." form. The twentieth-century English philosopher Gilbert Ryle proposed, in his book *The Concept of Mind* (Ryle 1949), that dispositions are nothing but the property of being the subject of a true if/ then statement. For example, according to Ryle to be fragile is simply to be something that would break if struck. To be irritable is to be someone that would become angry if provoked.

Whether Ryle was right or not about reducing dispositions to conditionals, there is obviously some important connection between the two. If we are going to get to the bottom of dispositions, we will have to achieve some clarity about the semantics of the relevant conditional statements. The first thing to note is that the kind of conditionals that we need are expressed in English (and in similar natural languages) by means of what is called the "subjunctive" mood, rather than the indicative mood. The subjunctive mood is the grammatical form we choose when expressing *counterfactual* conditionals, that is, conditionals whose "if"-clause (antecedent clause) is known to be contrary to actual fact.

Consider, for example, the following pair of conditionals (from David K. Lewis 1973):

(1) If Oswald did not shoot JFK in 1963, then JFK is still alive today.
(2) If Oswald had not shot JFK in 1963, then JFK would still be alive today.

Statement (2) is in the subjunctive mood. Using (2) would suggest that one believed that Oswald did in fact shoot JFK in 1963. Statement (1), in contrast, is in the indicative mood and has no such suggestion. Suppose that you think that Oswald shot JFK in 1963 and that he was solely responsible for JFK's death. In that case, it is very unlikely that you would agree with statement (1): you know perfectly well that JFK is not in fact alive today, and so if, contrary to your belief, Oswald did not shoot him, someone else must have. In contrast, you might agree with statement (2), depending on what you judge JFK's dispositions for longevity in 1963 to have been. The truth or falsity of (2) has nothing to do with whether JFK is in fact alive today, but only with his dispositions for long life in 1963 at the time of his assassination.

Subjunctive conditionals are not truth-functional compounds of their constituent clauses. Most of us agree, for example, that both the antecedent (the "if"-clause) of (2) is false (since Oswald did shoot Kennedy then) and that the consequent (the "then"-clause) of (2) is also false, since JFK is obviously not still alive. Nonetheless, some of us might think that (2) as a whole is true and others that it is false, depending on judgments about JFK's health and various other risks of death he might have subsequently faced. Given this lack of truth-functionality, the truth-value of subjunctive conditionals is not going to be reducible to the truth-values of categorical sentences in any simple way.

What then are the truthmakers for predications of dispositional properties and for the closely related subjunctive or counterfactual conditionals?

3.3   Four Metaphysical Theories

If there are such things as causes, there must be causal powers and dispositions. As we have seen, there is a close connection between predicating causal powers and dispositions and the truth of certain subjunctive or counterfactual conditionals. In addition, both causal powers and counterfactual conditionals seem to be linked to the laws of nature, especially the causal laws. For example, if some glass has the disposition or potentiality to break, then the laws of nature that govern the behavior of the particles and fields making up the glass ought to dictate that the glass will undergo certain changes when struck. Similarly, the truth of a counterfactual conditional has something to do with the derivability of the consequent of the conditional from its antecedent, together with the laws of nature and certain other relevant facts.

Take a subjunctive conditional like (3):

(3) If the white of this egg were heated, it would congeal.

In order for (3) to be true, we should be able to derive the proposition that the egg white congeals from the antecedent (the heating of the egg white), together with certain facts about the internal structure of the egg white and its current environment, and with the laws of nature that govern the evolution of the relevant physical and chemical systems.

Laws of nature, in turn, are obviously connected with the observation of certain patterns in nature. We believe in the law of gravity because we observe massive bodies accelerating at a rate that fits (at least approximately) the rate determined by the gravitational constant. We believe in the laws of chemistry because we consistently find chemical compounds changing in response to environmental conditions in a way that is consistent with those laws.

Thus, we have four kinds of phenomena – causal dispositions, counterfactual conditional truths, laws of nature, and patterns of actual changes – that are obviously connected. In fact, there is some hope that, given any one or two of these classes of phenomena, we could logically derive the truths in the other classes. If this is right, we can ask, which of the four kinds of dispositional phenomena is metaphysically fundamental?

1. Powers and dispositions only
2. Conditionals only
3. Laws of nature only
4. None of these three are fundamental: all can be derived from the patterns of purely categorical fact

There are thus four metaphysical theories, one corresponding to each of these possible answers: Powerism, Hypotheticalism, Nomism, and Neo-Humeism.

Before considering the merits and demerits of these four theories, we should stop to ask, What do we mean by "fundamental"? Historically, metaphysicians have been interested in discovering not only what is the case but which facts are truly fundamental. Let's consider some examples of what are widely considered to be non-fundamental facts. Consider the following pairs of statements:

(4a) There was a crowd in the marketplace.
(4b) The following 100 people were in the marketplace: P1, P2, ...
(5a) There is a shadow cast by the tree on the garden wall.
(5b) Part of the garden wall is not illuminated by the sun, due to the tree's obstruction of the light.
(6a) A spot of light is moving across the fence.
(6b) A spotlight is illuminating different parts of the fence at different times.

Let's suppose that all six statements are true. It seems unlikely that there are six distinct and metaphysically fundamental facts here. Crowds, shadows, and moving spots of light do not seem to be basic elements of reality, in the same way that substantial material objects are. It seems natural to say that the "b" truths above are more fundamental or closer to being fundamental than are the "a" truths.

There have been at least four theories about what this metaphysical fundamentality consists in:

1   The appeal to truthmaker theory. A fundamental truth is one that simply asserts the existence of a single, unique truthmaker. Non-fundamental truths take some other form: either having greater logical complexity, or by making some apparently simple assertion that requires the cooperation of many distinct truthmakers.

2   Grounding as a primitive relation (Fine 1994, 2001; Schaffer 2009; Rosen 2010). The fundamental truths are those that are not grounded in any other truths. Or, alternatively, the fundamental entities are those not grounded in more fundamental entities, and fundamental truths assert the existence of only fundamental entities.

3   The fundamental truths "cut nature at the joints," as Plato put it in the *Phaedrus* (265e) (see Sider 2012: 1–5, 44–66). That is to say, fundamental truths perspicuously express the true or real structure of the world, and others do not. For example, you might think that there are no deep facts of the matter about what counts as a cloud, even though it might be true that there are clouds in the sky. On the other hand, you might think there are deep facts of the matter about how water molecules are distributed in the sky. A representation of where the water molecules are located that didn't mention clouds at all would be a more adequate representation of the world's structure than a representation that mentioned clouds but no water molecules (or still more fundamental particles). The cloud truths, on this view, don't cut nature at the joints as well as the water molecule truths, and thus the cloud truths are less fundamental than the water molecule truths.

4   Only the fundamental truths are really or strictly true. "Derived truths" are really false, mere useful fictions. In some cases, a so-called *derived truth* may be used to express real truths, in which case we can offer a paraphrase of the literally false statement in terms of real or fundamental truths. In other cases, such a paraphrase may be impossible, but the derived truth may, despite its falsity, be a useful fiction, close enough to the truth in practical terms to make little or no difference outside of the context of philosophical inquiry.

We will focus in depth on the two most popular theories: Powerism and Neo-Humeism. Before getting to them, we will explain briefly why we are setting aside the other two, Hypotheticalism and Nomism.

3.3.1   Against Hypotheticalism

Hypotheticalism takes the fundamental truths about dispositions to be subjunctive conditionals. There are several reasons for rejecting this view.

First, there are truthmaker worries. How does the truthmaker of the whole conditional relate to the entities that are mentioned in the antecedent and the consequent? If we say that the truthmaker consists in a combination of properties of the participants, then we have adopted a form of Powerism. So, the hypotheticalist must deny this. But then there must be some mysterious and brute connection between the truthmaker of the conditional and the participants mentioned in its antecedent or consequent. To be concrete, let's consider a simple subjunctive conditional:

(7) If the glass vase were struck, it would break.

What is the relation between the vase itself and the truthmaker of (7)? If we suppose that the two are utterly separate, then we would have introduced a mysterious and brute connection between the two. Alternatively, if we suppose that the truthmaker of the conditional is the vase or some attribute of the vase, then it seems that the most likely candidate would be the predication of some disposition or power to the vase, which would lead us to Powerism, denying that the conditional really is the fundamental truth.

Second, it seems that powers and dispositions are not reducible to conditionals. Consider the relation between the conditional (7) and the predication of a corresponding disposition in (8):

(8) The glass vase is fragile.

There are four reasons for thinking that the two statements are not equivalent in all circumstances, which would have to be the case if we were going to ground the truth of (8) in the truth of (7). These four reasons have been given odd-sounding names: finks, reverse finks, mimics, and masks.

1   Fragility can be finked (Martin 1994; Lewis 1997; Lowe 2010). In this case, we have a vase that is fragile (so (8) is true), but it is false that the vase would break if struck, since a mechanism is in place that would alter the vase, making it no longer fragile, whenever something threatens to strike it (so (7) is false).

2   Fragility can be reverse finked. Now, we have a vase that is not fragile ((8) is false), but it would break if struck, since a mechanism is in place that would make the vase fragile whenever an event of striking the vase is imminent (making the conditional (7) true).

3   Fragility can be mimicked (Johnston 1992; Bird 1998). In this case, the vase is not fragile ((8) is false), but a mechanism is in place that would use a powerful sonic beam to break the vase whenever it is struck.

4   Fragility can be masked. The vase is fragile ((8) is true), but it is filled with an adhesive plastic in such a way as to prevent its breaking if struck ((7) is false).

3.3.2   Against Nomism

In the 1970s, three philosophers independently proposed that the laws of nature are fundamental, grounding both the attributions of dispositions and the truth of counterfactual conditionals. The view came to be known as the Dretske-Armstrong-Tooley account of laws (Dretske 1977; Armstrong 1983; Tooley 1977, 1987). If we know the laws of nature, we can decide when to attribute a power or disposition to something: a thing has the disposition to become F in circumstances C just in case it has some intrinsic properties, and the laws of nature dictate that a thing with those properties must (or at least might) become F in circumstances C.

Similarly, the laws of nature provide a basis for deciding the truth of many, if not all, subjunctive or counterfactual conditionals. Suppose that object V has never been and never will be struck, and we would like to evaluate the counterfactual conditional: if V were struck, it would break. We can look at the facts about V's intrinsic structure and the relevant features of V's environment and express these in a lengthy description of V. We then put together the following set of premises: the description of V and its environment, the generalizations that have the status of laws of nature, and the statement "V is struck." If this set of premises logically entails the statement "V breaks" (or something equivalent to this statement), then the conditional is true, and otherwise it is false.

What exactly is a law of nature? Every law of nature takes the form of a generalization: a law of nature dictates that every situation of one kind is accompanied or followed by a situation of a second kind. For example, the situation of being subjected to a certain force and having a certain mass is always accompanied by an acceleration in the direction of the force, an acceleration that is proportional to the ratio of the force and the mass (as dictated by Newton's law of motion, $F = ma$). It is also a law of nature that the gravitational force between two bodies is a function of their masses and the distance between them, a function determined by a certain constant (the gravitational constant).

However, it is clear that not every generalization is a law of nature. It may be, for example, that the name of every town in Wales has more than four letters. However, this is clearly not a law of nature: nothing prevents our introducing a three-lettered name. Similarly, it may be the case that nowhere in the universe is there a ball of pure aluminum weighing more than 100 tons, but nothing prevents our making such a ball.

This distinction is crucial, because the dispositions of objects and the truth-values of counterfactual conditionals depend on the laws of nature and not on accidental generalizations. Suppose, for example, that vases of a certain very valuable variety have never been broken and never will be. This accidental generalization would not legitimate our attributing the disposition of extreme durability to particular vases of that variety, nor would it license our asserting that any such vase, if struck, would not break.

Nomists propose that it is a basic or fundamental fact that certain generalizations are laws of nature and others are not. The status of being a law of nature is not conferred on the generalization by anything, but is simply a brute fact about it.

What's the difference between Powerism and Nomism? In both cases there is a real distinction between laws and mere accidental generalizations, and in both cases it is the laws plus certain categorical facts that determine the truth-values of conditionals. The difference lies in the way in which the laws of nature are supposed to be true. For Powerists, a law of nature is lawlike because of an *internal* relation between the properties involved, because of the powers and dispositions that those properties naturally confer on their bearers. For Powerists, it is of the very essence of the relevant properties that they be lawfully connected, as cause and effect. For Nomists, in contrast, the existence of a law consists in an *external* relation among the universals or properties.

The distinction between internal and external relations was first proposed by the British analytical philosopher G. E. Moore (1873–1958):

> R is an *internal* relation if and only if for every x and y, whether R holds between x and y depends only on the intrinsic properties of x and y (as separate individuals). (Moore 1922: 276–309)

Here are some traditional examples of internal and external relations. The relation of being twice as tall as is an internal relation between people, since height is an intrinsic property of people (a property that concerns how each person is, in himself or herself). Once we've fixed all of the intrinsic properties (including the height) of two people, the presence or absence of the being twice as tall relation will also be determined. In contrast, the property of being two miles apart is not internal. I can know all there is to know about the intrinsic qualities of two objects without knowing whether they are two miles apart or not.

In order to talk about internal and external relations among properties, we will have to introduce *second-order* properties: properties of properties. Then we can distinguish between the intrinsic and extrinsic properties of a given natural property. The property of being a property is a second-order property, as are such properties as being a spatial property, being a quality, having instances, belonging only to material things.

It seems reasonable to suppose that all of the intrinsic properties of a property are essential to it, in the sense that they are properties that the property could not lose or fail to have in any possible situation. If so, the difference between Nomists and Powerists comes down to this: for

Powerists, the laws of nature (at least, the causal laws) are all necessary, while for the Nomists, they are all contingent. That is, for Powerists, the laws of nature could not be other than they are, while for Nomists, the laws of nature could have been completely different.

This gives rise to three immediate commitments that raise the cost of Nomism as a theory:

1   We have to posit a new kind of external relation between universals, one whose holding constitutes a law of nature. In addition, this external relation's holding cannot itself be caused or scientifically explained, at least if scientific explanation must appeal to laws of nature.

2   Properties must themselves be fundamental entities, not reducible to facts about their instances. (Nomists must embrace the sort of realism about *universals* that we will discuss in the next chapter.)

3   We have to postulate a brute necessary connection between the existence of a law of nature and the truth of the corresponding accidental generalization. Bas van Fraassen labeled this the "inference problem" (van Fraassen 1989: 38–39). Why is it that just because the properties in a generalization stand in the *nomic* or law-making relation to each other, the generalization must be true? Why do particular situations have to conform to the law? The Nomists can have no informative answer to these questions. It is just a brute fact that laws of nature must be "obeyed" by their particular instances.

In addition, Nomists can't explain our preference for theories that posit relatively simple or elegant laws of nature. Since the lawfulness of each generalization is just a brute, unexplainable fact, there is no room in Nomism to offer any explanation for why the laws of nature should conform to any overall pattern, such as simplicity. Thus, an important part of our scientific practice is left without any justification.

3.4   Neo-Humeism

We now turn to the first of our two major theories of powers and dispositions: Neo-Humeism. On this view, no laws, no dispositions or powers, and no subjunctive conditionals are among the fundamental truths of the world. The only fundamental truths are categorical, truths about the distribution of qualities and other categorical features across the landscape of space and time.

Why is the position called "Neo-Humeism" or "Neo-Humeanism"? It is named after the eighteenth-century Scottish philosopher David Hume, who denied that there were any "necessary connections" among "separate existences" in the world. According to Hume, all *necessity* is logical, linguistic, or conceptual, not *out there* in the world of things. This idea of Hume's was revived in the twentieth century by Frank Ramsey (Ramsey 1978) and David K. Lewis (Lewis 1980, 1986, 1994).

The view we are discussing is called "Neo-Humeist" rather than "Humeist" because it diverges from Hume's own thinking in several respects. First of all, Hume himself was a skeptic, and especially skeptical toward metaphysical claims, while the Neo-Humeists offer their theory as a metaphysical account. Second, one could naturally interpret Hume as denying that causation or powers exist at all, while the Neo-Humeists are trying to give an account of causation and powers. They are trying to reduce these things to facts about the qualitative mosaic of the world; they are not denying the truth of propositions about causation, laws of nature, powers, or subjunctive conditionals.

The central task of Neo-Humeism is to provide an account of the difference between laws of nature and accidental generalizations. A law is an axiom of the best scientific theory of the world: the theory that has the best combination of simplicity, accuracy, and generality. A good scientific theory is one that encompasses as many particular facts as possible, with as few exceptions as possible, in the smallest and shortest set of axioms as possible.

For the Neo-Humeist, the fundamental facts consist only of the occurrent, categorical, or qualitative features of things, together with their arrangement in space and time. These features are not inherently powerful or dispositional. Instead, Neo-Humeists move from the qualitative mosaic to the laws of nature, and then from laws of nature to the truths of conditionals, attributions of powers, and particular causal connections. In contrast, the Powerists take attributions of powers to be fundamental and derive the truths of laws of nature and causal connections from them. Figure 3.1 illustrates the different structures of the two accounts:

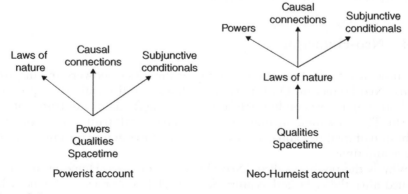

Figure 3.1

3.4.1   Advantages of Neo-Humeism

There are two main advantages to Neo-Humeism.

First, it is ontologically quite simple. There's no need to posit primitive powers, dispositions, or nomological or hypothetical facts. The fundamental facts are all categorical and actual, with no necessary implications about what could, would, or must occur.

Second, it justifies our preference for simpler theories in science. It is at least *prima facie* plausible to believe that the simplest generalizations that comprise all known data will resemble the simplest generalizations that comprise all particular fact, whether observed or unobserved. A simpler theory of the laws is more likely to be true simply because simplicity is one of the factors that makes a generalization be a law.

3.4.2   Objections to Neo-Humeism

There are five principal objections to Neo-Humeism: the objection from scientific realism, the problem of induction, the objection from "small" possible worlds, the problem of accounting for the linkage between particular causes and their effects, and the theory's difficulty in accounting for the asymmetrical direction of causation.

Objection 1: The Objection from Scientific Realism   Modern science, as it has developed in the last 300 years, seems to provide us with knowledge. Through science, we know a great deal more about how the natural world works than we once did. In particular, natural science provides us with insight about the natures of physical things: why they act as they do, and what is physically possible and impossible. These facts about the natures of things and the scope of physical possibility we encode in the assertions of the laws of nature.

If we take the pronouncements of scientists at face value, then, at least for the most part, we must take the growing body of scientific knowledge to be knowledge of nature as it really is. In contrast, if we were to suppose that all scientific theories, including theories about the very small, the very large, and the very old, are really about our own practices and preferences, then we would have to discount quite radically our pretensions to knowing and understanding nature.

Scientific realism is the view that we should take science at face value, as constituting an impressive body of knowledge about the propensities of nature. Scientific realists don't have to suppose that we have infallible knowledge, or that the practices of science are never influenced by extraneous social and cultural factors. However, they do suppose that our established scientific enterprises do succeed with some reliability at uncovering truths that are entirely about the non-human world. Neo-Humeists have to deny that this is ever so, a view that comes at some cost, given the apparent success of science and the technologies it engenders.

There is at least some significant tension between Neo-Humeism and scientific realism, since Neo-Humeism makes the facts about what the laws of nature are depend on our own practices and preferences, since whether a generalization counts as a genuine *law* depends on whether it would be part of what we would count as the *best* scientific theory of the world, given an accurate inventory of all of the particular facts. Therefore, when we *discover* that it is a law of nature that the force of gravity is inversely proportional to the square of the distance between two bodies, what we come to believe is at least in part about our own preferences for theories of a certain kind and not entirely about the physical world itself.

The subjectivity or conventionality of laws enters in at least two ways, on the Neo-Humeist account. First, there is the problem of defining exactly what counts as the *simplest* theory of nature. There are a number of different ways to measure *simplicity*, and none of them applies to every possible inter-theory comparison. Other things being equal, a postulate is simpler if it involves fewer constants or parameters (like the speed of light, Planck's constant, or the gravitational constant). At the same time, a theory also counts as simpler if its basic vocabulary is smaller, making reference to fewer basic properties or forces. (A theory that reduces the four fundamental forces to just three is thereby simpler.) In addition, a theory is simpler if it postulates fewer entities, a small number of fundamental particles. These various criteria of simplicity can conflict with each other. Making an overall judgment of which theory is simpler in cases of conflict can thus appear to involve a more or less arbitrary preference on our part.

Second, simplicity is not the only criterion. We are also supposed to prefer theories that encompass a wider domain of fact, as well as theories that deviate as little as possible from universality – theories that minimize the number of exceptions. These criteria are even harder to apply when dealing with probabilistic theories, since now we should prefer theories that make actual facts as probable as possible, and that minimize cases of extreme improbability. Once again, these three criteria (simplicity, scope, and accuracy) will often conflict. We will have to choose between the simpler theory and the theory with the wider scope, or between a wider scope and fewer exceptions, or between fewer exceptions and greater simplicity. There is no way to get nature herself to make these choices for us – we must simply consult our own preferences, in something like the way we might choose between different flavors of ice cream.

From the point of scientific realism, the laws of nature are what they are, independently of our preferences. Neo-Humeists have to deny this plausible assumption. If our preferences were different, a different theory (postulating different laws) might be the *best* theory (relative to those new preferences). If so, then the actual laws of nature depend on our arbitrary preferences concerning theory choice, which seems an uncomfortably radical conclusion.

It is possible for Neo-Humeists to escape this consequence. Following David K. Lewis (1994: 481), they could "rigidify" their definition of the *laws of nature*. Instead of saying that in each possible scenario S, the laws of nature in S are the axioms of the theory that people would (if S were actual) judge to be the best, Neo-Humeists could instead stipulate that the laws of nature in S would be the axioms of the theory that we (in the actual world, with our actual world) judge to be the best theory, given the actual *mosaic* of particular facts in scenario S. That is, we rigidly build our own present, actual preferences into the definition of the "best" theory, and then use that rigidified conception of what's best in defining the laws of nature. Now, the fact that our scientific-theory preference might have been different in different possible scenarios (or at different times in the past or future) is no longer relevant to the laws of nature in those scenarios. It would only be relevant to what people in those scenarios would *call* "the laws of nature."

If we rigidify the reference of "law of nature" in this way, then the fact that at other times, in other cultures, or in possible scenarios, scientists have different standards of good theories is completely irrelevant. The only standards that matter are those that we have right now, in the actual situation. The point is similar to one that Abraham Lincoln once made, in the form of a riddle. Lincoln asked, "How many legs would a horse have, if we called the tail of a horse a 'leg'?" The correct answer is, four. Horses would remain four-legged animals, regardless of how we might come to use the word "leg." The anatomical structure of horses does not depend on how we use English words. Similarly, the Neo-Humeist can argue, the laws of nature do not depend on how we use the phrase "good theory."

Nonetheless, the fact remains that there is something problematically anthropocentric (people-centered) about the Neo-Humeist's account of the laws of nature. Why, from the point of view of metaphysics, should we treat these generalizations as more important or significant than those, if the only intelligible difference makes some reference to our own arbitrary standards of theory preference? Although Lewis's rigidification makes the laws of nature modally independent of our preferences (in the sense that they wouldn't have varied had our standards been different), the laws remain *explanatorily* dependent on our preferences: what *makes* these generalizations laws of nature is in part our actual, current preferences.

In addition, if we take the rigidification seriously, it seems that our attunement to the actual laws of nature is a matter of sheer, dumb luck: the fact that our actual standards happen to fit the standards in terms of which "law of nature" is defined. As a result, our reliability as detectors of the laws of nature is very fragile or insecure: had our scientific standards or preferences been different than what they are, we wouldn't have been attracted to the real laws of nature (rigidly defined by the practices and preferences of the actual). This would seem to undermine our ability to claim that we know what the laws of nature are like even in the actual world. Real knowledge must be grounded in a secure and robust reliability at finding the relevant truth, not in some lucky coincidence.

Objection 2: The Problem of Induction   In order to learn from our past experience, we have to assume that what we have not yet observed (including all future events) will be relevantly similar to what we have observed. The task of justifying or defending this assumption is known as "the problem of induction." According to the Neo-Humeist, any pattern or distribution of qualities in space and time is possible. The vast majority of these distributions are very chaotic, obeying no simple generalizations at all. In fact, the ratio of chaotic to orderly patterns in a universe as large and complex as ours is a number of absolutely staggering size. Even if we restrict ourselves to patterns that conform to the observed generalizations within the space-time bubble that represents our actual history so far, the number of possible extensions of that history in which the observed order breaks down vastly outnumbers those in which things continue in much the same way.

There is a principle of probabilistic reasoning, the Principle of Indifference, which dictates that the probabilities of two hypotheses should be proportional to the number of possibilities in which each of the two hypotheses would be true. Applying the Principle of Indifference to the problem of induction, given Neo-Humeist assumptions about possibility, leads to a catastrophe of skepticism. We would have to include that the probability that any generalization we have observed so far would continue to hold just in the near future and in our local neighborhood would be so small as to be negligible. This would be true even of the probability that those observed generalizations would continue to hold with some approximation.

Here's an illustration. Suppose I know that an urn contains millions of black balls for every white ball, and that each ball has an equal chance of being selected on each occasion. Now, suppose that I pick five balls, and each turns out to be white. Will that increase my expectation that the next ball will also be white? No, it shouldn't. It was very unlikely that I should pick five white balls in a row, but it is still more unlikely (by a wide margin) that the sixth ball should also be white. Similarly, no matter how orderly the universe appears to be so far, the Neo-Humeist would seem to have overwhelmingly good reason to expect that future observations will deviate widely from the rigorous patterns seen so far.

It's as if, for the Neo-Humeist, all possible spacetime mosaics have been assembled at random, and our actual world-mosaic has been randomly drawn from this urn. Even if some simple pattern has been realized in the so-far observed part of that mosaic, this does not increase at all the probability that the unobserved part fits the same pattern, since there is no real connection between the two parts.

In response, the Neo-Humeist must simply assert that it is not reasonable to apply the Principle of Indifference in this way. It must be something like a self-evident axiom of reason that we prefer simpler theories, other things being equal, even if the number of possible universes that conform to such simple theories is vanishingly small.

Such an appeal to a new first principle is a permissible move for the Neo-Humeist, but it must come at a significant cost. If the Powerist can account for the rationality of induction without such a new principle, that should count in favor of the Powerist theory.

Objection 3: The "Small Worlds" Objection   It seems possible for one event to cause another, even if these two events were the only events in the world's history. This is because our notion of causation is that of a local or *intrinsic* fact, involving just the cause and the effect (and, at most, their immediate environment). It just doesn't seem reasonable to suppose that whether an event A is the cause of event B could depend on facts about the occurrence of other events remote in time and space from A and B. And yet this is just what Neo-Humeism entails: according to that theory, the existence of a causal connection between two events depends on the world's laws of nature, and the actuality of those laws simply consists in the existence of a global pattern of succession, across the whole of space and time.

Objection 4: The Problem of Causal Linkage   According to Neo-Humeism, whether one event is the immediate cause of another event depends on just three things: the internal qualities of the two events, their relation to each other in space and time, and the actual laws of nature. However, there are a number of apparently possible cases in which it seems that these three factors are not sufficient for the existence of a real causal connection. These apparent counter-examples to the Neo-Humeist theory all involve an element of *over-determination* of the effect by a collection of possible causes. Given the laws of nature and the proximity of the potential causes, any one of the potential causes would be sufficient to produce the effect.

There are two cases to consider, depending on whether the causal laws in question are deterministic or probabilistic. A deterministic law of nature dictates that, if the potential causes are present, a suitable effect must occur. A probabilistic law requires only that there be some finite probability of the effect's occurrence, with some probability lower than 100%. For example, in some interpretations of quantum mechanics, there is a 50% probability that a radium atom of a certain kind (isotope 226) will result in a decay event within 1600 years.

In the deterministic case, let's suppose that a possible effect E is over-determined by two possible causes, C_1 and C_2. That is, there are two deterministic laws of nature, one of which dictates the events C_1 type are always followed by E-type events, and another of which dictates that C_2-type events are also followed by E-type events. Let's consider a world in which all three events occur, C_1, C_2, and E. It seems that there are three possibilities. First, it could be that the events C_1 and C_2 in such a case somehow cooperated in producing the E event. Second, it could be that the C_1 event caused the E event alone, pre-empting the disposition of the C_2 event to cause such an event. Third, it could be that the C_2 event alone caused the E event, pre-empting the action of the C_1 event. However, the Neo-Humeists cannot acknowledge the possibility of the second or third case. They must suppose that all cases of over-determination are cases of cooperative causation.

The problem is perhaps clearer in a scenario involving probabilistic laws. Now let's suppose that each of the two potential causes, C_1 and C_2, has just a 50% chance of producing an E-type event, and let's suppose that in the scenario in question an E-type event does in fact occur. When both C_1 and C_2 events occur, the probabilistic laws will dictate that there is a 75% chance that an E event will follow. Now, it seems very clear that, when an E event does occur, there was a one-third chance that it was caused only by the C_1 event, a one-third chance that it was caused only by the C_2 event, and a one-third chance that it was jointly caused by the two of them. However, the Neo-Humeists must again deny that the first two cases are possible at all. They must say that, when the E-type event does occur, it is certain (with probability 100%) that it was caused by both potential causes, since there is nothing occurring in such a world that could discriminate between this possibility and the other two.

Objection 5: The Problem of Accounting for the Asymmetric Direction of Causation   Causation has an asymmetric direction: for A to cause B is something entirely different from B's causing A. Neo-Humeists have to give an account of causation that refers only to three factors: arrangements in space and time, the intrinsic qualities of the events, and the laws of nature. However, each of these seems to be reversible. There's a gap between the metaphysical resources of Neo-Humeism and a crucial fact about causation.

For example, it sometimes happens that the laws of nature entail that an effect will occur, given its causes. But it also can happen that the laws entail that a cause must have happened, given the effect. For example, the laws of nature entail that a flagpole will cast a shadow of a certain length, given its height and the angle of the sun, but it is equally true that they entail that the flagpole have a certain height, given the length of the shadow and the angle of the sun.

It's tempting for Neo-Humeists to do as David Hume himself did, which is to base the asymmetry of causation on the asymmetry of time. We could define an effect as a later event whose occurrence is entailed by the occurrence of the cause, given the laws of nature. However, there are two problems with this suggestion. First, it seems possible for causes and effects to be simultaneous with each other: my decision to think a certain thought might be simultaneous with the thought itself, for example. In fact, it is not obvious that there couldn't be cases in which the effect occurs before the cause, as might happen in cases of precognition. And some interpretations of quantum mechanics involve such temporally reversed causal sequences.

Even more significantly, Hume's suggestion just pushes back the problem one step: how can the Neo-Humeist account for the asymmetry of time? The direction of time and the direction of causation seem to be intimately connected. In most cases, and in all ordinary cases, the two directions coincide.

There have been several attempts by Neo-Humeists to account for the asymmetry of temporal direction. The three most popular attempts are the appeal to the increase in entropy, the appeal to *open conjunctive forks* (Reichenbach 1958; Salmon 1984), and the appeal to the relatively rare temporal asymmetries in fundamental physics, especially the temporal asymmetry in the decay of the kaon particle (Dowe 2000: 202–204). There are technical difficulties with each of these. In the case of the necessary increase in entropy (the Second Law of Thermodynamics), modern physics does not take this to be a fundamental law of nature, but merely the by-product of the fact that our universe happened to start out in a state of extremely low entropy (see Price 1996 for more details). In a similar way, the appeal to open conjunctive forks relies on the fact that we observe a relatively large number of common causes but few *common effects*. Like entropy, this is not the result of any fundamental law of physics but depends on the apparently contingent fact that our universe began in a relatively uncorrelated initial condition. In the case of kaon decay, we can reverse the direction of time, so long as we also reverse the negative/positive polarity of electrical charge.

In addition, all three accounts run afoul of "small-worlds" thought-experiments. It is relatively easy to imagine a world in which entropy decreases, in which open conjunctive forks point backwards, or in which kaon decay is oriented in the opposite direction.

David Lewis proposed a different solution to the problem of causal asymmetry, one that does not depend on assuming any prior asymmetry of temporal direction. He argued that causes can be distinguished from effects on the basis of a sophisticated, Neo-Humeist account of the semantics of counterfactual conditionals. According to Lewis, event A is the immediate cause of event B just in case, had A not occurred, B would not have occurred.

This relation of counterfactual dependency is at least non-symmetric, in the sense that conditional (9) does not entail conditional (10), nor vice versa:

(9) If A had not occurred, B would not have occurred.
(10) If B had not occurred, A would not have occurred.

However, this non-symmetry of counterfactual dependency is not the same thing as asymmetry. To get asymmetry, we would have to show that (9) and (10) are *inconsistent*: that they cannot be true together. In order to show that causation is asymmetric (at least in most, ordinary cases), Lewis attempts to show that counterfactual dependency does define a temporal direction, since most true counterfactuals are forward-tracking rather than backward-tracking. A conditional is forward-tracking when its consequent refers to an event that occurs later than the event that is referred to by its antecedent. Backward-tracking conditionals have the reverse relation between the times: the time of the event mentioned in the consequent is earlier than the time mentioned in the antecedent.

Lewis suggests that we evaluate counterfactual conditionals using the idea of a possible world. We invite the reader to consult Chapter 7 for more details, but roughly, a possible world is a possibility, a way the world might be. First, we find the "closest" possible world in which the antecedent is true, or the closest worlds in which it is true (more on the idea of *closeness* presently). Then, we simply check if the consequent is also true in that closest world, or true in all those closest worlds. If it is, the conditional is true; otherwise, it is false.

Obviously, the success of this account depends on defining the relation of being a "closest possible world" in a way that is consistent with the resources of Neo-Humeism. Here are Lewis's four criteria for determining the closest possible worlds, for the purposes of evaluating counterfactual conditionals (Lewis 1979):

1. It is of the first importance to avoid big, widespread, diverse violations of causal law.
2. It is of the second importance to maximize the spatiotemporal region throughout which perfect match of particular fact prevails.
3. It is of the third importance to avoid even small, localized violations of law.
4. It is of little or no importance to secure approximate similarity of particular fact.

Lewis argues that, using these criteria and his definition of causation, we will typically find (in a world like ours) that causes are earlier than their effects, which matches common sense and which imposes a direction on time. Lewis argues that it is easier to find a world that exactly matches our world in respect of its past than it is to find a world that exactly matches our world with respect to its future. Consequently, when evaluating a conditional with a counterfactual antecedent A, we should select a world that exactly matches the actual world with respect to the past, which includes a small, localized "miracle" in order to verify A, and which thereafter obeys exactly the same laws of nature as the actual world. This will make many events count as causes of later events, since in worlds in which the causes are absent, the later events will be quite different, while few if any events will count as causes of earlier events.

However, as Alexander Pruss has pointed out (Pruss 2003), Lewis never provides good reason to think that it is easier in a logical or metaphysical sense to find a world that matches our world in the future but not the past. It may be psychologically easier to imagine or computationally easier to describe such worlds, but those subjective factors are not sufficient to ground a real, objective difference in the direction of time. Consequently, there is no reason to think that Lewis's counterfactual account of causation provides an explanation of causal direction that comes anywhere near our actual conception of it.

3.5   Powerism

3.5.1   Powers and Properties

The theory of Powerism takes the attribution of causal powers and dispositions to be metaphysically fundamental. The laws of nature and the truth-values of subjunctive conditionals are both grounded in the actual powers of things.

There are several kinds of causal powers or dispositions. First, there are active powers. One thing has an active power when it is disposed to bring about a certain kind of change in other things. Fire, for example, has the active power to heat things in its vicinity. Certain foodstuffs, like wheat or rice, have the active power to nourish certain organisms when ingested.

There are also passive causal powers. A thing has a passive causal power when it is disposed to undergo change of a certain kind under certain circumstances. Water has the passive power to begin to boil when heated to 100° C at one atmosphere of pressure. Ice has the passive power to melt when heated above 0° C. Bodies have the passive power to accelerate when subjected to forces.

Typically, active and passive powers are exercised jointly. The fire heats the water, making it boil, as a result of a combination of an active power on the side of the fire and various passive powers on the side of the water.

In addition, in most cases two entities in close proximity will act upon each other, with some active power of each engaging with a passive power of the other. For example, when a billiard ball collides with a stationary ball, the first ball exercises the active power of causing the first ball to move, and the second exercises the active power of altering the momentum of the first ball.

There may also be fundamental powers that are immanent to a single entity. For example, a musically inclined person may be disposed to sing at regular intervals, in a way that doesn't require any external stimulus. Similarly, certain atoms of radioactive isotopes may be disposed to decay spontaneously with a certain probability over time.

When one thing (the *agent*) exercises an active causal power on another thing (the *patient*, which has a complementary passive causal power), then two things happen simultaneously: the patient undergoes a certain change, and a new relation is established between the agent and the patient: an irreducibly causal relation, which makes it true that the agent was the cause of the change in the patient. For Powerists, there is a necessary connection between these two facts: changes cannot occur in the absence of a causal connection, and causal connections cannot be established except when the relevant change ensues. This necessary connection between changes and causal connections is an unavoidable cost of the Powerist theory.

Powers are properties of concrete, particular things, like particles, material bodies, organisms, and artifacts. We find powers bundled together in fairly regular ways, resulting in a definite number of natural kinds. For example, every electron seems to have exactly the same active, passive, and immanent powers as any other electron. We can say that the property of being an electron "confers" those powers on each individual electron.

For Powerists, the relation between a property or kind and the powers it confers will be an *internal relation* (in G. E. Moore's sense). It will be part of the very essence of that kind to confer the powers it does on its members. The laws of nature, then, will simply be our way of expressing the essences of the world's natural kinds, cataloguing the powers conferred on the members of those kinds.

3.5.2   Nothing but Powers?

Powers are properties, but are they the only properties? Causal or power *structuralists* say yes: every real or natural property is nothing but a bundle or conjunction of causal powers. Powerists who are not structuralists insist, to the contrary, that there are some properties that confer powers without being powers or bundles of powers.

As we have seen, all Powerists believe that properties confer the powers they do as a matter of necessity. It is essential to each real property that it confer on its instances a certain set of causal powers. Power structuralists believe that this necessity runs in the other direction as well: any set of powers that is conferred by a property is necessarily conferred by just that property and no other. This makes sense for structuralists, since for them every property is either a power or a bundle of powers. Hence, it would be impossible for two different properties to confer exactly the same powers on their instances.

Another way to put this point is to say that, according to structuralists, each property is *individuated* by the set of powers it confers. If property X confers a set of powers S, and property Y confers exactly the same set S of powers, then property X and property Y must be identical, one and the same property.

Anti-structuralists deny this individuation of properties by powers. According to anti-structuralists, it is possible for two different properties to confer exactly the same causal powers. What, then, can make these two properties distinct from each other? Anti-structuralists must suppose that some natural properties have intrinsically a kind of qualitative character or "thusness" (*sicceity*, in Latin),[1] which is not reducible to the causal powers that a property confers, and which can individuate such a property from its causal "twins."

Sidney Shoemaker (1980, 1998) has offered three arguments in favor of structuralism: a semantic argument, an epistemic argument, and an appeal to simplicity or parsimony (Ockham's Razor).

Argument 1: The Semantic Argument for Structuralism   Suppose that there are in fact two properties in nature, which confer exactly the same causal powers on their bearers. For instance, we can suppose for the sake of argument that there are two properties, electron-1 and electron-2, that confer exactly the same causal powers that we associate with electrons (e.g., the power of repelling other negatively charged particles, of attracting positively charged ones, of exerting a certain amount of gravitational attraction on other bodies, of accelerating in response to external forces in a way indicative of the electron's rest mass, and so on). We are able to recognize whether a particle is or isn't an electron by testing its causal powers. Hence, if there were two properties that conferred the same set of causal powers, we could never tell whether any given particle had one property or the other.

This inability to distinguish between the two properties would make it impossible for us to refer to one property or the other. The only label we could use, the "electron" label, would in such a case be perfectly ambiguous between the two possible meanings (electron-1 and electron-2). Our scientific vocabulary would be infected with an incurable case of indeterminacy.

If it's possible for two or more properties to share the same *causal profile* (that is, if causal structuralism is false), then this sort of semantic indeterminacy might be ubiquitous, making every part of our scientific language massively ambiguous. Shoemaker argues that we should prefer structuralism, on the grounds that it would rule out such a Babel of linguistic confusion.

However, as John Hawthorne (2001) has pointed out, Shoemaker's argument moves too quickly. It is possible for a name like "electron" to become attached to a single property through the particular facts of linguistic history, even on the supposition that there exist other properties with the same causal profile. Suppose that the discoverer of electrons (Robert Milliken) was observing a case of electron-1 when he introduced the term "electron." The historical fact that his introduction of the term was causally connected with an instance of the electron-1 property would suffice to give his term the unambiguous meaning of referring to that very property, despite the existence of a causal "twin."

Argument 2: The Epistemic Argument In response to Hawthorne's objection to the semantic argument, the defender of structuralism could point out that the anti-structuralists might be able to secure an unambiguous language, but they can do so only at the cost of throwing us into a hopeless case of scientific skepticism. Even if our scientific vocabulary is unambiguous, if each term refers to a property with one or more causal duplicates, then we could never know whether we are really observing things to which our scientific terms genuinely apply. If, as a result of historical happenstance, our term "electron" refers to the electron-1 property and not the electron-2 property, we would be unable to tell whether a given particle is or is not really an electron (as we use the term), since particles of the electron-2 kind would not be electrons but would perfectly mimic the behavior of electrons (electron-1) in every observable circumstance.

However, Hawthorne points out that this argument fails to compel us, since the mere possibility of undetectable error is not sufficient to deprive us of genuine knowledge. I might be unable to tell whether or not I am currently a disembodied brain in a vat, being fed electrical impulses that perfectly mimic real sense perception, but this mere possibility is not enough to refute the claim that I can know many things via my senses. Epistemologists generally agree that the possibility of error must be relatively close to the actual situation in order to count against knowledge.

If that's true, then we might still be able to detect the presence of electrons (despite the existence of those perfect electron mimics, the members of the electron-2 kind), so long as there are no cases of electron-2 in our nearby environment in the actual world. In order to secure real scientific knowledge, we do not have to suppose that causal mimics or twins are impossible or entirely absent from the real world: we only have to suppose that they are rare in our interactions with the world.

Argument 3: The Appeal to Ockham's Razor   In metaphysics, as in other sciences and in everyday life, we prefer those theories that provide the simplest and most economical explanation of the observed facts. William of Ockham, the thirteenth-century English philosopher and theologian, first articulated such a principle of simplicity or economy, and, consequently, it is often named "Ockham's Razor." The mental picture involves using the Razor to slice off unnecessary complications and elaborations from our theory.

Structuralism is a simpler theory than anti-structuralism, since it enables us to dispense with all properties except for powers and bundles of powers, while the anti-structuralist must also believe in further properties that are disjoint from all powers. In addition, the anti-structuralist has to suppose that these non-power properties are necessarily connected with the powers that they confer on their bearers. Structuralists have no such connection in their theory, since each bundle simply confers its members on the objects that bear it.

Objection: The Symmetry Argument against Structuralism   The best argument against structuralism (again, due to Hawthorne) makes reference to the possibility of a causally or nomologically symmetrical world. Suppose, for example, that there were only four properties in the world: *A*, *B*, *C*, and *D*. If structuralism is true, each of these properties must be a mere bundle of powers. Let's suppose that this list gives us the relevant powers:

A = {the power, when combined with property *B*, of producing a change from *D* to *C*; the power, when not combined with *B*, of producing a change from *C* to *D*}

B = {the power, when combined with *A*, of producing a change from *D* to *C*; the power, when not combined with property *A*, of producing a change from *C* to *D*}

C = {the power of producing a change from *B* to *A*; the power of producing a change from *A* to *B*}

D = {the power of producing a change from *B* to *A*; the power of producing a change from *A* to *B*}

The picture is this: when a body has both properties *A* and *B*, it has the power to change another body from *D* to *C*, but not vice versa. When a body has either property *A* or property *B*, but not both, it has the power to change another body from *C* to *D*, but not vice versa. The properties *C* and *D* have powers that treat *A* and *B* equivalently. In such a world, there must be a difference between the two properties (or supposed power-bundles) *A* and *B*, since there is a real causal difference between having just one of the properties and having both of them simultaneously. However, if we try to identify the two properties with their power-bundles, we face a kind of vicious circularity: the only difference between the two bundles depends on there being a difference between *A* and *B*: if we substitute *A* for *B* and *B* for *A*, we transform the *A*-bundle into the *B*-bundle, and vice versa. Figure 3.2 illustrates the symmetry of the situation. The horizontal arrows between *A* and *B* and between *C* and *D* represent possible changes, and the diagonal and vertical arrows represent the causal powers of the five relevant combinations of properties: *C*, *D*, (*A*&*B*), (*A*& ~ *B*), and (~*A*&*B*).

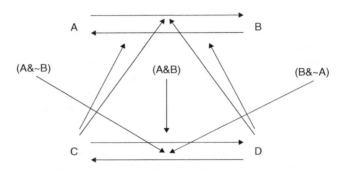

Figure 3.2

Thus, it seems that there must be something in addition to the powers themselves (a difference in qualitative characters or *sicceities*) that accounts (in a non-circular way) for the difference between *A* and *B*. Only by accounting for the difference between *A* and *B* can we account for the difference between the power of instantiating two properties and the power of instantiating just one of them.

3.5.3   Advantages of Powerism

Advantage 1: Powers and Scientific Knowledge (Induction)   The Powerist account of scientific or inductive knowledge reflects a very different model of how such knowledge is acquired from the one relied upon by Neo-Humeists. The Neo-Humeists, following Frank Ramsey and David K. Lewis, focus on our choice of the grand theories of fundamental physics, assuming that the scientist's job is one of choosing the simplest theory that fits available data. What the Neo-Humeists overlook is the active, experimental side of science, reflected in the work of Nancy Cartwright (1983, 1994), Judea Pearl (2009), and Alexander Bird (2010). For Powerists, the key to our discovery of natural powers is good experimental design: isolating small interactions from the influence of outside forces, and actively prodding natural things to reveal their hidden dispositions and tendencies.

The Powerist picture also fits better with a post-Gettier, causal account of knowledge. We come to know the powers of things by actively engaging with those powers, allowing them to act upon us and upon our instruments. By so doing, we make the skeptic's worries about a wildly chaotic landscape, just beyond the reach of our current data, into a groundless fantasy, one that has no relevance to the legitimacy of our claims to knowledge, so long as it is true, in the actual world, that we have successfully based our beliefs on the manifested powers of the things in our environment.

This is not to say that the Powerist has no epistemological vulnerabilities, relative to the Neo-Humeist. The Powerist has to admit that our ability to observe or detect real powers through experimental interaction is fallible. There is always the possibility that we have mis-identified the samples we are probing (e.g., we're trying to study water but accidentally obtained a sample of hydrogen peroxide instead), or that we have failed to identify and neutralize all interfering factors in the environment. In addition, if we are trying to measure something's propensity to cause or to undergo certain effects, we may unluckily observe a frequency that deviates from the true objective propensities. Our empirical investigations of powers can never attain 100% certainty, and this opens the door to the skeptic, who worries that we cannot rule out the possibility that we are always wrong. However, the Powerist can plausibly respond that it would be unreasonable to be paralyzed by mere possibilities of error, without specific reason to suspect that we are in error in this particular case. In addition, the Neo-Humeist also faces similar skeptical challenges, since our observations of the categorical qualities of things are also fallible.

Advantage 2: Token Causal Connections and Causal Direction   Powerists believe in real causal connections between things, causal connections that are not reducible to the Humean mosaic of qualities in spacetime. Instead, Powerists can rely upon the existence of causal processes, temporally extended things that unite cause and effect into a single, undivided whole. When one thing exercises an active causal power, introducing a process of change in the patient, there exists a single process that begins with the agent's active power at the time of the action and that includes the subsequent process of change in the patient. (For more details on this issue, see Chapter 9, especially 9.1–9.3.)

Where there is symmetric over-determination (whether deterministic or probabilistic), the question of which potential cause is a real cause is simply the question of which potential agent is actually connected, by a real process, with the effect. This may be impossible for us to determine empirically, but there will always be a fact of the matter in the things themselves.

Similarly, Powerists can appeal to the intrinsic nature of processes to fix the direction of causation. The exercise of an active power is always found at the beginning of an appropriate process in the patient, never at the end. That is, agents with appropriate active power are always joined to a process of an appropriate kind in the patient at the beginning of that process. Which terminus of the process counts as the beginning and which the end is also fixed by the nature of the active and passive powers involved. So, for example, since fire has the power to heat water, exposure to fire will typically be found at the beginning of a process of the water's becoming hotter, that is, at the terminus of the process with the lowest water temperature. We learn whether a power is one of heating or cooling by interacting with its bearer in well-designed experiments.

3.5.4   Objections to Powerism

We will look briefly at four principal objections to Powerism: the objection to necessary laws of nature, the *mystery* of natural intentionality, the problem of establishing a natural concord between separate active and passive powers, and the problem of *negative* causation (especially, causation by absences).

Objection 1: Necessity of the Causal Laws of Nature   First, it is a consequence of Powerism that all causal laws of nature are metaphysically necessary – there is no causal law that could have failed to be a law. This is because the relation between a property and the causal powers it confers is an internal one, and since properties do not seem to have any contingent intrinsic properties, each property confers the powers it does essentially – simply by being the property it is.

This consequence runs afoul of the fact that we can easily imagine (as David Hume pointed out) a world in which the laws of nature are very different: a world, for example, in which fire freezes and water runs uphill. We must take imagination as at least a fallible guide to real possibility, or else we would have few if any resources for knowing possibilities. However, the Powerists can plausibly respond that imagination need only be a fallible guide. We can imagine these impossible scenarios only because we do not rightly conceive of the relevant properties. If we really understood what fire, water, and heating are, we would clearly see the impossibility of fire that fails to heat water.

Objection 2: The Mystery of Natural Intentionality   Intentionality is a common feature of mental states. A mental state is typically about something, and the things it is about need not be immediately present – in fact, they need not exist at all. I can think about my mother, even if she is thousands of miles away, and I can even think about vampires, efficient bureaucracies, and other non-existent entities. The Austrian philosopher Franz Brentano (Brentano 1973: 88–89; orig. pub. 1876) suggested that intentionality is the "mark" of the mental: that all and only mental states are intentional in this way.

However, as George Molnar pointed out (Molnar 2003: 61–66), if Powerism is true, then intentionality is much more widespread than Brentano thought. Each and every causal power involves a kind of intentionality. For example, electrons can have the power to attract protons, even if the closest proton is millions of light-years away. In fact, it seems that electrons could still have that power, even if there were no protons at all.

Many philosophers, even as early at Parmenides in the 6th century BC, have found intentionality mysterious. Philosophers who are naturalistically or materialistically inclined have attempted to reduce intentionality to more basic and non-intentional facts, including facts about behavior (behaviorism) or evolutionary history – the "teleo-semantics" of Fred Dretske (1995), Ruth Garrett Millikan (1984), or Karen Neander (2011). If Powerism is true, such a project cannot ultimately succeed, since intentionality is a metaphysically fundamental feature of the world. However, this could be turned into an advantage for Powerism, suggesting that intentionality isn't as mysterious or odd as we might have thought. Having quasi-intentional causal powers at the fundamental level of reality might well make the task of understanding mental intentionality more tractable.

Objection 3: Pairing Active and Passive Powers   If the world contains both active and passive causal powers as basic or fundamental facts, this would seem to involve an amazing coincidence. If, for example, fire had the basic causal power of heating water, this would seem to entail that water have the basic passive power of being heated by fire. But how can one metaphysically fundamental fact logically entail another fundamental fact? How can there be a logical necessity connecting two separate facts?

The best answer to this problem involves carefully distinguishing between a causal power and our descriptions of it, or, to put it more precisely, between those descriptions that capture the true essence of the power, considered in isolation, and those descriptions that tacitly take into account the existence of other powers.

Here's a suggestion about how this disentangling might go. Let's suppose that water has the passive power of being capable of being heated, period. This fact about water doesn't entail that fire, in particular, should have the active powers of heating water, but only that there could be properties that confer such an active power. At the same time, fire might have the active causal power of heating anything with the passive power of being capable of being heated, or perhaps, of heating anything with this passive power together with certain other characteristics. Fire could have this active power, regardless of whether water, in particular, has the passive power of being capable of being heated. The two facts together entail that fire can heat water: that is, these two fundamental facts entail the two derived facts that fire has the active power of heating water, and water has the passive power of being heated by fire. No circularity or unexplained coincidence is required.

Objection 4: Negative Causation – Causation by (and of) Absences   We've saved the most difficult problem for the last. We often speak about events being caused by absences. In fact, as Jonathan Schaffer (2004) has pointed out, such negative causation is extremely common. Every time one fires a gun, for example, there is a case of negative causation: pulling the trigger removes an obstacle between the firing pin and the bullet. It is the absence of the obstacle that causes the gunpowder to be ignited. Every time a nerve signal passes through the brain, a case of negative causation is involved: it is the absence of certain chemicals in the synapse between two neurons that causes an electrical impulse to be transmitted. Many cases of death (perhaps all) involved negative causation: the absence, for example, of oxygen in the bloodstream to the brain, for example.

We can also speak of absences as effects. The causation of an absence is a case of prevention. We can prevent an explosion by cooling a chemical compound, thereby causing the absence of an explosion. One can prevent a stampede by calming a jittery steer, or prevent an accident by swerving one's car to the right.

How is this a problem for Powerists? The Powerist account of causation requires that we attribute causal powers to absences. But only things can have powers (whether active or passive), and absences aren't things!

Here's another way to put the point: Powerists conceive of causation as a real connection between things. If absences are nothing, then they cannot be connected to other events, either as causes or as effects.

The Powerists have three options. First, they could deny that negative causation is a real phenomenon. Second, they could give a disunified or disjunctive account of causation – employing causal powers for positive causation, but using something like the Neo-Humeist account for negative causation. Third, they could reify absences, allowing them to possess real properties and causal powers. Each option comes at a significant cost.

Concerning the first option, it would be hopeless to deny entirely that absences play any significant role in causation. However, Powerists can plausibly make a distinction between the role of positive things and their causal powers, on the one hand, and the role played by mere absences, on the other. Whenever an absence does play a role in causing a change or initiating a new process, it always does so in collaboration with some positive entities possessing appropriate active and passive causal powers. For example, when a gun is fired, the absence of the obstacle does play a role, but only in the presence of a spring or other mechanism with the active power of producing the appropriate motion in conjunction with the absence. Even when death is produced by an absence of water or oxygen, there is always a living organism with the capacity to produce, in those circumstances, an unliving corpse.

It would, therefore, be tempting for the Powerist to embrace the second option, and to reduce the causal role of the absence to the fact that a certain result can be deduced from the proposition that something is absent, when that proposition is combined with propositions about the laws of nature and about the states of the other, positive participants in the causal interaction. Even if absences don't exist, there do exist propositions to the effect that certain things are absent, and we can always consider what follows logically from such propositions, either alone or in conjunction with others. The Powerist could distinguish between causes and enabling conditions, arguing that absences can never be causes (in the strict sense) but only conditions that enable something else to act as a cause.

However, this maneuver comes at a significant cost, since it threatens to deprive the Powerist of the argument from causal linkage as a weapon against Neo-Humeism. This problem emerges when we focus on the other form of negative causation: prevention, or causation of absences. Consider again the case of two, symmetrical potential causes C_1 and C_2 of some event E, but now suppose that the effect E is an absence, the absence of an event of type K. It still seems to make sense to ask, on each particular occasion, whether it was C_1 alone, C_2 alone, or C_1 and C_2 jointly that produced the absence. However, we will always be able to give a causal explanation of the proposition that no event of type K occurred that refers to both C_1 and C_2. How then can we distinguish the three possibilities?

The answer to this problem might lie in hypothesizing that effects always consist in some change or absence of change in a persisting patient. When we prevent some event from happening, this always involves our preventing some thing (the *patient*) from changing in certain ways. We could now suppose that the continuing existence of any patient is a temporally extended *process* of a certain kind. (We'll explain more about what this means in Chapter 9.) The causal linkage between the agent and the absence of change in the patient consists in some powerful state of the agent's being an integral part of the process of the patient's continued, unchanging existence. If C_1 causes the absence and C_2 does not, then some state of C_1's power will be literally a *part* of the patient's continued and unchanging existence, while no such state of C_2 will be contained in that process of continuing existence.

The third option, reifying the absences, also comes at a theoretical cost – indeed, at what might seem to be a prohibitively high cost. If we reify all the absences in the world, we will end up with the thesis of Truthmaker Maximalism, which we discussed in the last chapter. Not only does Truthmaker Maximalism's addition of an infinite number of negative facts weigh against the theory by way of inflating its ontology, but also it requires (as we saw in Chapter 2) a huge number of mysterious necessary connections between the positive and negative facts. It must be impossible, for example, for the presence of water and the complete absence of water to coexist in the same place and time, and it must also be impossible for both the presence and the absence to be absent!

John Haldane has suggested that the Aristotelian and scholastic idea of *privation* might be helpful for the Powerist (Haldane 2007). Privations are those absences that do make a causal difference, due to the nature of the causal powers instantiated in a particular situation. If, for example, a spring in the gun has the power to expand in the absence of an obstacle, then the absence of such an obstacle could count as a privation in that situation. Similarly, if an organism requires water or oxygen in its environment in order to survive or in order to function normally, then the absence of such water or oxygen in that organism's immediate environment would also count as a privation. In contrast, absences that have nothing to do with the exercise of active or passive causal powers of any actual entity would be *mere absences* and not privations. Given this distinction, the Powerist has the option of supposing that privations exist and enter into real causal relations, but mere absences do not. This doesn't eliminate the cost of reifying absences entirely, but it might reduce that cost to a manageable level. The relevant necessary connections could be grounded in the positive powers relative to which the privations exist.

3.6   Conclusion

We've seen that there are two metaphysical camps on the issue of powers, the Neo-Humeists and the Powerists (assuming that we set aside old-fashioned Humean doubts about whether causes or powers exist at all). Neo-Humeists have the advantage of a remarkably lean theory, with few categories of things and few (if any) necessary connections.

The Neo-Humeists pay a price for this theoretical parsimony. They introduce an element of anthropocentricity (human-centeredness) into all of our basic causal notions. The laws of nature are what they are in part because of our own preferences concerning scientific theories. The direction or asymmetry of causation is not some universal and objective feature of the world, but only a by-product of our own perspective or of the contingencies of cosmic history. Induction is justified, but only by virtue of an inherent bias toward simple and uniform theories embedded in rationality itself. Causal linkage is not, despite our natural inclinations to think so, an intrinsic feature of pairs of events, but only a consequence of global patterns of repetition.

The Powerists can claim with reason that their theory does more justice to the centrality and weight of causation in our view of the world. It fits nicely with a post-Gettier emphasis on the causal element in knowledge, and a post-Kripke emphasis on causation as the ground of reference. It also accords with the practice of experimental science, with its active determination to isolate and measure the powers and capacities of natural things. All of these advantages come with a commensurately high price, including the multiplication of a kind of natural intentionality, and (possibly) with the reification of a large number of absences.

Note

1   The scholastic philosopher John Duns Scotus introduced the term "haecceitas" or thisness, referring to a supposed property that is necessarily unique to each concrete particular, distinguishing it from all other possible particulars. Anti-structuralist Powerists need an analogous term, the "thusness" or "so-ness" of a property, as a way of distinguishing it from all other properties. Many contemporary philosophers (like John Hawthorne) have used the term "quiddity" ("whatness") for this intrinsic, qualitative distinguisher, but that term already has a well-established use in scholastic philosophy, referring to a thing's essence – for example, Socrates's quiddity is humanity, as is yours. Thus, we use "*sicceity*."

4

Properties

There are *things*, and there are *the ways those things are*. The objects in the
world have a certain character, certain features, attributes, *properties*. There
are particular trees, and then there's the shared attribute of *being a tree*.
There are particular balls, and there are attributes like *being spherical*, *being
red*, and *having a mass of one kilogram*. Further, there are the relations that
things stand in, like the relation of *being the same color as*, *together forming
a circle*, and *being more massive than*. What we are gesturing toward is the
fact that the world is made up of both particulars and the properties and
relations that those particulars *exemplify* or *instantiate*. The categories *particular* and *property* are each menageries. Among the particulars are dogs
and people, mountains and lakes, electrons and electromagnetic fields,
bookbags and tables, angels and God, and many other things besides.
Among the properties are shapes, colors, spins, masses, various mental
states, relations of spatial distance or comparative size, and on and on.

We will spend the next two chapters investigating the shared natures of the
things in these two categories. In this chapter, we will consider the nature of
properties, and in the next, of particulars. There is substantial disagreement
among philosophers about what particulars and properties are like. For
example, there are some who believe that both are fundamental, that there
are certain things in each category that are not derived from or dependent on
anything in the other category. Such philosophers are "Realists" about both
categories. Realism about properties will be the first view we consider below.
"Bundle" Theorists, on another hand, take properties to be fundamental
while denying that particulars are: particulars are just "bundles" of properties. We will engage the Bundle Theory in the next chapter. On a still different

Metaphysics: The Fundamentals, First Edition. Robert C. Koons and Timothy H. Pickavance.
© 2015 Robert C. Koons and Timothy H. Pickavance.
Published 2015 by John Wiley & Sons, Ltd.

hand, Nominalists deny that properties are fundamental; instead, Nominalists insist that properties, if they exist at all, are derivative of particulars. We will consider four varieties of Nominalism later in this chapter.

Amidst all the disagreement, however, there are two notable points of near-unanimous agreement. First, many paradigmatic cases of properties are *shareable*. In other words, the sorts of attributes that have long gotten philosophers exercised are attributes that more than one object can exemplify. It is well nigh obvious that many objects exemplify the property of *being a tree*, for there are many trees. Likewise the property of *being green*, as there are many blades of green grass, among all the other green things as well. While it may not be clear how to account for this sharing, it is undeniable that the sharing is done.

Second, the exemplification of properties is intimately related to the satisfaction of linguistic predicates. Consider the sentence, "Lyle is tall." The word "Lyle" in that sentence picks out Lyle, and ought to be true just in case Lyle satisfies the predicate "is tall." But what does it take for something to satisfy that predicate? One answer is this: an object satisfies a predicate just in case one generates a true sentence if one combines, in a grammatically appropriate way, a name or unique description for that object with the predicate. But this answer is not satisfying, as that just looks like a definition of predicate satisfaction. A more satisfying answer appeals to properties: an object satisfies a predicate just in case the object exemplifies the property that is correlated with that predicate. The sentence "Lyle is tall" is true, then, whenever the object correlated with the name "Lyle" exemplifies the property correlated with the predicate "is tall." Which is to say, that sentence is true whenever Lyle exemplifies the property of *being tall*. No doubt this simple-minded account needs refinement and clarification, but the general point is, we believe, true: objects satisfy predicates because those objects exemplify properties correlated with those predicates.

4.1   The Theoretical Role of Properties

One might already be thinking that properties are rather puzzling, strange objects. They're meant to be correlated somehow with linguistic predicates; they're meant to be connected somehow to, maybe even to *explain*, the character of things; they're meant to be shared among various particulars. One might, therefore, be wondering why one should believe in properties at all. As we will see below (in Section 4.2.1), some philosophers think we should not believe in properties. However, a great many philosophers have suggested that we believe in properties *precisely because* the best theory of the fundamental structure of the world is one according to which there are properties. These philosophers think that we should believe in properties because they are theoretically useful.

It is worth noting that theoretical usefulness is very often taken to be a reason to believe in something. Many physicists, for example, believe that there is so-called "dark matter" and "dark energy," and they do so because they need to explain certain observable facts. There are a number of views about just what dark matter and energy are, but these views are constrained in important ways by the explanatory role that dark matter and energy play. In other words, one cannot go in for a view of dark matter that prevents it from explaining what it is that dark matter is meant to explain.[1] At any rate, arguments for the existence of an object on the basis of its explanatory usefulness are common, not only in physics, but in other sciences, and in philosophy as well. Properties are examples of something that most philosophers believe in because of their explanatory usefulness. In light of this, it is worth stepping back to consider directly the explanatory role of properties in a broader philosophical theory. This will constrain the sort of thing that properties can be, in just the way that the explanatory role of dark matter and energy constrains the sort of things those can be.

We will here be focused on two interrelated aspects of the classical theoretical role of properties. Properties ground *similarities* or *resemblance* by grounding *character*.[2] Character and similarity are two phenomena that have been central to the debate about the nature of properties. Indeed, we have already gestured at these issues, but it will be useful to dwell a bit more. Consider three objects, one of which is yellow and triangular, the second of which is yellow and rectangular, and the third of which is orange and triangular. Let's call these objects YelTri, YelRect, and OrTri, respectively. Each of these objects have a certain character. For example, YelTri is yellow, and it is triangular. Similarly for YelRect and OrTri. Further, YelTri and YelRect are exactly similar in color; in particular, they are both yellow. YelTri is also exactly similar to OrTri, but in shape, not in color; they are both triangular. And YelRect and OrTri are not exactly similar in either shape or color. So there are different sorts of similarities that obtain between different pairs of this trio. These similarities do not come from nowhere: one is tempted to explain the similarities by reference to these objects' character. It is *because* YelTri and YelRect are both *yellow* that they are similar in color. Character grounds similarity. And properties are, at the very least, intimately related to the character of things. Where there is character, there are properties exemplified. It's natural to think that YelTri is yellow because it exemplifies the property of *being yellow*, or anyway that its being yellow *just is* its exemplifying that property. OrTri, on the other hand, exemplifies the property of *being orange*, and so is orange rather than yellow. On the heels of this observation, we can explain why YelTri and YelRect are similar to one another, but dissimilar from OrTri, with respect to color: the former two objects exemplify a property that the latter fails to exemplify. Likewise for the shape similarities and dissimilarities. Further examples aren't far to seek.

Importantly, character and similarity are not the only bits of data that a theory of properties must explain, though they are the historically central bits, and the ones that will occupy us most in what follows. Among the other facts that a theory of properties must go some way toward explaining is, for example, the connection between property-having and predicate satisfaction discussed above. There are also the various *categorial* relations among properties.[3] In the last chapter, we discussed one type of categorial relation: that that obtains between determinables and determinates. There are others. For example, certain pairs of properties F and G are such that, if an object exemplifies F it cannot exemplify G. (Example: if something is more than five feet tall, it cannot also be exactly four feet tall.) In such a case, we say that F precludes G. At any rate, one interesting feature of categorial relations is that they hold of necessity. Given that two properties stand in some categorial relation, it is not possible that they fail to do so. Therefore, a theory of properties on which these relations are brute facts would be less desirable than one on which these relations can be explained.

One final comment, before we get to the theories themselves. As we noted in the Introduction, there are very rarely knock-down arguments in philosophy, and so there is almost always a number of views that might be true. Further, one cannot judge the truth of a philosophical view in isolation from its competitors: we must weigh the costs and benefits of the various views on offer, and then judge which one is *best*. It is the best view – not the only possible view, and not just some view that does the relevant work – that we hunt for. This is true in the context of properties no less than in other areas; the reader would do well to bear this in mind, and to delay delivering a final verdict, insofar as he or she is able, until we have completed our survey.

4.2   Realism

Realism is the first view we will consider. There are two characteristic Realist commitments. First, the character of ordinary objects is explained by their properties, in the way canvassed above. Which is to say, objects have character *in virtue of*, or *because of*, their properties.[4] And second, properties are universals. Which is to say, properties are just as fundamental as the fundamental things that have them, whether those things are particulars or other properties.[5] If one's view of properties demands both of these, then one's view is Realist.

Admittedly, the idea that properties are just as fundamental as the things that have them may not, at this stage, be clear. It may help to contrast Realism with Nominalism. Nominalism is the view that the universals, if they exist at all, do not ground ordinary objects' character. (Indeed, some Nominalist views deny that the character of ordinary objects is grounded at all!) *Class* Nominalism, for example, is the view that properties are classes. In general, the property *F* is just the class of *F* things. The property of *being red* is just the class of red things; the property of *being a tree* is just the class of trees; and so on. In an important sense, classes are less fundamental than their members, since classes depend on their members in an asymmetric way. Consider: the class containing just THP exists in virtue of the existence of THP, but THP does not exist in virtue of the existence of the class containing just THP. Therefore, if Class Nominalism is true, properties are less fundamental than the things that exemplify them. And therefore, if Class Nominalism is true, properties are not universals.

It is fairly clear that Realists accept the need to explain both character and similarity, and that they offer an explanation something like the one outlined above. The idea is that universals, in paradigm cases, ground the character of multiple objects, and in that way account for similarities among those objects. For example, the universal BLACK is exemplified by a number of things, including THP's phone, his car key fob, and the keys on his computer's keyboard. These things, according to Realism, are similar because they exemplify one and the same universal. The universal BLACK that is exemplified by THP's phone is identical to the universal BLACK that is exemplified by the "Y" key on THP's keyboard. The similarity between these two things is to be explained by the fact that each exemplifies *the very same property*. Further, the reason why the exemplifying of the very same property makes for similarity, according to Realism, is that shareable properties, like the universal BLACK, ground character. THP's phone is black because it exemplifies the universal BLACK; likewise, the "Y" key on THP's keyboard is black because it exemplifies the universal BLACK. According to Realism, universals ground character, and thereby ground similarity. The picture the Realist paints appears promising, at least when it comes to the central phenomena properties are meant to explain.

Three Problems for Realism

The sailing for Realism, however, may not be smooth after all. We will consider three prominent problems for Realism. The first, Bradley's Regress, presses on the central Realist idea of exemplification. The second, Russell's Paradox, presses on the central Realist idea that character is always grounded by universals. And the third, a challenge from Ostrich Nominalism, presses on the central Realist idea that character is even sometimes grounded by universals. The progression from one to the next of these problems is intentional: each pushes further one and the same complaint, namely that the Realist story about character cannot be universally applied. The Ostrich Nominalist goes furthest, suggesting that because the Realist story cannot be universally applied, it ought to be universally rejected. Let's start swirling the waters, and see if we can build a storm.

Problem 1: Bradley's Regress One central Realist commitment is that objects have their character in virtue of the universals they exemplify. Thus, they are plausibly taken to be committed to a principle called, by Michael Loux (2006), "Platonic Schema": If object *o* is *F* (or, *o Fs*), then *o* exemplifies the universal *F-ness*. F. H. Bradley (1930: 27–29; orig. pub. 1893) insisted that a commitment to something like Platonic Schema produces a regress. There are at least two ways a regress might occur; we will take them in turn.

Regress 1. Consider:

(1) Lyle is tall.

This is a true claim about the character of THP's son, Lyle. (1) has a simple, subject-predicate form; it says that an object *o* (Lyle) is *F* (tall). Given Platonic Schema, then, the Realist must say that (2) is also true:

(2) Lyle exemplifies the universal TALL.[6]

(2), however, is also of a form to which the Realist must apply Platonic Schema, since it says that an object *o* (Lyle) *Fs* (exemplifies the universal TALL). Thus, the Realist will have to say that (3) is true as well:

(3) Lyle exemplifies the universal EXEMPLIFIES-THE-UNIVERSAL-TALL.

Like (2), (3) can be run through Platonic Schema, and on and on. This is one version of a Bradley Regress.

Regress 2. The second type of Bradley Regress is closer to the original version Bradley offered, and begins with the idea that, according to Realism, there is a need for a relation of exemplification or instantiation to *bind*, as it were, universals to objects. In other words, if Realism is true, exemplification seems to be a relation that objects stand in to universals. We can see this commitment in Platonic Schema: when something has a property, that something *exemplifies* the relevant universal. We can generalize this point. When a universal is exemplified, there must be an instance of the exemplification relation that relates the universal to the thing that has it or the thing(s) that have it.

Consider (1) again. If we let "l" pick out Lyle, "t" pick out the universal TALL, and "E" pick out the relation EXEMPLIFICATION, we can, given Platonic Schema, note that (1) commits us to (2*):

(2*) E(l,t)

(2*) simply says what (2) says, in a bit more formal way. But if Realism is true, EXEMPLIFICATION seems to be a universal, since many objects exemplify many properties! The Realist must, therefore, say that for (2*) to be true, there must be an instance of EXEMPLIFICATION binding Lyle and TALL. But since EXEMPLIFICATION is a universal, something must bind this instance of EXEMPLIFICATION to Lyle and TALL. And that is the job of EXEMPLIFICATION. So we need yet another instance of EXEMPLIFICATION, and we are committed to (4):

(4) E*(E,l,t)

Of course, another regress looms, as the new instance of EXEMPLIFICATION needed for (4) will itself need to be bound to the things it relates (namely, EXEMPLIFICATION, Lyle, and TALL), and so on.

Responding to Regresses 1 & 2. There are, speaking generally, two ways Realists might respond to these two regresses. They might admit that there really are regresses here, but deny that they make trouble for Realism, or they might resist the claim that there really are regresses here. The second strategy will likely involve rejecting, or at least restricting, Platonic Schema.

The first strategy, accepting the regresses but denying the trouble, might seem sunk from the outset. After all, these are *infinite regresses*. How could they *not* be problematic? As it happens, things aren't so simple. There are infinite sequences of things that almost no one objects to. For example, consider the natural numbers: 0, 1, 2, 3, 4, ... Almost everyone admits that this sequence is infinite and is not, for that reason, problematic. But there is a regress here, for if you admit one number in the sequence, the principles of mathematics dictate that you have to accept the next member in the sequence. Every natural number, after all, has a successor. By committing to 0, and the successor principle, you are thereby committed to the infinite sequence. This is regressive no less than the two regresses above.

However, there are certainly some infinite regresses that are problematic, namely so-called "vicious" infinite regresses. Regresses are vicious when they involve *dependence* relations. If, in an infinite sequence, one *explains* the first member of the sequence by the second, and explains the second by the third, and the third by the fourth, and so on; or if the first member of sequence *depends* on the second, the second on the third, and so on; then the regress involved is vicious. This type of regress is problematic because, given that the sequence is infinite, one can never complete one's explanation of the first member of the sequence.

The difference between vicious and non-vicious regresses is on display with the two versions of Bradley's Regress. In Regress 1, there are no relations of dependence as one moves along the sequence. (3) is not meant to explain or ground (2). Anyway, Realists don't tend to think so. Despite the fact that the Realist is committed to (3), and the further members of the sequence, they are *not* committed to the claim that later members of the sequence ground or explain earlier members of the sequence. Thus, Regress 1 is not vicious.

Regress 2, however, is vicious. The thought that drives Regress 2 is that universals have to be bound to things; given that the thing doing this binding will itself be a universal – namely, the universal EXEMPLIFICATION – one will need binders for one's binders, and binders for one's binders' binders, and so on. Notice, though, that each stage depends on the later stages in this regress. (1), for example, is *explained* by (2*), (2*) is explained by (4), and so on. Think of it this way: Lyle can't exemplify TALL unless the latter is bound to the former by the universal EXEMPLIFICATION. And EXEMPLIFICATION can't do that work of binding without a further instance of EXEMPLIFICATION binding the first instance of EXEMPLIFICATION to Lyle and TALL. And so on. Because the earlier members of the sequence are explained by the later members, this regress is vicious.

The Realist is not, though, without recourse. She may, for example, deny or restrict Platonic Schema. One way to do this is to deny that there really is any such universal as EXEMPLIFICATION. That is, one might be a Nominalist about that relation, by insisting that facts of exemplification or instantiation are fundamental, rather than explained by appealing to universals. If one goes this way, one is right to insist that Platonic Schema cannot be applied to sentences like (2). A second way to restrict Platonic Schema is to deny that relations themselves need to be bound to the things they relate. It is, after all, the *job* of relations to relate. The thought that they must be related to things is, then, odd. One can then accept that (1) is grounded in (2*), but deny that (2*) must be grounded in (4).

Later, we will return to the question whether these moves on behalf of the Realist are sustainable, though, importantly, they seem reasonable at this stage. It is enough for now to note that Bradley's Regress demands certain concessions by the Realist: her explanation for similarities, captured by Platonic Schema, cannot be applied in every case. One is left to wonder whether it ought to be applied in any case.

Problem 2: Russell's Paradox   The second problem for Realism, Russell's Paradox, presses in a different way on the idea that similarities are grounded in the sharing of universals. It will be helpful at this stage to recall the connection, noted above, between a thing's satisfying a predicate and it's exemplifying the property correlated with that predicate. The Realist, for example, will say that Lyle satisfies the predicate "is tall" because he exemplifies the property that is correlated with that predicate, namely the property of *being tall*. If one is a Realist, this is just the universal TALL. Russell's

Paradox purports to show that this sort of account simply *cannot* be applied in every case.

As a start, consider the fact that Lyle is not short, and thus that he satisfies the predicate "is not short." If we stick with the above thought about properties and predicates, one will say that Lyle satisfies that predicate because he exemplifies the property of *not being short*. (If one is Realist, one will say this property is the universal NOT-SHORT. But its being a universal isn't important here, so we won't bother making this further step below.) More generally, it seems like every property is going to have a *negation*, where the negation of a property *F* is just the property something has when it doesn't have *F*; it is the property *not-F*. Since Lyle doesn't have the property of *being short*, he must have the property of *not being short*.

On a different front, some properties seem to exemplify themselves. Consider, for example, the property of *being a property*. This is a property that every property exemplifies, and so, in particular, the property of *being a property* must exemplify the property of *being a property*. The property of *being a property*, therefore, is self-exemplifying. Likewise, the property of *not being short* is not short, and so it is self-exemplifying. (Other examples aren't far to seek.) All of these self-exemplifying properties are similar in that they are self-exemplifying. The Realist will want to explain these similarities by appealing to the property of *being self-exemplifying*. But there are other properties that aren't self-exemplifying. These are easier to come by: the property of *being green* is not itself green; the property of *being tall* is not itself tall; the property of *being human* is not itself a human; and so on. These properties are all non-self-exemplifying. The Realist will want to explain these similarities by appealing to the property of *being non-self-exemplifying*, just as with the property of *not being short*.

However, this strategy waltzes the Realist into Russell's Paradox. For, consider the property of *being non-self-exemplifying*. Is the sentence, "The property of *being non-self-exemplifying* does not exemplify itself," true or false? That sentence is true, on the standard Realist account, if and only if the property of *being non-self-exemplifying* fails to exemplify itself. As we have seen, whenever a property fails to exemplify itself, it has the property of *being non-self-exemplifying*. Evidently, then, the property of *being non-self-exemplifying* fails to exemplify itself if and only if it has the property of *being non-self-exemplifying*. But that means that the property of *being non-self-exemplifying* does not exemplify itself if and only if it does exemplify itself! On the other hand, by similar reasoning, we can show that "The property of *being non-self-exemplifying* exemplifies itself" is false if and only if it both lacks and has itself. Either way, one gets a contradiction. That is Russell's Paradox.[7]

What we learn from this is, at the very least, that there cannot be a property that correlates with every predicate. And this is true even if there are similarities that such a property could explain. The Realist explanation of similarities cannot be absolutely general. What is needed, therefore, is a principled restriction of that explanation, one that allows the Realist to do away with the problematic properties but keep as much of her preferred explanation as possible. One initially attractive thought is to commit only to logically simple properties, like the property of *being tall*, the property of *being green*, the property of *being human*, and so on. Then one might say that a thing satisfies, for example, the predicate "is not tall" whenever that thing fails to exemplify the property of *being tall*, rather than whenever that thing does exemplify the property of *not being tall*. Similarly, a thing satisfies the predicate "is tall and green" not when it exemplifies the property of *being tall and green*, but when it both exemplifies the property of *being tall* and exemplifies the property of *being green*. (Similarly for other logically complex predicates.) This strategy would allow one to deny that there exist logically complex properties, and thus one will be able to deny that there is a property of *being non-self-exemplifying*.

If one adopts this strategy, one must deal with the question of how many universals are needed. The answers to that question will put one's view on a spectrum from *sparse* to *abundant* theories of universals. Sparse theories of universals commit to comparatively fewer universals, whereas abundant theories of universals commit to comparatively more universals. Super-abundant theories, for example, will entail that there is a property for more or less every predicate, whereas super-sparse theories will entail that very few predicates go with a property. We will not pause to take up this question in detail, but it is a question worth taking up.

Returning to Russell's Paradox, then, conceding that not every predicate correlates with a property may not seem particularly troubling. But as with the concessions needed to elude Bradley's Regress, it may be worse than it seems. For the Realist wants to account for similarities in terms of universals, but here seems to be conceding that this needn't always happen. For example, non-green things are similar in being non-green, but there may be no universal shared between them. So there are similarities that don't require universals. One is left to wonder whether the Realist has undermined her fundamental motivation. If some similarities require no universal, why not say that *no* similarity requires universals? Why not opt for the sparsest possible theory of properties: the theory according to which there are *no* properties. This is precisely the tack of the Ostrich Nominalist, to whom we now turn.

Problem 3: Ostrich Nominalism   Nominalism, recall, is just the view that universals do not ground character. Most versions of Nominalism go further, denying that there are any universals at all. The Ostrich Nominalist (Armstrong 1978; Devitt 1980) goes still further by denying that facts of similarity and resemblance need to be explained or grounded in any general way. Detractors from Ostrich Nominalism gave the view its name, accusing Ostrich Nominalists of, as it were, sticking their head in the sand when faced with facts of similarity.

We can say a bit more about the Ostrich Nominalist view of similarity. According to most theorists, YelTri and YelRect are similar in color because they both exemplify the property of *being yellow*, and YelTri and OrTri are similar in shape because they both exemplify the property of *being triangular*. Ostrich Nominalists deny these claims. They do not invoke properties to explain the color similarity between YelTri and YelRect, or the shape similarity between YelTri and OrTri, or the similarity along any other dimension between any other things. Instead, Ostrich Nominalists simply point to the character of these objects. So, they say that YelTri and YelRect are similar in color because YelTri is yellow and YelRect is yellow, YelTri and OrTri are similar in shape because YelTri is triangular and OrTri is triangular, and so on. Further, Ostrich Nominalists insist that these character facts are metaphysically fundamental, that we should not account for them by appealing to properties any more than we appeal to sharing of properties to account for similarities. In general, then, the Ostrich Nominalist will explain similarities by appealing to pairs of metaphysically fundamental character facts. What they do not do, indeed *cannot* do, is say that similarities are grounded by shared properties. They want to avoid talking about properties at all! Because of this, they must take each similarity on its own. Each similarity will be explained by different metaphysically fundamental facts. And so the Ostrich Nominalist denies that we ought to give a general explanation of the similarity facts.

We've already gestured toward the fact that not all Nominalists are Ostriches. Some Nominalists, though they deny that universals ground character, accept that we can give a general account or explanation of the similarity facts. Speaking broadly, then, there are two types of Nominalism, Ostrich and Reductive. Reductive Nominalists are just Nominalists who think that there is a general explanation of similarity. We consider Reductive Nominalism in the next section.

Our immediate concern, however, is with a principal objection to Ostrich Nominalism. In order to work toward that objection, we will consider a putative advantage of Ostrich Nominalism over Realism. Ockham's Razor would seem to demand that we prefer Ostrich Nominalism to Realism because Ostrich Nominalism requires a commitment to far fewer fundamental entities. The Realist, for example, believes in universals and also in fundamental particulars. And there are a great many universals, even on relatively sparse versions of Realism. To give ourselves something to work with, let's suppose there are m particulars, and that there are n types of things (that is, there are n dimensions of similarity among the particulars). Realism requires, in such a case, that there are $m + n$ things, because there are the universals, one for each dimension of similarity or each type, in addition to the particulars. Ostrich Nominalism, by contrast, requires only that there are *m* things, since it rejects the need for universals in addition to particulars. The more kinds of similarities there are, the more universals are needed, and therefore, the more strongly Ockham's Razor cuts against Realism in favor of Ostrich Nominalism. For the more universals the Realist needs, the less economical her theory becomes.

There are, though, two types of theoretical economy. The first type of theoretical economy is quantitative economy. To measure a theory's quantitative economy, one simply counts the number of fundamental things required by the theory. The second type of theoretical economy is qualitative economy. To measure a theory's qualitative economy, one counts the number of fundamental *types* of things required by the theory. Quantitative economy is a straightforward notion, and it is clear that Realism fares worse than Ostrich Nominalism on this measure. Qualitative economy may not be so clear, but we can illustrate the idea by considering the contrast between Realism and Ostrich Nominalism. The Realist believes in two, possibly three, fundamental types of things. There are fundamental particulars, universals, and possibly a fundamental relation of exemplification or instantiation between them. Green things, according to Realism, are not a fundamental type of thing; rather, something is a green thing if it exemplifies the universal GREEN. Likewise, cubes are not fundamental; rather, something is a cube if it exemplifies the universal CUBE. Fundamental particulars need not be of different fundamental types, so the Realist can do with particulars of just one fundamental type, PARTICULAR. The character of various types of particulars is then accounted for on the basis of those particulars standing in exemplification relations to various universals. The Ostrich Nominalist, on the other hand, must say that particulars come in many fundamental types. Indeed, it is just the Ostrich Nominalist view that cubes, spheres, green things, red things, humans, dogs, trees, and on and on, are of different fundamental types. If, as we assumed above, there are *n* types of fundamental things, then Ostrich Nominalism requires *n* fundamental *types* of things, one for each dimension of similarity among fundamental particulars.[8] Even by relatively sparse accountings of dimensions of similarity, this is a great many fundamental types of things. Anyway, it's far more than the three fundamental types required by Realism. Ostrich Nominalism, therefore, scores far worse than Realism when it comes to qualitative economy. Here is the big picture, then: Ostrich Nominalism has a distinct advantage over Realism when it comes to quantitative economy, but a distinct disadvantage when it comes to qualitative economy.

Whether this situation ultimately cuts against Ostrich Nominalism, Realism, or neither view turns on whether one kind of economy is more important than the other. Philosophers, and theorists in other fields as well, have typically regarded qualitative economy as more important than quantitative economy. Adding more of the same type of thing simply seems less troubling than adding new types of thing. For example, scientists have been able to reduce the number of types of fundamental things by insisting that the over 100 elements are really just different combinations of a relatively few subatomic particles. Taking all the elements to be fundamental requires believing in fewer things, but more fundamental types of things. Scientists take the qualitative advantage to outweigh the quantitative advantage.[9] There are many other examples of this kind of preference. The upshot, then, is that qualitative economy is more important than quantitative economy, other things being equal.

Notice, though, that the Daltonian view, according to which the elements are fundamental types, stands to atomic physics in the way that Ostrich Nominalism stands to Realism. The Daltonian view and Ostrich Nominalism both go for fewer things but more fundamental types, whereas atomic physics and Realism go for more things but fewer fundamental types. If atomic physics is preferable vis-à-vis the Daltonian view in virtue of its qualitative simplicity, despite its disadvantage in terms of quantitative economy, then Realism is preferable vis-à-vis Ostrich Nominalism as well.[10] This is a surprising twist, as Ostrich Nominalists have taken their view to be far simpler than Realism. Indeed, that is taken to be one of the main advantages of the view. It turns out, however, that Ockham's Razor cuts in just the opposite direction, if the foregoing is correct.

We led into this consideration of Ostrich Nominalism in the following way: given that Bradley's Regress and Russell's Paradox reveal that the Realist cannot always account for similarity in terms of universals, why not just say that no similarities are grounded in universals? We are now in a position to answer that question, if only partially. One reason to believe in universals is that Realism is simpler than Ostrich Nominalism. Maybe, though, there are other versions of Nominalism that do better than Ostrich Nominalism, and will thus fare better vis-à-vis Realism. We turn, therefore, to Reductive Nominalism.

4.3 Reductive Nominalism

Reductive Nominalism is the view that Nominalism is true, but Ostrich Nominalism is false. That is, Reductive Nominalism is the view that, if there are universals, they don't ground the character of ordinary objects, but that there is nonetheless a general explanation of resemblances between and among particulars. There are many varieties of Reductive Nominalism, but we will focus our attention on two that have been popular of late, namely Class Nominalism and Resemblance Nominalism.

4.3.1   Class Nominalism

Class Nominalism is that version of Reductive Nominalism according to which things resemble in virtue of belonging to a common class. These classes *just are* the properties, on this view. So, for example, the property of *being a cube* is just the class of cubes, the property of *being grey* is just the class of grey things, the property of *being tall* is just the class of tall things, and so on. Exemplification is just class membership. What it is to exemplify the property of *being grey* is to be a member of the class of grey things. Grey things have their grey character in virtue of exemplifying the property of *being grey*, which is to say grey things have their grey character because they are member of the class of grey things. Two grey things resemble, then, simply because they are members of a common class, namely the class of grey things, the property of *being grey*.

We will highlight a trio of problems for Class Nominalism. The first two, the contingent predication and companionship problems, are *extensionality* problems. Which is to say, these problems stem from the fact that classes have their members essentially. The third problem, the problem of super-abundancy, will point us toward Resemblance Nominalism.

Problem 1: Contingent Predication   According to standard theories, classes have extensional identity conditions. This means that class C_1 is identical to class C_2 if and only if everything that is a member of C_1 is a member of C_2, and vice versa. If C_1 has a member that C_2 doesn't have, or if C_2 has a member that C_1 doesn't have, then C_1 is not identical to C_2. A consequence of the fact that classes have extensional identity conditions is that classes have their members essentially. Consider, for example, the class that contains THP's left shoe, the Eiffel Tower, and Alpha Centauri. Call this class, "Random." If the Eiffel Tower were destroyed, Random would be destroyed as well. Random *just is* the class containing THP's left shoe, the Eiffel Tower, and Alpha Centauri, so if there is no Eiffel Tower, there can be no such thing as Random. Once there is no Eiffel Tower, Random cannot be the class that contains just THP's left shoe and Alpha Centauri (for example). For that class doesn't have a member that Random has, namely the Eiffel Tower. By the extensional identity criterion noted above, then, Random simply does not exist if there is no Eiffel Tower.

Consider, then, the class that contains all the actually existing dogs, BigDog. Suppose there are n dogs. Then BigDog is a class containing dogs $d_1, d_2, d_3, \ldots d_n$. By the same reasoning as we applied to Random, this class cannot exist if even one of these dogs is destroyed. Suppose, for example, that d_n died. Then one of BigDog's members no longer exists, and so BigDog no longer exists either. Here, the Class Nominalist is up against a serious problem. The Class Nominalist says that the property of *being a dog* is *identical to* the class of dogs. That is, the property of *being a dog* is identical to BigDog. If these two are identical, though, then one cannot exist without the other; there is, after all, just one thing here! Therefore, if even one dog is destroyed, so is the property of *being a dog*.

Similarly, if another dog comes to be, then there is a dog that does not exemplify the property of *being a dog*. The property of *being a dog*, again, is identical to BigDog. But BigDog cannot add members because classes have extensional identity conditions. When a new dog comes to be, BigDog still has the same members. But this means that, when a new dog comes to be, the property of *being a dog* has the same members. If exemplification is just class membership, when a new dog comes to be, there is a dog that doesn't exemplify the property of *being a dog*. Strange indeed!

What this points to is a deep tension between thinking of properties as classes and exemplification as class membership, on the one hand, and standard, if not inevitable, constraints on property exemplification. The extension of a property is the class of things that exemplify the property, and properties have their extensions contingently. On the other hand, classes have their extensions necessarily. It seems, therefore, that properties cannot be classes.

Problem 2: Companionship[11]   The Companionship Difficulty is another extensionality problem for Class Nominalism. Some pairs of distinct properties have identical extensions. For example, everything that has a heart has a kidney, and vice versa, so the class of things with a heart is coextensive with the class of things with a kidney. Thus, the property of *having a heart* is coextensive with the property of *having a kidney*. Similarly, everything that is triangular is also trilateral, so the property of *being triangular* is coextensive with the property of *being trilateral*. But the property of *having a heart* is not the property of *having a kidney*, nor is the property of *being triangular* identical to the property of *being trilateral*.

The trouble for Class Nominalism is that, again, classes are identical if they have the same members. The class of triangles is identical to the class of trilaterals; this is just what it is for the property of *being triangular* to be coextensive with the property of *being trilateral*. However, the Class Nominalist says the property of *being triangular* is identical to the class of triangles, and the property of *being trilateral* is identical to the class of trilaterals. Since the class of triangles is identical to the class of trilaterals, the property of *being triangular* is identical to the property of *being trilateral*. But we just noted that these are distinct properties! Class Nominalism requires an identity where there doesn't seem to be one.[12]

Problem 3: Super-Abundancy   A third problem for Class Nominalism is that it is a super-abundant theory of properties, and such theories have undesirable consequences. If properties are just classes of objects, then every unique class corresponds to a unique property. Random, for example, is a property, as is any other random collection of objects. This is the sense in which Class Nominalism requires super-abundancy. And since no class is metaphysically more fundamental than any other class, no property is metaphysically more fundamental than any other property.

In light of the foregoing, Class Nominalism has an especial trouble with Nelson Goodman's (1954) "new riddle of induction." Goodman asks us to consider the color property *grue*. Something is grue if and only if (a) it is green and first observed before or during the year 2020 or (b) it is blue and first observed after the year 2020. All the emeralds we've observed to this point were, of course, green, but they were also all grue. Given that we should expect the future to resemble the past and present, we have good evidence that in the future emeralds will be green. But it turns out we have equally good evidence that in the future emeralds will be grue. All the evidence we have for the claim that emeralds will continue to be green is equally good evidence for the claim that emeralds will continue to be grue. Indeed, we have no reason to prefer one of these expectations to the other. But, of course, if the emeralds we discover after the year 2020 are green, they are not grue, and vice versa. So the expectation for future green emerald observations differs from the expectation for future grue emeralds.

There are related problems. We expect that the thoughts, beliefs, desires, and other mental attitudes that we express using sentences involving the word "green" have to do with the property of *being green*, not the property of *being grue*. Likewise, we expect that sentences we express using the predicate "is green" predicate the property of *being green*, not the property of *being grue*. But again, why? Why not think that the predicate "is green" is correlated with the property of *being grue* rather than the property of *being green*? And why not think that the thoughts (etc.) we express with "green" have to do with the property of *being green* rather than the property of *being grue*? For up to this point, every experience of a green thing is equally an experience of a grue thing, every thought prompted by a green thing is a thought that is equally prompted by a grue thing, every true sentence having to do with a green thing is equally to do with a grue thing. If these relations are a significant part of what give our mental states and words content, as many philosophers think, then we have no reason to expect that those mental states and words are correlated with the property of *being green* rather than the property of *being grue*.

Obviously, we expect emeralds to be *green*, not grue, and that our thoughts express propositions involving green. But, why? Why not think emeralds will be grue, and that our thoughts express propositions involving grue? Presumably, the answer has something to do with the conceptual simplicity of green when compared to grue. This conceptual simplicity seems to point to a kind of *naturalness* had by the property of *being green* but lacked by the property of *being grue*. The property of *being grue* seems to be gerrymandered, made up, somehow false or unreal, or at least dependent in some way on more fundamental properties. The Class Nominalist, though, cannot say these things. There is a class of things that are green and first observed before or during 2020 or blue and first observed after 2020. That class just is the property of *being grue*. And, as we noted, there is no metaphysical priority of the properties of *being green* and of *being blue* over this class. The Realist, on the other hand, can opt for a sparse theory of universals, deny that there is a universal GRUE, and give a complicated account of why it is that something satisfies the predicate "is grue" on the basis of the exemplification of the universals GREEN and BLUE, the relation of OBSERVED BY, and so on.

A promising solution to this predicament is to distinguish between *natural* and *unnatural* classes. The Class Nominalist can then insist that the natural classes are able to sustain inductive inference and are more eligible to be correlated with predicates, thoughts, etcetera. The class of green things is, according to this strategy, more natural than the class of grue things. This explains why induction is appropriate when it has to do with the property of *being green* but not with the property of *being grue*, and why our thoughts and sentences have to do with the property of *being green* but not the property of *being grue*.

But there is an important question that is yet to be answered: *why is it* that some classes are natural and others are not? The most plausible answer to this question is quite simple. To work our way to that answer, notice that some things in the class of grue things don't resemble with respect to color in any interesting way: they are variously green and blue. In the class of green things, on the other hand, all the members of the class resemble with respect to color, for they are all green. Natural classes, then, are made up of members that resemble one another. Or maybe better, the more the members of a class resemble one another, the more natural the class.

This resulting view, however, appears to abandon Class Nominalism. After all, the Class Nominalist says that things resemble in virtue of their shared character, and that character is had by virtue of class membership. But the resemblances to which we are now appealing must be metaphysically more fundamental than class membership; otherwise they cannot mark the differences among more and less natural classes. This move, then, while it looked like it would salvage Class Nominalism, turns out to undermine it, and move us in the direction of Resemblance Nominalism.

4.3.2   Resemblance Nominalism

Resemblance Nominalism is the view that Nominalism is true (either no universals, or universals don't ground character) and that resemblances among particulars are metaphysically fundamental. The idea is that there are just particulars, and the resemblances among particulars ground character. If shareable properties exist at all, they must be built out of these more fundamental particulars. The usual Resemblance Nominalist view of shareable properties is that they are classes or the particulars that resemble. This is a similarity between Resemblance Nominalism and Class Nominalism. According to both, shareable properties are classes of particulars. The difference concerns what grounds similarity. For the Class Nominalist, common class membership grounds similarity (by grounding character), whereas for the Resemblance Nominalist, fundamental resemblance relations ground similarity.

Further, Resemblance Nominalists do not believe that class membership grounds character. A red ball, for example, is not red because it is a member of the class of red things. Rather, Resemblance Nominalists say that character is grounded in the metaphysically fundamental resemblance relations. Consider two balls, b_1 and b_2. Balls b_1 and b_2 stand in a fundamental resemblance relation. In virtue of this, they are members of the resemblance class of balls, where the resemblance class of balls is, intuitively, that class containing all and only the balls. More precisely, a resemblance class of objects is a class such that all the members of that class resemble one another more or differently than they resemble anything not in the class. (Note that the Extreme Resemblance Nominalist *cannot* give a definition of resemblance classes that makes use of the character of particulars. That would make the view circular.) The fact that b_1 and b_2 have ball-ish character is explained by the fact that b_1 and b_2 stand in fundamental resemblance relations to all and only the members of a certain resemblance class, namely the resemblance class of balls. It's not the class membership that is doing the work, but the metaphysically fundamental resemblance relations.

The idea is a bit more complex than we've so far been letting on, because particulars resemble one another in different respects. To get a little clearer, consider a possibility, a possible world, in which the only particulars are a red dog RD, a blue dog BD, a red cat RC, and a white cat WC. RD and BD resemble each other, in that they are both dogs; RD and RC resemble each other, in that they are both red; and RC and WC resemble each other, in that they are both cats. The commas in that sentence are important, since we cannot yet appeal to the redness, doghood, and cathood of these particulars; we are trying to account for that character by using the more fundamental resemblance relations. Notice, though, that while RD resembles both BD and RC, BD and RC don't resemble each other. Similarly, while RC resembles both RD and WC, RD and WC don't resemble each other. Consider, then, the class containing only RD and BD. This is a resemblance class because the members of this class resemble one another differently than they resemble anything outside the class, since only RD resembles RC. Likewise, the class containing only RD and RC is a resemblance class because RD and

RC resemble one another differently than they resemble anything outside the class, since only RD resembles BD. These two resemblance classes, in such a world, are the property of *being a dog* and the property of *being red*, respectively.

Despite that class membership does not ground character or similarity, the shareable properties that are classes of resembling particulars are implicated in a general account of similarity. For the Resemblance Nominalist thinks that two things are similar in some respect if and only if they are members of some one resemblance class, which class is made of up of all the particulars that are exactly alike in that respect. Thus Resemblance Nominalists are not Ostriches, but Reductive Nominalists.

There are two varieties of Resemblance Nominalism. Traditionally, Resemblance Nominalists have said that ordinary objects – chairs, trees, people, and so on – are the things that stand in fundamental resemblance relations. Any view that accepts this traditional commitment is a version of Extreme Resemblance Nominalism. Resemblance Nominalists who reject this claim are committed to a certain kind of Trope Theory. We turn to Trope Theory in Section 4.4, below, where we will clarify the view by considering what sort of particulars Trope Theorists say stand in fundamental resemblance relations. Our target in this section is Extreme Resemblance Nominalism.

Extreme Resemblance Nominalism faces the two extensionality worries, the contingent predication and companionship problems, we discussed in connection with Class Nominalism above. We leave it to the reader to articulate why this is so. Extreme Resemblance Nominalism faces a third extensionality worry, the problem of Imperfect Community.[13] Once we press that argument against Extreme Resemblance Nominalism, we will consider a different objection, the Hochberg–Armstrong Objection.

Problem 1: Imperfect Community   Suppose that there are three natural properties, being Large, being Green, and being Cubical. Now consider the class of things that have at least two of these three properties. This class, call it At-Least-Two, will contain particulars of the following kinds:

Large Green Cubes
Large Non-Green Cubes
Large Green Non-Cubes
Small Green Cubes

Intuitively, there is no real or natural or *sparse* property that all of these things have in common. Nonetheless, the class At-Least-Two does satisfy the comparative definition of a resemblance class: any two members of At-Least-Two do resemble each other to a certain degree (by having two or three of the properties in common), and nothing outside the class resembles every member of the class to that same degree. At least, it seems plausible that we can find cases like this that do satisfy that condition.

The most plausible Nominalist solution to this problem abandons Extreme Resemblance Nominalism in favor of Trope Theory. We will consider the nature and merits of Trope Theory below. We sketch the Trope Theorist's response to the Problem of Imperfect Community here, but the reader may need to return to this sketch after reading about Trope Theory below. For the Trope Theorist, resemblance relations obtain in the first place between singly charactered tropes rather than between multiply charactered particulars. Multiply charactered particulars resemble in virtue of having resembling tropes. This allows Trope Theorists to build more fine-grained resemblance classes, constituted by tropes rather than multiply charactered particulars. This has the potential to dissolve the Problem of Imperfect Community.[14]

Problem 2: The Hochberg–Armstrong Objection   There is a further difficulty for Extreme Resemblance Nominalism, raised by both Herbert Hochberg (1999) and David M. Armstrong (2004). The Extreme Resemblance Nominalist, according to Hochberg and Armstrong, must say that one fact can be the truthmaker for distinct propositions, propositions that seem to require different states of the world to be true. Consider, for example:

(5) Particulars p_1 and p_2 are exactly similar,

and

(6) p_1 and p_2 are distinct particulars.

The Extreme Resemblance Nominalist must say that it's just the existence of p_1 and p_2 that make both (5) and (6) true. Indeed, if Extreme Resemblance Nominalism is true, the truth of (5) and (6) must be grounded in just the existence of p_1 and p_2. The pair $\{p_1, p_2\}$ makes both (5) and (6) true. The Realist, on the other hand, can say that while that pair makes (6) true, (5) is made true by the fact that p_1 and p_2 share some one universal.

But what is the *objection*? The objection is that (5) and (6) seem to require different things of the world, and this is made clear by the fact that (6) could be true even if (5) were not. For p_1 and p_2 might have existed and been distinct, without being exactly similar. This is, at the very least, uncomfortable for the Extreme Resemblance Nominalist, since in such a case the truthmaker for (6), namely the pair $\{p_1, p_2\}$, would still exist! But further, and more troublingly, the relations expressed to hold between these two particulars by (5) and (6) are distinct. (5) says that p_1 and p_2 stand in a relation of similarity, while (6) says they stand in a relation of distinctness. These two relations have different extensions, not just possibly but actually. Given that these two relations are distinct, it is natural to require separate truthmakers.

Suppose that the Resemblance Nominalist accepts this requirement for different truthmakers where there are different relations. She can then postulate that there is a particular relation of resemblance that holds between p_1 and p_2, and insist that this particular resemblance relation is the truthmaker for (5), whereas the pair is the truthmaker for (6). The problem here, as Bertrand Russell (1959) emphasized, is that the Extreme Resemblance Nominalist thereby takes on an infinite regress. For one must ask what makes this particular relation a *resemblance* relation. The answer, of course, has to be that it resembles other such particular resemblance relations. But these relations resemble as well, and so we will need further resemblance relations to ground the fact that the resemblance relations are *resemblance* relations. And these relations doing that bit of explaining will need further resemblance relations to make them resemblance relations. And so on. This regress is vicious, since each new set of resemblance relations grounds the fact that the resemblance relations earlier in the sequence are able to do their work.

These are significant hurdles for the Extreme Resemblance Nominalism. It will be worth investigating whether the alternative Resemblance Nominalist Theory, Trope Theory, fares better.

4.4   Trope Theory

The problems for Extreme Resemblance Nominalism are the result of the fact that the particulars that stand in fundamental resemblance relations have what we might call "thick character." To say that an object has thick character is to say that one and the same thing has more than one dimension of character. A red ball, for example, has both reddish character and ballish character. It is, therefore, a thickly charactered object. The objects that we experience every day are thickly charactered. And the Extreme Resemblance Nominalist says that it is these objects that stand in metaphysically fundamental resemblance relations. In order to see how this commitment creates trouble for the Resemblance Nominalist, we need to contrast Extreme Resemblance Nominalism with Trope Theory.

Trope theory is, at bottom, the view that tropes directly ground the character of ordinary, thickly charactered objects. A trope is a property that is also a particular. They are, like universals, related to only one dimension of the character of an ordinary object, and they ground that dimension of character. Tropes are, in that sense, properties. A red ball, for example, has a redness trope that grounds its being red and a ballish trope that grounds its being a ball. The thick character of an ordinary object is, then, the result of its having a number of different tropes. However, unlike the properties we've been concerned with up to this point, tropes are not shareable. A trope can be exemplified by only one object. They are, in that sense, particulars. The similarity that obtains between thickly charactered objects is grounded in the sharing of exactly resembling tropes. A red ball resembles a red dog because both objects have their own red trope, and these red tropes exactly resemble. The general picture, then, is this. Tropes stand in relations of resemblance; in virtue of being related to a number of different tropes, ordinary particulars have thick character; further, ordinary particulars resemble in some respect when they exemplify exactly resembling tropes.

All versions of Trope Theory are Nominalist, since tropes ground the character of ordinary objects. However, some versions of Trope Theory are committed to the existence of universals. According to this version of Trope Theory, tropes exactly resemble in virtue of being related to one and the same universal. More commonly, Trope Theorists are Resemblance Nominalists. According to this version of Trope Theory, tropes, rather than thickly charactered particulars, stand in metaphysically fundamental resemblance relations. Shareable properties are classes of exactly resembling tropes. We will focus on the Resemblance Nominalist form of Trope Theory in the sequel, though not much turns on this focus.

Why believe in tropes? One reason is we can avoid the pitfalls of Extreme Resemblance Nominalism. For example, consider the companionship problem. The Trope Theorist faces no trouble here, for the class of triangular tropes is distinct from the class of trilateral tropes. Thus, there are two properties here, rather than just one. There is a similar solution to the problem of imperfect community. Likewise, the Hochberg–Armstrong objection is diffused, because the truth of sentences like (5) is grounded in the tropes had by particulars like p_1 and p_2, whereas the truth of sentences like (6) is grounded in the mere existence of the relevant particulars. But further, tropes can serve in roles that Realist universals cannot. Trope Theorists say, for example, that tropes can serve as the relata of causal relations and, relatedly, as the immediate objects of sense perception. Things have causal powers in virtue of their properties, and tropes seem fit to serve in that role. A red ball causes certain wavelengths of light to reflect off its surface, for example, because of the red trope it has. Further, Trope Theory offers a potentially attractive account of the metaphysics of ordinary objects: they are bundles of tropes. (We return to this view in the next chapter.)

In the remainder of this section, we will do two things. First, we will distinguish two ways of thinking about tropes, which give rise to two different versions of Trope Theory. This is necessary to undertake the second thing, evaluating Trope Theory, for the two versions of Trope Theory face different problems. Our evaluation of Trope Theory will, however, bleed into the next chapter, in which we will consider the metaphysics of substance.

4.4.1   Two Versions of Trope Theory

First, then, to the task of distinguishing between two versions of Trope Theory.[15] The question that divides these versions is this: do tropes have the character they ground? If tropes do have the character they ground, then they are modular tropes; if they do not have the character they ground, then they are modifier tropes. Consider the redness trope, r_1, had by a red ball, RB. On all versions of Trope Theory, r_1 grounds the redness of RB. That is, RB has its red character in virtue of having r_1. The question we are now concerned to answer is whether r_1 itself has this red character, or not. Is r_1 itself red? If yes, then tropes are modular tropes. If no, then tropes are modifier tropes. Modifier tropes ground character that they lack, whereas modular tropes ground character that they have.

Modular Trope Theory is that version of Trope Theory according to which tropes are modular tropes. Modifier Trope Theory is that version of Trope Theory according to which tropes are modifier tropes. These are the two versions of Trope Theory. They are importantly different. If Modifier Trope Theory is true, then tropes don't have even this thin character. Red tropes are not red, and ball tropes are not ballish. A red trope grounds the redness of something else without itself being red, and a ball trope grounds the character of something else without itself being ballish. Modifier tropes only have *formal* character; that is to say, modifier tropes only have properties like *being a trope*, *being-self-identical*, *being particular*, and so on. We will return to this in the next chapter, where we will directly criticize Modifier Trope Theory. By way of preview, the worry will be that Modifier Trope Theory is explanatorily identical to Realism but quantitatively less economical. Therefore, one ought to prefer Realism.

On the other hand, if Modular Trope Theory is true, then tropes are thinly charactered particulars. Modular tropes are thinly charactered because they have only one dimension of character. A red trope, for example, is merely red. It is not ballish, or cubical, or human, or what-have-you. Similarly, a ball trope is merely ballish. It is not reddish, or human, or tree-ish, or what-have-you. This commitment, while it solves certain problems, creates others. Indeed, there is a dilemma for Modular Trope Theory.

4.4.2   A Dilemma for Modular Trope Theory

As we have just seen, modular tropes are thinly charactered particulars. They are *merely* red, or *merely* ballish, or *merely* human, and so on. They are, therefore, just like ordinary particulars except for having only one dimension of character. Modular Trope Theory, then, is just like Extreme Resemblance Nominalism except on the question of whether the things standing in fundamental resemblance relations have more than one dimension of character.[16]

This conception of tropes is, however, troubling. Robert Garcia has articulated what he calls "Thickening Principles." Here are two:

Color Thickening: Every colored object is shaped.
Shape Thickening: Every shaped object is extended.

The basic idea here is that it is metaphysically impossible for something to be colored without also being shaped, or to be shaped without being extended. The having of some type of thin character seems to require the having of some other type of thin character. Which is to say, thin character sometimes requires thick character. Further, these principles are *very* plausible. How something could have a color without having a shape is difficult to imagine. One wants to say that colors are distributed over regions, and these regions have a certain shape. Similarly, it difficult to see how something could be, for example, spherical, without having a certain diameter. These relationships seem to be at the heart of our understanding of what it is to have character of these sorts. Modular Trope Theory, however, is committed to denying these Thickening Principles. A red trope, recall, is *merely* red. It is not also shaped. Likewise, a spherical trope is *merely* spherical. It does not have an extension. This is just *what it is* to be a modular trope.

Either the Modular Trope Theorist will have to give up these extremely plausible Thickening Principles, or she will have to admit that modular tropes have multiple dimensions of character. Giving up the Thickening Principles is a significant cost. Again, it's hard to even understand what it would be to have a color without a shape, for example. But saying that modular tropes have many dimensions of character appears to abandon Modular Trope Theory. For example, the Trope Theorists' solutions to the extensionality problems would no longer be available. Indeed, one wonders whether modular tropes would wind up looking just like the Extreme Resemblance Nominalist's ordinary particulars. Give a red module trope a definite shape and size, and it looks like one just has a red ball!

The situation at this stage is this: If one is a Trope Theorist, one must be a Modifier Trope Theorist or a Modular Trope Theorist. If one is a Modular Trope Theorist, then one is in danger of collapsing into Extreme Resemblance

Nominalism, unless one is willing to violate Garcia's Thickening Principles. On the other hand, if one is a Modifier Trope Theorist, then one's view is less attractive than but explanatorily identical to Realism. Either way, one ought to give up Trope Theory. Admittedly, we have only canvassed one horn of this dilemma. In the next chapter we will develop the other horn.

Stepping back a bit, we have in this chapter covered some major theories of properties, from Realism to Class and Extreme Resemblance Nominalism to Trope Theory. Each theory has its strengths and weaknesses, and it is a difficult question which view comes out ahead in the end. No wonder the question of the nature of properties has been, and will continue to be, a lively area of metaphysical inquiry.

Notes

1 See, for example, http://science.nasa.gov/astrophysics/focus-areas/what-is-dark-energy/. Accessed July 30, 2014.
2 As will become clear, there are disputes about whether properties do either of these things. In large measure, this is because there are disputes about whether there is really something here that needs to be explained or grounded. Regardless, though, a theory of properties will have something to say about the character of ordinary objects as well as about resemblance.
3 "Categorial" is not a typo! These relations are categorial in that they are relations among the categories, among properties themselves.
4 Importantly, we are here thinking of properties as *shareable* properties. This is important, for otherwise certain varieties of Trope Theory would count as Realist, despite that they are decidedly *not* Realist. This way of thinking applies as well to the second characteristic feature of Realism.
5 More technically, we might say that universals are as fundamental as substances. Since we don't take up a discussion of substances until the next chapter, we have chosen the formulation above.
6 Here and in the next chapter, we will use italics to speak generically of properties and all-caps specifically for universals.
7 Anyway, that's the *intensional* version of Russell's Paradox, the version of the paradox applied to properties. See Russell (1956: 59–60).
8 Note well: we are *not* saying that Ostrich Nominalists are committed to some additional entities, called "types." That's wrong, and it would in any case be relevant only to the question of quantitative economy. Even if the Ostrich Nominalists deny that types exist, they can still compare two theories in terms of qualitative economy by referring to the number of fundamental and irreducible kinds of things distinguishable in the two theories. If Ostrich Nominalism were not able to accommodate comparisons of qualitative economy, this would be a devastating problem in its own right.
9 No doubt there are other reasons to prefer the qualitatively simpler theory that appeals to subatomic particles rather than fundamental elements, but the qualitative simplicity is a reason in its own right.

10   The argument we have just given against Ostrich Nominalism is taken from Mantegani (2010), Pickel (2010), and Pickel and Mantegani (2012).

11   Goodman (1951: 160–161) developed this worry.

12   The Concretist about modality has an out here, at least with respect to certain of the trouble cases, because she believes in the existence of merely possible things as well. Thus, the extensions of properties are much larger than someone who doesn't think merely possible things exist. See Chapter 7 for more. We chose the triangular-trilateral case because Concretism doesn't seem to help in that case, since those properties are not just coextensive, but *necessarily* coextensive.

13   Due again to Goodman (1951: 162–164).

14   As Manley (2002) points out, Trope Theory can solve the problem of imperfect community only if it posits tropes of determinable properties (like color), and not just of determinate (perfectly specific) properties. See Wilson (2012) for a defense of determinable properties as fundamental.

15   The ensuing discussion of Trope Theory, both in this chapter and the next, is due almost exclusively to Robert Garcia. See, for example, Garcia (2010). We owe him a great debt, both for his written work, and for a great many invaluable conversations.

16   The dilemma we put to Modular Trope Theory holds equally well on the version committed to universals. The problem is just easier to see when one focuses on the Resemblance Nominalist version of Modular Trope Theory.

5

Particulars

Our discussion of properties, both in the last chapter and the chapter on powers, leads to a different question about properties, one that will take us away from the nature of properties themselves. The question, nonetheless, is rather simple: Is there anything more to say about the relationship between properties and particulars than just that the latter exemplify the former? The discussion is split into two parts. First, we will briefly consider the nature of facts (Section 5.1). The bulk of the discussion focuses on the metaphysics of substances (Section 5.2).

5.1 Facts

Facts have shown up repeatedly in our discussion to this point, often at important moments. Truthmakers are quite naturally taken to be facts. The truthmaker for the sentence, "Lyle is tall," for example, is plausibly the fact that Lyle exemplifies the property of *being tall* (if it has a truthmaker at all). Indeed, atomic sentences like this are plausibly true in virtue of some fact that a certain individual exemplifies a certain property. We have, though, seen reasons to wonder about the existence of truthmakers of this sort. The theory that Truth Supervenes on Being, for example, doesn't deploy facts in this way. Only if one were committed to Classical Truthmaker Theory would it be wise to motivate the idea that there are facts on the basis of a consideration of truth. But more importantly, it's not clear that we are able to make any progress getting at the nature of facts by considering truthmakers.

Metaphysics: The Fundamentals, First Edition. Robert C. Koons and Timothy H. Pickavance.
© 2015 Robert C. Koons and Timothy H. Pickavance.
Published 2015 by John Wiley & Sons, Ltd.

The most we can say, it seems, is that facts are something to do with an object exemplifying a property.

Trope Theory, however, may offer more guidance, for tropes seem closely related to facts. Tropes are individualized properties or property instances, and many facts seem to be the same. Causal statements are clear places where this connection is apparent. We often say things like, "The fact that Tom is clumsy caused him to trip," or alternatively, "Tom's clumsiness caused him to trip." In these kinds of cases, we are appealing to one fact to causally explain, at least in part, some other fact. In this case, the fact is that Tom is clumsy. But notice that in the second sentence, we seem to be accounting for the same causal relation in terms of a particular trope, in this case, Tom's clumsiness. The reader will recall that one reason Trope Theorists have given for believing in tropes is that one can thereby give an account of the relata of causal relations. It is just this sort of idea that Trope Theorists have in mind. One view of facts, then, is just that they are tropes.

If facts are tropes, they must be modular tropes, for modifier tropes are unfit to be the relata of causal relations. Things have the causal powers that they do because they have a certain sort of character, and it is the things with powers that are the relata of causal relations. Tom, for example, has his propensity to trip because he himself is clumsy. It's the charactered thing that has the causal powers, not (in typical cases) that which does the characterizing. Compare Realism: universals *confer* causal powers by grounding character; it is not the universals themselves that have the causal powers (in typical cases), but the things that exemplify the universals. Therefore, if one is a Modifier Trope Theorist, one should not think that the tropes themselves are the relata of causal relations, since they don't have the sort of character that could supply tropes with causal powers. Rather, it is the things that exemplify modifier tropes that have causal powers. Tom's clumsiness trope is not itself clumsy, and so does not possess the causal powers that come along with clumsiness. Only Tom has that sort of character, if Modifier Trope Theory is true. On the other hand, Modular Trope Theorists *can* say that tropes are the relata of causal relations. Modular tropes, after all, do have the sort of character that is associated with causal powers. If Modular Trope Theory is true, Tom's clumsiness trope is itself clumsy, and therefore must have the powers that come along with clumsiness. Thus, modular tropes, but not modifier tropes, can serve as the relata of causal relations. And modular tropes, but not modifier tropes, might be facts.

Realists might try to substitute states of affairs for tropes in giving an account of facts. A state of affairs is the exemplification of a property by a particular, or the holding of a relation between or among particulars.[1] Unlike the view that facts are tropes, this view maintains that facts are complex particulars. Tropes are metaphysically simple and fundamental, while states of affairs are constituted by a universal, a particular or particulars, and (possibly) some sort of tie or nexus that holds between the universal and the particular (or particulars). The state of affairs of Tom's being clumsy, for example, is constituted by Tom, the universal CLUMSINESS, and (possibly) the tie between the two. Other than the difference having to do with complexity, states of affairs and tropes are quite similar, and play similar roles in their respective Realist and trope theoretic ontologies.[2] States of affairs, unlike the thick particulars of everyday experience, have their constituents necessarily. The state of affairs of Tom's being clumsy could not have failed to have either Tom or CLUMSINESS as constituents. (Compare: a whiteness module trope could not have failed to be white.) Tom, on the other hand, might have failed to be clumsy, and so might not have been related to CLUMSINESS in the way he in fact is related. This fact is important, for it allows for states of affairs to serve not only as the relata of causal relations and as facts, but also as truthmakers for atomic sentences. For given that the state of affairs of Tom's being clumsy exists, Tom and CLUMSINESS have to be related in the relevant way, namely the way that makes it true that Tom is clumsy. States of affairs are, therefore, truthmakers. We leave it to the reader to consider whether this is a virtue or a vice!

This is an admittedly cursory survey of the metaphysics of facts. We must, however, turn our attention to a more thorough discussion of the relationship between properties and substances.

5.2   Substances

Prior to thinking about how substances relate to their properties, we need some sense for what our target is. We need some sense for what substances are. Traditionally, philosophers have taken substances to be, among particulars, fundamental. Substances are those particulars that aren't metaphysically grounded, at least in other particulars. They are also commonly taken to be the ultimate subjects of properties, and the things in the world fundamentally capable of surviving through change. But philosophers have also disputed what sorts of things have these features, whether substances need have them all, and whether anything even *could* have them all. But philosophers have also tended to begin their discussions of substance with a list of particulars in mind, a list which itemizes those things of which we're looking for a metaphysically analysis. This list usually includes (i) living things, from viruses and shrubs, to dodos and dinosaurs, whales and humans, and angels and God; (ii) artifacts like telephones and armoires and espresso machines and apartment complexes; and (iii) naturally occurring inanimate objects from quarks, electrons, and water molecules, to rivers and glaciers, hills and mountains, and planets and stars and galaxies. These two approaches may not dovetail, for it may be that the list of particulars includes nothing that has the list of features. We are more interested in getting at the metaphysics of the particulars included in that three-fold list, rather than in identifying things that have the features commonly associated with substance. Our targets, in other words, are living things, artifacts, and naturally occurring inanimate objects. We leave open the question whether, and the degree to which, the two coincide.

That our targets are living things, artifacts, and naturally occurring inanimate objects will become more clear as we proceed through our discussion of particulars. Those categories will play more centrally in later chapters, where we will consider the relation of things to their parts (Chapter 6), the metaphysics of change and persistence (Chapter 9), and the metaphysics of possibility and necessity (Chapter 7). Here, we are interested in a more abstract, foundational question: To what extent can we give a metaphysical analysis of substance in terms of properties? What we mean by this question may yet be unclear, but it will become clearer as we proceed. It is an old question, and we will canvass some of its most popular answers.

Let's start, as ever, with a simple observation: substances are thickly charactered. Each substance has multiple dimensions of character. Our clumsy friend Tom is not only clumsy but also blue-eyed and red-haired, weighing in at 95 kilograms, and standing just under two meters tall. In addition to exemplifying the property of *being clumsy*, then, he exemplifies the properties of *being blue-eyed*, *being red-haired*, *having 95kg mass*, and *being less than two meters tall*. Additionally, he exemplifies a number of properties that every other human does as well, including the properties of *being human*, *being capable of rational thought*, and so on.

One natural thought to have in light of this observation is that the properties that ground a substance's thick characteredness do so by, in some sense, being parts of the substance. Consider, for example, a red ball. It's clear that the ball exemplifies the property of *being red*, but it is tempting to think that the property of *being red* somehow characterizes the ball by being a part of it. The redness of the ball is *there in the ball*, after all. Where there is redness, there must be the property of *being red*, or anyway *a* property of *being red*, if one is a Trope Theorist. Any view that accepts that properties are parts of the substances that exemplify them is a version of Constituent Ontology (Wolterstorff 1970). Properties, if Constituent Ontology is true, are what we might call "metaphysical" parts, which give substances metaphysical structure.[3] (Whether Constituent Ontologists ought to think that substances have metaphysical parts that are not properties will be a question we take up below.)

Constituent Ontology offers to give an account of the metaphysics of substance at least in part in terms of properties by offering an account of exemplification in terms of parthood. Relational Ontologists deny Constituent Ontology, and so insist that properties are not parts of substances in any sense and that exemplification is a fundamental relation between properties and substances that cannot be analyzed in terms of parthood. Many Relational Ontologists resist the idea that we can even make sense of the Constituent Ontologist's fundamental claim, that exemplification is a kind of parthood. We will assume that Constituent Ontology is at least comprehensible, though we don't mean to be dismissive of this worry. We will simply not take it up here, for Constituent Ontology has a long and distinguished history, tracing back (at least) to Aristotle (see Koslicki 2008). That is enough to warrant taking various versions of the view seriously.

To be clear, the issue that divides Constituent and Relational Ontology is whether exemplification is a kind of parthood. This means, though, that with the exception of Trope Theorists, Nominalists are not party to the present discussion. This is unsurprising, since non-Trope Nominalists want to give an account of the metaphysics of properties in terms of particulars, rather than vice versa. Since non-Trope Nominalists don't think properties (whether shareable or tropes) ground character, they wouldn't be interested in the question of whether properties ground character by being parts of the things whose character is grounded. Thus, in what follows, we will ignore non-Trope Nominalism.

5.2.1   Relational Ontology

We turn first to Relational Ontology, the view that exemplification is a fundamental relation that cannot be analyzed in terms of parthood. Because of this commitment, Relational Ontologists must deny that substances have any metaphysical structure. Substances may have physical structure, and maybe even non-physical structure, if there is immaterial "stuff," but substances cannot have a structure that is determined by properties, the exemplification relation, or other metaphysical parts. The view is just that substances have no such parts! Relational Ontology must therefore take exemplification as a primitive of their theory. This is a cost in qualitative economy relative to Constituent Ontology, because Constituent Ontology analyzes exemplification in terms of parthood. Where the Constituent Ontologist needs one parthood relation, the Relational Ontologist needs both parthood and exemplification. Further, though, the fundamentality of exemplification requires that both Class and Resemblance Nominalism are false, since these views analyze exemplification in terms of parthood. And Ostrich Nominalism is out, since there is no exemplification on that view. Thus, there is a cost in terms of qualitative economy relative to these views as well. If other things are equal, Ockham's Razor demands that we prefer Constituent Ontology or some kind of non-Trope Nominalism. What is to be determined is whether other things are equal. We have already canvassed reasons to think that other things may not be equal in the case of Ostrich,

Class, and Resemblance Nominalism. Here, we will concern ourselves only with the relative merits of Relational and Constituent Ontology.

In order to work toward the needed comparison, we must distinguish between two types of Relational Ontology. The distinction comes down to whether Relational Ontology gets combined with Realism or with Trope Theory. If one combines Relational Ontology with Realism, one gets Classical Relational Realism. On this view, fundamental particulars stand in a fundamental relation of exemplification to the universals that ground their (thick) character. This view, given that it involves both fundamental particulars and universals, is a form of Realism. If one combines Relational Ontology with Trope Theory, one gets Trope Relational Ontology.

Trope Relational Ontology comes in two varieties, depending on whether tropes are modifier tropes (without the character they ground) or modular tropes (with the character they ground). Modular Trope Relational Ontology is problematic, however. Substances have character in virtue of standing in a fundamental relation of exemplification, but modular tropes also have character. This means that whenever a substance has character of a certain sort, there is a wholly distinct thing – a modular trope – that has exactly that sort of character. Our red ball (from earlier) itself has red character. But if there are modular tropes, then there is also a modular trope that has red character. The ball has red character in virtue of standing in a fundamental exemplification relation to its modular trope with red character. On this view, the red character of the modular trope is not identical to the red character of the red ball. So two things have red character! Modular Trope Relational Ontology is thus committed to a problematic sort of character duplication.

Better for the Trope Relational Ontologist to go for modifier tropes. For if tropes are modifier tropes, they do not have the character they ground, and thus we will not encounter character duplication. When a redness modifier trope is instantiated by a particular, only the particular has red character. The way for the Trope Relational Ontologist to avoid character duplication, then, is by opting for modifier tropes.

The solution to the problem of character duplication, however, exacts its own cost. As we saw in the last chapter, because modifier tropes lack the character they ground, they have only formal character, properties like *being a trope*, *being-self-identical*, and *being particular*. One might wonder, then, what guarantees that modifier tropes can be exemplified by only one thing. There seems to be nothing in their nature that would preclude them being exemplified by more than one thing at the same time. Modifier Trope Theorists will, of course, have something to say about this. In particular, they tend to say that tropes are individuated by their spatiotemporal locations. To be the trope that it is, a trope must occupy a certain place in space and time. Further, tropes are exemplified by things with which they share a location. In order to be exemplified by more than one thing, then, tropes must be wholly located in more than one place. But this is impossible, so tropes can only be exemplified by one thing. The problem here, though, is that this combination of views – modifier tropes only have formal character, but they are individuated by their spatial location – is incompatible with a plausible Thickening Principle:

Location Thickening: Spatially located objects have a definite size and shape.

If Location Thickening is true, then either tropes aren't individuated by their spatiotemporal location, or they have more than formal character. While it is true that Location Thickening is not as plausible as Color and Shape Thickening, it still carries significant plausibility. Giving it up counts as a cost of a theory.

In order to keep from paying this cost, the Modifier Trope Theorist might opt for a different view of the individuation of tropes. They might, for example, say that tropes are just primitively distinct, that there is nothing that individuates them. In effect, this option simply stipulates that tropes are not shareable. This is fine so far as it goes, but it's unclear what is being gained. Suppose the Realist went for the view that there are multiple primitively distinct REDNESS universals, and that it just so happened that each universal was exemplified by just one object. There would appear to be no substantive difference between this sort of Realism and Modifier Trope Theory. But one would be right to wonder why the Realist thought that there were many REDNESSes, and would be right to think that a more Classical Realist picture was to be preferred, in light of Ockham's Razor. It would seem, then, that the Modifier Trope Theorist ought to just embrace this Classical Realist picture as well.

It is important to emphasize that these troubles for Modifier Trope Theory were not the result of combining the view with Relational Ontology. They are problems for Modifier Trope Theory whether or not Relational Ontology is embraced as well. This is worth bearing in mind, as there will be additional problems for Constituent Ontologists who embrace Modifier Trope Theory, as we will see below.

Maybe Classical Relational Realism fares better than Trope Relational Ontology. According to Classical Relational Realism, substances stand in a fundamental exemplification relation to universals, which universals ground the character of the substances that exemplify them. This view happens to be the only version of Relational Ontology that has been defended in the literature, and it has had its fair share of advocates.[4] The view, however, faces a well-known and powerful problem: the Extrinsicality Objection.

The Extrinsicality Objection purports to show that, if Classical Relational Realism is true, then substances have no intrinsic properties. An intrinsic property is a property that something has just in virtue of it or its parts; the idea is that a property F is intrinsic when o's having F-ish character (for any object o) is grounded in o and its parts. It is problematic if Classical Relational Realism precludes substances' having intrinsic properties because it is plausible that substances do have intrinsic properties; in particular, the fundamental natural kinds of substances, their colors and shapes, their masses, and so on, are all plausibly intrinsic. The intrinsic makeup of a substance guarantees that it has those features. Classical Relational Realism, on the other hand, is just the view that a substance's properties *aren't* parts of the substance. But, given that the view is a *Realist* one, it is also part of the view that the universals exemplified by a substance ground the substance's character. Thus, it would follow that none of a substance's character is grounded by the intrinsic structure of the substance. If that is so, though, substances have no intrinsic features. This, goes the objection, is problematic, since so many of a substance's features do seem to be intrinsic.

The most promising responses to this objection are to either deny that we have gotten the right notion of intrinsicality, or to deny that is really problematic for all of a thing's properties to be extrinsic. If one were to go the first way, one might, for example, insist that a property F is intrinsic when a thing's having F-ish character is grounded in the thing, its parts, and the universals it exemplifies. This strategy may over-generate intrinsic features, though. If one's theory of universals is relatively abundant, for example, it might include relational universals like BEING-10-METERS-FROM-A-TREE.[5] Consider, then, a substance s that is ten meters from a tree. This ought to be paradigmatically extrinsic; something has that feature not just in virtue of it or its parts. But if universals ground character, then the new definition of intrinsicality is in danger of classifying this property as intrinsic, since the exemplification of BEING-10-METERS-FROM-A-TREE by s is enough to guarantee that s is ten meters from a tree.

This discussion of the Extrinsicality Objection, and Relational Ontology more generally, is all too brief, but is enough to give one a sense for why one might want to avoid Classical Relational Realism. We turn, then, to Constituent Ontology. The question is whether it fares better than its Relational cousin.

5.2.2   Constituent Ontology

Constituent Ontology is the view that substances exemplify properties by having properties as parts. Exemplification is, then, a kind of parthood. Substances may or may not have ordinary parts (see Chapter 6) – for example, hands that are parts of bodies, oxygen atoms that are parts of water molecules, and tabletops that are parts of tables – but even if they do, properties are not parts in the same sense as these other parts. In order to facilitate our discussion, and to mitigate certain confusions, we will reserve the term "constituent" to refer to a substance's metaphysical parts, parts like their properties. The term "part," from here out, will be used to refer more particularly to the ordinary parts of substances. Nothing hangs on this terminological choice. The Constituent Ontologist, then, thinks that a substance's character is determined by its metaphysical structure, which metaphysical structure is determined by the interrelations of its constituents.[6]

Constituent Ontologists are generally interested in giving an account of a substance in terms of its constituents. They think that one can say *what a substance is* by identifying its constituents and their interrelations. Insofar as one has given an *assay* of a substance, in this sense, one has said what the substance is. In other words, the substance *just is* that set of constituents standing in those relations. Thus, Constituent Ontologists are committed to the Principle of Constituent Identity, or PCI. PCI says that no two substances have exactly the same constituents standing in exactly the same relations to one another. If substance S_1 has all the same constituents as substance S_2 (and those constituents stand in all the same relations)[7], then S_1 and S_2 are the very same substance; "they" are identical. If one can say *what a substance is* by identifying its constituents, then no non-identical substances can have the same constituents.

In light of the Constituent Ontologist's commitment to both PCI and the view that properties are among a substance's constituents, one might wonder whether the *only* constituents of a substance are its properties. Bundle Theorists say that the properties of a substance are its only constituents. Substrate Theorists deny the Bundle Theory; they think that each substance has at least one constituent other than its properties. We will, in turn, examine each of these views.

Bundle Theories   Bundle Theorists, by virtue of being Constituent Ontologists who think that a substance's properties are its only constituents, think that substances just are a bundle of properties. This is a simple, straightforward account of the metaphysics of substance. On the supposition that one is already committed to the existence of properties, Bundle Theory requires no new theoretical posits. This is unlike Substrate Theories, which require a substrate of a different fundamental than properties. So, if one is a Constituent Ontologist, Bundle Theory is the most plausible place to begin the hunt for a theory of substance.

Depending on whether one combines Bundle Theory with Trope Theory or Realism, one gets either Trope Bundle Theory or Classical Bundle Theory. Trope Bundle Theory, as the name suggests, combines Bundle Theory with the idea that tropes ground character; accordingly, substances are bundles of tropes. Trope Bundle Theory, therefore, reduces the category of substance to the category of trope, trading one type of particular for another. Classical Bundle Theory, on the other hand, combines Bundle Theory with the idea that universals ground character; accordingly, substances are bundles of universals. Classical Bundle Theory, therefore, reduces the category of substance to the category of universal, trading one type of particular for a type of non-particular.

Trope Bundle Theory comes in two sub-varieties, since tropes can be modifier tropes or modular tropes. Modular Trope Bundle Theory, just like Modular Trope Relational Ontology, faces the problem of character duplication if substances, in addition to modular tropes, are thought to be charactered.[8] Going for character duplication might seem like the natural avenue, given that tropes are meant to *ground the character of substances*. If one gives up the idea that substances are charactered, then one seems to have given up the idea that tropes ground character at all. But maybe this isn't quite right in the case of Modular Trope Bundle Theory. The Bundle Theorist, after all, is hoping to *reduce* substances to bundles, and to characterize exemplification in terms of parthood. Thus, the Modular Trope Bundle Theorist might say that substances are "charactered" simply by having charactered constituents. We needn't go in for duplication; having a modular trope as a constituent is enough. This is a less robust account of the sense in which substances are charactered, but it is not obviously problematic just for that reason. It is not as if the view says that there is nothing that is really and truly red, for example; it's just that the thing that is really and truly red isn't what one thought it was. Unfortunately for the Modular Trope Bundle Theorist, there is a problem in the neighborhood. If one thinks that substances have character only by having charactered constituents, then one must deny that there are thickly charactered things. That is, one must deny that there are things with many dimensions of robust character. Modular tropes only have one dimension of character, so if Modular Trope Bundle Theorists are to avoid character duplication, they must say that nothing has more than one dimension of character. This is troubling, for it seems that there are thickly charactered things. Indeed, it is thick character that tropes are meant to ground. But it appears that Modular Trope Bundle Theory, if it is to avoid character duplication, cannot accept that there are thickly charactered things.

Given that this trouble is created by the need to avoid character duplication, it might be that Modifier Trope Bundle Theory fares better than its modular brother. Because modifier tropes don't have the character they ground, there is no need to deny that substances themselves have character in the robust sense. No character duplication will result. However, given that Modifier Trope Bundle Theory wants to say that substances are just bundles of tropes, one might wonder what, exactly, modifier tropes are meant to modify. Since the only constituents of a substance are tropes, it must be that tropes characterize other tropes. Nothing else is around to characterize! But as we saw in Chapter 4, modifier tropes can only have formal character. These two commitments are at odds with one another, for if modifier tropes are characterizing one another, then these tropes will have more than formal character. There are two ways to push back against this problem. First, the Modifier Trope Bundle Theorist might simply insist that there *is* something else around to characterize, namely the bundle itself. Tropes don't characterize other tropes; rather, they characterize the bundle. Just because one has built the bundle out of tropes doesn't mean that the bundle doesn't exist to be characterized. A house is not a brick just because it's made of bricks. Second, the Modifier Trope Bundle Theorist might go for a constituent that is not a property, which constituent can be modified by the modifier tropes. This, though, constitutes an abandonment of Bundle Theory in favor of Substrate Theory, for if the needed constituent is not a property then it must be a substrate. We will take up Substrate Theories below.

First, though, we turn our attention to Classical Bundle Theory, the view that substances are bundles of universals. Classical Bundle Theorists tend to opt for relatively sparse theories of universals. If one has an abundant theory of universals, then each substance exemplifies very many – even innumerably many – universals. For example, suppose that one's theory of universals admitted disjunctions of universals to be universals themselves. Then, if a substance exemplifies two universals, F and G, then it must also exemplify the disjunction of these, a universal we can call H. But then, there will also be the disjunction of F and H, and the disjunction of G and H, and the substance will exemplify these as well. These two further universals can be disjoined with the other three to supply six more universals that the substance must exemplify, and so on. Supposing, as Classical Bundle Theory does, that universals are constituents of substances, an abundant theory of universals requires that substances have a great many, even innumerable constituents. Most Classical Bundle Theorists – indeed most Constituent Ontologists more generally – have thought this view outfitted substances with an unhelpful and unpalatable metaphysical complexity. A relatively sparse theory of universals solves this problem. We assume, therefore, that Classical Bundle Theory is committed to a sparse theory of universals. We will consider certain details to do with the Classical Bundle Theorist's sparse theory of universals below, in connection with an objection to Classical Bundle Theory.

It should be clear that Classical Bundle Theorists should not say that just any set of universals will be a substance. There is a simple reason for this: not all sets of universals accurately describe the character of a substance. First of all, some sets of universals aren't thick enough. Consider the unit set of the universal BLUE. There is no substance that is just blue. Whether or not one is committed to the thickening principles we've discussed previously, no *substance* is just blue. Second, some sufficiently thick sets of universals don't correspond to a substance either. For example, there are no orange elephants. Thus, any set containing the universals ORANGE and ELEPHANT doesn't correspond to a substance. Not just any set of universals will do.

Instead of thinking of substances merely as sets of universals, the Classical Bundle Theorist might think that substances are sets of *co-instantiated* universals.[9] The idea is that among all the sets of universals, some of them (that is, some of the sets, not some of the universals) have a special feature, namely co-instantiation. A set of universals is co-instantiated, roughly, when there is some one thing that exemplifies just the universals in the set. The Classical Bundle Theorist, then, can identify substances with these special sets of universals. A substance *just is* a particular set of co-instantiated universals.[10] On this view, which we'll call the Simple Bundle Theory, for every set of co-instantiated universals U, there exists a substance s that exemplifies a universal F just in case F is in U.

There are two problems for Simple Bundle Theory. First, Simple Bundle Theory seems incompatible with the possibility of change. Lyle is 45 inches tall. Further, Lyle is identical to a set of co-instantiated universals. Among those universals, given his height, must be a certain height universal, namely BEING-45-INCHES-TALL. The set that is Lyle does not include, for example, the universal BEING-48-INCHES-TALL. But Future Lyle will be 48 inches tall. Future Lyle will have to be identical to a set of co-instantiated universals, namely that set that includes all and only the universals that he exemplifies. Future Lyle will exemplify BEING-48-INCHES-TALL, not BEING-45-INCHES-TALL, so the set of universals he will be identical to will have to include BEING-48-INCHES-TALL and not BEING-45-INCHES-TALL. But sets, as we saw in Chapter 4, in connection with Reductive Nominalism, have extensional identity conditions. Different members, different set; same members, same set. The set of co-instantiated universals to which Lyle is identical is, therefore, non-identical to the set of co-instantiated universals to which Future Lyle is identical. Thus, Lyle and Future Lyle cannot be identical to one another. If Lyle grows even a hair, whether in height or on his head, he will cease to be, and some other thing will replace him. Simple Bundle Theory is incompatible with change.

Nuclear Bundle Theory attempts to rectify this problem.[11] Roughly, Nuclear Bundle Theory identifies a substance with a special subclass of its properties, rather than with all of its properties. Doing so requires distinguishing between nuclear co-instantiation and peripheral co-instantiation. Sets of universals that are nuclearly co-instantiated are "nuclei." The idea is that nuclei are sets of co-instantiated universals that are essential to some substance, where a universal is essential to a substance just in case that substance could not exist while failing to exemplify that universal. Nuclear Bundle Theory identifies substances with nuclei. Further, each set of nuclearly co-instantiated universals will be a subset of some peripherally co-instantiated set of universals. Every universal exemplified by the substance is a member of that peripherally co-instantiated set. So long as the nucleus remains, so does the substance, even if the peripherally co-instantiated set of universals changes. Thus, Nuclear Bundle Theory is compatible with change. Here is an example. Consider THP's daughter, Gretchen. Suppose, for simplicity, that Gretchen has only two essential features: HUMANNESS and GRETCHENHOOD. She has a number of features that she might have lacked, like BEING-30-INCHES-TALL and IMPISHNESS. Let's assume, for simplicity, that these are her only two accidental features. Nuclear Bundle Theory says that Gretchen is identical to the nuclearly co-instantiated set of universals, {HUMANNESS, GRETCHENHOOD}. There is also a peripherally co-instantiated set of universals, {HUMANNESS, GRETCHENHOOD, BEING-30-INCHES-TALL, IMPISHNESS}, which set contains all of Gretchen's characterizing universals. Suppose that Gretchen grows an inch. Then the relevant peripherally co-instantiated set is no longer peripherally co-instantiated; instead, there is a new peripherally co-instantiated set, {HUMANNESS, GRETCHENHOOD, BEING-31-INCHES-TALL, IMPISHNESS}. But this is compatible with Gretchen's continuing to be, since {HUMANNESS, GRETCHENHOOD} is still a nucleus (that is, is still nuclearly co-instantiated). That nucleus *just is* Gretchen.

The fundamental cost associated with Nuclear Bundle Theory vis-à-vis Simple Bundle Theory is the addition of an additional primitive property. Whereas Simple Bundle Theory required only co-instantiation, Nuclear Bundle Theory requires both nuclear and peripheral co-instantiation. Nuclear Bundle Theory is, therefore, qualitatively less economical than Simple Bundle Theory. However, its compatibility with a robust view of change is a great benefit to the view. It is probably better to pay this cost than to pay the cost associated with being incompatible with change.

There is, though, a further worry, not just for Nuclear Bundle Theory but also for all varieties of Classical Bundle Theory.[12] Classical Bundle Theory combined with PCI entails that indiscernible substances are impossible, where two substances are indiscernible if they have the same thick character. To see why, suppose that two substances could be indiscernible. In a Realist setting, indiscernibility requires sharing all the same universals. So, suppose there are two indiscernible substances, a and b, and that these two exemplify just the universals F and G. If Classical Bundle Theory is true, then a is identical to the co-instantiated set of universals $\{F, G\}$, and b is identical to the co-instantiated set of universals $\{F, G\}$. Therefore, a is identical to b. There is just one substance, rather than two, which contradicts our initial assumption that there were *two* indiscernible substances. Classical Bundle Theory is, therefore, incompatible with indiscernible substances.

Classical Bundle Theory is committed to a version of Leibniz's principle of the Identity of Indiscernibles. The Identity of Indiscernibles says that distinct but indiscernible substances are impossible. It says that if a substance s_1 has all the same properties as a substance s_2, then s_1 is identical to s_2. More carefully, the Identity of Indiscernibles says that if substance s_1 exemplifies a property if and only if substance s_2 does, then s_1 is identical to s_2. The Identity of Indiscernibles should not be confused with a different principle, the Indiscernibility of Identicals. The Indiscernibility of Identicals says that if s_1 is identical to s_2, then s_1 and s_2 must exemplify the same properties, that s_1 exemplifies a property if and only if s_2 does. That is, it says that identical substances must share all "their" features. The Indiscernibility of Identicals is accepted by almost all philosophers; indeed, it is a constraint on identity itself, in its strict, philosophical sense. It would be hard to know what "identity" meant if it did not entail the Indiscernibility of Identicals. The Identity of Indiscernibles, on the other hand, is more controversial, as we will see.

We must take care with how we formulate the Identity of Indiscernibles. Indeed, how one formulates the principle will turn on how sparse or abundant one's theory of properties is. The more abundant one's theory of properties, the more difficult it is for distinct substances to be indiscernible. For the more properties there are, the more properties a thing will exemplify, and thus the harder it will be for two substances to have all properties in common. Likewise, the more sparse one's theory of properties, the easier it is for distinct substances to be indiscernible. Where there are fewer properties, it is easier for substances to have all the same properties. For example, in our discussion of Nuclear Bundle Theory, we deployed the universal GRETCHENHOOD. This is what we might call an "identity property," a property that requires that anything that has it be identical to a certain object, namely Gretchen. Nothing could have GRETCHENHOOD and fail to be identical to Gretchen. To have this property just is to be identical to Gretchen. If there are universals like this, then the Identity of Indiscernibles will be true. These identity properties, by their very nature, cannot be shared. There are other properties that are this way, as well. For example, the property of *being the youngest daughter of THP*, or the property of *being the elder author of this book*, or the property of *being the first husband of JKP* each could be exemplified by only one substance. In the context above, appealing to identity properties, or any other property that can have but one possessor, is fine; we were simply illustrating how Nuclear Bundle Theory works. The question now, though, is what sorts of properties ought to be involved in our formulation of the Identity of Indiscernibles. As we noted above, Classical Bundle Theorists ought to be committed to a relatively sparse theory of universals, in order to avoid supplying substances with over-rich metaphysical structure. The question is, then, how sparse should they go?

We can work toward an answer to this question by starting with the idea of a *qualitative* property. Qualitative properties are those that are associated with a thing's fundamental character; they make for the qualities of things. A couple of examples might help. The property of *being green* is qualitative, while the property of *being grue* is not. Mass properties are qualitative, but disjunctive properties are not. We would like, though, to have more than a list, since any such list is likely to not be exhaustive. A plausible way to identify which properties are qualitative is this: properties are qualitative if and only if they are "natural," in something like David Lewis's (1983) sense.[13] Natural properties are those that make for objective resemblances or fundamental causal powers. If a property can explain an objective resemblance between or among things, then it is natural. Likewise, if a property can explain why something has a fundamental causal power, then it is natural. Importantly, a property needn't do both of these, though it might; it need only do one or the other. Classical Bundle Theorists can then say that a universal exists if and only if it is a natural property. This, then, requires a particular formulation of the Identity of Indiscernibles, which we can call Restricted Identity of Indiscernibles: if substance s_1 exemplifies a natural property if and only substance s_2 does, then s_1 is identical to s_2.

We are now positioned to articulate the problem for Classical Bundle Theory toward which we've been working. Restricted Identity of Indiscernibles seems false. Since Classical Bundle Theory entails Restricted Identity of Indiscernibles, Classical Bundle Theory must be false as well. The trouble for Restricted Identity of Indiscernibles comes in the form of thought experiments. Simply put, we seem to be able to imagine possibilities in which there are two qualitatively indiscernible substances. These worlds are often called Max Black worlds, after a philosopher, Max Black, who famously argued that there are such possibilities. Consider, for example, a world with just two homogeneous iron globes of exactly the same dimensions. Or a world with two disembodied minds with all the same thoughts, memories, beliefs, desires, and so on. Or a world with just two electrons eternally orbiting a fixed point on exactly the same path. Or we might imagine a world that is temporally symmetrical. For example, Friedrich Nietzsche imagined a world of "eternal recurrence" in which the same types of event are repeated over and over again in different temporal epochs. In such a situation, there could be a substance in one epoch that is indiscernible from a substance in every other epoch. Distinct but indiscernible Napoleons, or Beethovens, or Obamas. In each of these cases, there are two or more substances with all the same natural properties. If these scenarios are possible, then Classical Bundle Theory must be false.

This argument relies on imagination being correlated with possibility. From the fact that a certain scenario can be imagined, we must be able to infer that it is possible. If these scenarios are merely imaginable, but aren't in fact possible, then there is no trouble here for Classical Bundle Theory. The argument requires that these scenarios are really possible. In general, philosophers reject the claim that every scenario that is imaginable is also possible, and they reject the claim that every scenario that is possible is also imaginable. For example, I can imagine that Woody Allen is not Allen Konigsberg, but the two are identical, so it is not possible that Woody Allen were not Allen Konigsberg. Further, I cannot imagine a subatomic particle that fails to have a definite location or velocity, but (if quantum mechanics is true), there are actual, and so possible, situations in which subatomic particles fail to have a definite location or velocity. However, philosophers also tend to think that what we can imagine is a reliable guide to what is possible. Therefore, they think that imaginability is evidence, indeed very good evidence, of possibility. It is just evidence that can be overridden in certain cases, namely cases where one has good reason to deny the imaginable is possible. All this is to say that the inference from imaginability to possibility is a good, yet defeasible, inference. Therefore, Classical Bundle Theorists must find a way to override the evidence against their view supplied by the imaginability of the sorts of scenarios highlighted above.

Classical Bundle Theorists are here faced with what philosophers have called the problem of individuation. The problem of individuation consists in a challenge to identify a constituent of substances in virtue of which two substances are distinct, rather than identical. Since Classical Bundle Theory identifies substances with co-instantiated sets of universals, and since universals are natural properties and natural properties seem to all be shareable, the Classical Bundle Theorist seems to have no way to account for the distinctness of indiscernible substances. However, the problem of individuation is not unique to Classical Bundle Theory. Any Constituent Ontology committed to both PCI and Realism must respond to it. The problem of individuation is related to the Hochberg–Armstrong objection to Extreme Resemblance Nominalism. The reader might recall that the Hochberg–Armstrong objection pressed the Extreme Resemblance Nominalist to find distinct truthmakers for facts of similarity and facts of distinctness. The Extreme Resemblance Nominalist conflates the truthmakers for these types of fact in a problematic way, according to the objection. What we now see is that Classical Bundle Theory is up against a similar problem because they are using the same constituents of substances to account both for similarity and distinctness. The problem of individuation is a challenge to separate the metaphysical ground for similarity facts and distinctness facts.

There are at least three ways to overcome the problem of individuation.[14] Each gives up on Classical Bundle Theory as we have been characterizing it, but some of the revisions are more radical than others. First, one might go for primitive identity. Second, one might go for haecceities. Third, one might go for substrates. Let's consider each of these in turn.

Primitive Identity. Proponents of Primitive Identity claim that pairs of substances are self-individuating. A pair of substances a and b is self-individuating if and only if the metaphysical ground for the distinctness of a and b is just the pair itself. Primitive identity is, therefore, a kind of rejection of the problem of individuation as a *problem*. Its proponents say we don't need to do what the problem of individuation says we need to do. The idea is that one doesn't need to find a new constituent to individuate indiscernible substances; the pair of substances can simply be self-individuating. Primitive identity, therefore, also either rejects PCI or fails to overcome the objection from Black worlds. If a commitment to PCI is maintained, then indiscernible substances simply *can't* be self-individuating: PCI entails that two substances cannot have identical constituents, since it says where there is sameness of constituents, there is sameness of substance. If the commitment to Primitive Identity is to do any work in our present context then, it must be taken as a rejection of PCI. This rejection of PCI is also the chief trouble for Primitive Identity. For as we saw above, PCI is very difficult to escape if one is a Constituent Ontologist. Michael Loux (2006) has gone so far as to call it a "framework constraint" on Constituent Ontology. Which is to say, a commitment to PCI is part of what it means to be a Constituent Ontologist. It is not surprising that Robert M. Adams, the most prominent defender of Primitive Identity, rejects not just PCI but also Constituent Ontology.[15]

Haecceities. In order to maintain a commitment to PCI, Constituent Ontologists must identify a type of constituent that will be unique to every substance. Some have opted to go in for haecceities. A haecceity is a property that can only be exemplified by a particular substance. They are, or are equivalent to, identity properties, properties of being identical to such-and-such object. More precisely, where s is a substance, then s's haecceity $H(s)$ is that necessarily existing universal that is exemplified by s and which nothing but s could possibly exemplify. Above, we used GRETCHENHOOD to illustrate Nuclear Bundle Theory. If this property is taken to be one that only Gretchen could even possibly have, then it is a haecceity. If there are haecceities, then we can maintain the Bundle Theory's advantage of giving a theory of substance that appeals only to properties, a Constituent Ontology that is fully committed to PCI, while also overcoming the problem posed by Black worlds. For if substances have haecceities, then Classical Bundle Theory is compatible with the falsity of Restricted Identity of Indiscernibles. Substances that are indiscernible with respect to natural properties need not be identical, for haecceities are non-natural properties that are constituents of substances. Given that every substance has a haecceity, there will always be a constituent to individuate one substance from any other substance. There is an associated cost: Classical Bundle Theorists must admit that there are non-natural properties. This doesn't sit particularly well with Constituent Ontology, and is a cost in terms of quantitative economy.

Many philosophers, though, have thought that haecceities are creatures of darkness, or at least that, if they exist, they cannot solve the problem of individuation. Robert M. Adams (1981), for example, complains that we cannot even understand what haecceities are. Take Gretchen's haecceity, GRETCHENHOOD. This haecceity, if we know what it is at all, we know because it is the property of *being identical to Gretchen*. But suppose Gretchen had never come to be; maybe THP and JKP decided to have but one child, rather than two. Then it's a challenge to understand, according to Adams, how there could be a property of *being identical to Gretchen*. For in such a case, there is no Gretchen to which to be identical! But haecceities are meant to be necessarily existent; they must exist even when the substance they are associated with does not. Maybe worse, though, it's not clear that haecceities are up to the job of solving the problem of individuation. If we understand haecceities as properties of identity – for example, if we understand GRETCHENHOOD as the property of *being identical to Gretchen* – then it is tempting to think that they are a type of relational property. A relational property is a property that something exemplifies in virtue of standing in some relation to some object or objects. For example, the property of *being ten meters from a tree* is a relational property because it is had by something in virtue of that thing's standing in the *ten meters from* relation to some tree or other. If haecceities are relational properties in this sense, then they are exemplified in virtue of a thing's standing in identity relations to certain things, namely themselves. Therefore, a substance must stand in the identity relation metaphysically prior to its exemplifying a haecceity. But this means that a substance must be individuated prior to its exemplifying a haecceity, for a thing cannot be self-identical unless it already exists, and it cannot exist if it is not individuated. Haecceities, then, cannot ground individuation. So goes the argument, anyway.

Substrates. If one is dissatisfied with both Primitive Identity and haecceities, one might opt for substrates. Substrate Theories are a more radical departure from Bundle Theory and require a more sustained discussion.

Substrate Theories   Substrate Theories require that each substance have a constituent, a substrate, in addition to the properties that characterize it. Importantly, substances are in a different fundamental category than properties; this is a matter that will receive fuller attention below. According to Substrate Theory, then, a substance is a metaphysically complex particular that has both properties and a substrate as constituents. There are different varieties of Substrate Theory, as we will see. But a fundamental motivation for Substrate Theory in all its forms is that it purports to solve the problem of individuation. No matter what sort of substrate one opts for, no two substances can share a substrate.[16] Recall, though, that Modifier Trope Bundle Theory faced a problem of accounting for what, exactly, a substance's constituent tropes were characterizing. There is a similar problem for Classical Bundle Theory: it is not clear what a substance's constituent universals are meant to characterize, since universals are generally taken not to have the character they ground.[17] Sometimes substrates are offered to solve this problem in addition to the problem of individuation.

Substrate theory comes in two varieties, depending on whether tropes or universals ground character. (The reader might sense a pattern!) According to Trope Substrate Theory, there are substrates and tropes ground character, while according to Classical Substrate Theory, there are substrates and universals ground character. Trope Substrate Theory in turn comes in two varieties (surprise, surprise!), depending on whether tropes are modifiers or modules. We will not take up the two varieties of Trope Substrate Theory in any detail, since the troubles with each variety parallel the troubles for the two varieties of trope Bundle Theory. In particular, Modifier Trope Substrate Theory appears to be theoretically identical to Classical Substrate Theory while also being quantitatively less economical. Modular Trope Substrate Theory, on the other hand, faces the dilemma between character duplication and having to deny that there are thickly charactered objects. We will, therefore, focus on Classical Substrate Theory.

There are two main varieties of Classical Substrate Theory, and they are distinguished by their respective views on whether a substrate has character independent of the properties that are constituents of the substrate's substance. The question that distinguishes different varieties of Classical Substrate Theory, then, is whether a substrate has character *in itself*. According to Modular Substance Theory, each substrate has one dimension of character in itself, that is, independent of the properties that are constituents of the substrate's substance. This view is *Modular* Substance Theory because substrates are, on this view, roughly akin to modular tropes. According to Bare Particular Theory, each substrate has no character in itself. *Bare* particulars have no character in themselves.

The acute reader may have noticed that we have passed over views according to which substrates have more than one dimension of character in themselves. This is not an oversight, for such views face a crippling dilemma. For suppose a substrate b has two dimensions of character. (The use of two dimensions of character is incidental, and serves as a simplification. The dilemma would go the same way were the substrate to have three or more dimensions of character.) Either there are tropes or universals that ground b's character or there are not. On the one hand, suppose there are no such properties. Then b seems to be a thickly charactered object, and one will need to appeal to an account of b's character in Class or Extreme Resemblance Nominalist terms, or deny that such an account is needed, in keeping with Ostrich Nominalism. Regardless, one has thereby undercut a central motivation for Realism and Trope Theory. If Realism and Trope Theory are not needed as an account of the thick character of b, then Realism and Trope Theory are needed as a more general account of the thick character of substances. But we only need substrates if Realism or Trope Theory is true. On the other hand, suppose that one does need tropes or universals to ground b's character. Either b's characterizing properties are constituents of b or not. If they are, then one faces the problem of individuation, but for b. Given that we have embraced Substrate Theory, b will itself need a substrate. But this just sets us off down an infinite regress. If b's characterizing properties are not constituents of b, then one has abandoned Constituent Ontology in favor of Relational Ontology. Since Substrate Theory presupposed Constituent Ontology, this view is incoherent. Therefore, b, and substrates generally, cannot have more than one dimension of character.

Let's return, then, to Modular Substance Theory. We noted earlier that Modular Substance Theory is *modular* in that substrates have only one dimension of character; substrates are just modular tropes. The view is Modular *Substance* Theory because substrates, on this view, are meant to be thinly characterized with substance kinds. Substance kinds are kinds like MOUNTAIN, HUMAN, OAK-TREE, and so on, kinds that supply a thing with its characteristic species.[18] Substrates are *merely* mountains, *merely* humans, *merely* oak trees. A substrate, then, has only one dimension of character, but it is character that determines the kind of the substrate's substance. In order to avoid character duplication, Modular Substrate Theory is best combined with modifier tropes or universals as the ground of a substance's non-substance-kind character. This also displays the sense in which substrates are of a different fundamental kind than the rest of a substance's characterizing properties, despite that substrates are charactered. Further, because modular tropes need not be limited to having formal character, they can be characterized by other properties without incoherence. However, Modular Substance Theory combined with Modifier Trope Theory faces a worry that troubles all versions of Modifier Trope Theory. In particular, Modular Substance Theory with modifier tropes may be a quantitatively bloated version of a Realist Modular Trope Theory. We leave it as an exercise for the reader to develop this worry.

There is an additional trouble, one to do with Thickening Principles, for all varieties of Modular Substance Theory. Because there are no color or shape modular tropes, according to Modular Substance Theory, the thickening principles we've considered before, Color Thickening and Shape Thickening, do not plague Modular Substance Theory. However, consider:

Oak Tree Thickening: Everything that exemplifies the kind *oak tree* has a definite shape and size.

If Oak Tree Thickening is true, then Modular Substance Theory must be false. For Modular Substance Theory requires the existence of substrates that exemplify the kind *oak tree*, but that have no definite size or shape, at least not in themselves. (If one doesn't think *oak tree* is a fundamental substance kind, then substitute your favorite example to produce the right sort of thickening principle. The choice of the kind *oak tree* is not essential to the worry.) This worry, however, may not be so troubling as that facing Modular Trope Theory more generally. First of all, the connection between substance kinds and the other features that substances exemplify aren't so clear as that between, for example, color and extension. It is inconceivable that something can be blue without being extended in at least two dimensions. While it is difficult to conceive of an unshaped oak tree, the connection here doesn't seem quite so demanding. But, more importantly, it's not clear that the Modular Substance Theory has to commit to the claim that there are oak trees without a definite shape and size. For the modular trope that is an oak tree's substrate also might exemplify a number of modifying tropes or universals. In this case, the substrate has many dimensions of character. Modular Substance Theory requires only that substrates have one dimension of character *in themselves*. It is possible that they have many dimensions of character, so long as they have the other dimensions in virtue of exemplifying other properties. If this is right, then there is no incompatibility between Oak Tree Thickening (and other thickening principles of this sort) and Modular Substance Theory. Modular Substance Theory emerges, therefore, relatively unscathed.

We have one final view to consider: Bare Particular Theory. Bare particulars are substrates that have no character in themselves; they are, in that sense, property-less. They are, however, often taken to be the peg on which their substance's properties hang, as it were. That is, bare particulars are sometimes taken to be *tied to*, one might even say they *exemplify*, the properties of the substance of which they are a constituent.

This duality famously led Wilfrid Sellars (1963: 282), and others, to object that bare particulars are self-contradictory. Bare particulars are meant to have properties, but also meant to be property-less. In the context of Classical Substrate Theory, we might put the objection more forcefully. Bare particulars are not meant to be similar to one another, for they are property-less. But they also exemplify universals, and in virtue of this they very well may be similar to one another. The Bare Particular Theorist ought to say, in response to this objection, that bare particulars are only meant to be property-less *in themselves*. However, they very well may have character when taken in conjunction with the properties they exemplify as part of their role as the substrates of substances. This is similar to the way in which Modular Substance Theory involves modular tropes that do not violate thickening principles because they have one dimension of character in themselves but many when taken together with the rest of a substance's properties. In the context of a Truthmaker Theory, we might understand the sense in which

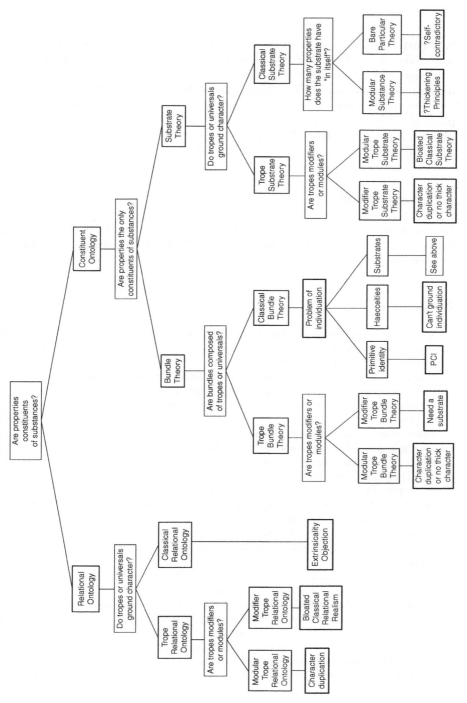

Figure 5.1

bare particulars have no properties in themselves in the following way. The truthmaker for a claim that some bare particular is similar to another bare particular will involve more than the pair of bare particulars themselves; it must involve some universal or trope. The truthmaker for the distinctness of two bare particulars, on the other hand, will involve just the pair of bare particulars themselves. It is not, therefore, clear that Sellars's incoherence objection is fatal to Bare Particular Theory. Bare Particular Theory, like Modular Substance Theory, emerges relatively unscathed.

5.3   Conclusion

No doubt there is much more to say about all of the views we have canvassed in this section on theories of substance. But the results of our preliminary investigation are summarized in Figure 5.1.

Notes

1   We are here using "state of affairs" in the way David M. Armstrong (1997) does. There are important differences between this usage and others; see, especially, Plantinga (1974) and Chapter 7.
2   One does, for the reasons canvassed in connection with tropes, have to think of states of affairs as charactered in the right sorts of ways, *à la* modular tropes. Whether this picture of states of affairs is sustainable is not a question we take up here.
3   Philosophers have sometimes used the modifier "non-mereological" where we use "metaphysical." Constituent Realists can hold, we think, that the metaphysical and ordinary material parts of a substance are all *parts* in the same sense. See Paul (2012) for a sophisticated defense of this point.
4   See, especially, Loux (1978) and van Inwagen (2011).
5   As we noted in the previous chapter, we use all-caps to speak of universals and italics to speak generically of properties.
6   Some philosophers say that Constituent Ontologists think of properties as immanent in substances. We take ourselves to be expressing the same idea in the foregoing.
7   We will generally drop this parenthetical remark. The reader is invited to assume that it holds, in the cases we are interested in.
8   Modular Trope Bundle Theory also faces the worries for Modular Trope Theory in general, discussed in Chapter 4. We won't rehearse those arguments here.
9   Our talk of "sets" in this section shouldn't be taken too literally. It's easier to talk about a set of universals than to keep talking about "some universals" (in the plural). However, the latter is closer to what Bundle Theorists really think: a substance is (somehow) some universals that stand in a single co-instantiation relation to each other.

10 Or, to be more precise, it just is the members of that set, taken together.
11 See Simons (1994) and Paul (2002, 2006).
12 See especially Black (1952) and Adams (1979).
13 Cf. Pickavance (forthcoming). Our use of "natural" is close to Lewis's use of "perfectly natural," though differences may emerge in the details.
14 There are, in fact, even more than three. We have chosen to focus our attention on the three most prominent responses. For more on the other strategies, see Koons and Pickavance (forthcoming).
15 See especially Adams (1979).
16 This is intentionally ambiguous among readings that prohibit just temporally synchronic sharing, temporally synchronic and temporally diachronic sharing, and temporally synchronic and diachronic as well as trans-world sharing. All versions of Substrate Theory prohibit temporally synchronic sharing of substrates. Most defenders of Substrate Theory do not explicitly take up this question, though things they say suggest that they mean to prohibit all three forms of sharing. But some do not; Pickavance (2009), for example, is explicitly agnostic about this question. See also Pickavance (2014).
17 We have not directly taken up the question of whether universals have the character they ground, but it is a matter of some historical importance. Plato was famously taken by Aristotle to believe that universals have the character they ground, and Aristotle's "Third Man" argument is an attempt to refute that aspect of the theory Aristotle attributes to Plato.
18 "Species" need not mean biological species. We are not overly concerned with the specifics here, since they don't matter to the issues we're targeting.

6

Composition

In the last chapter, we looked at the metaphysical structure of particular things. In this chapter, we turn to another aspect of the world of particulars: the ways in which ordinary, material things can be parts of larger, more inclusive wholes. When some material things form a whole in such a way that they are parts of it, we shall say that they *compose* that whole. The first question to ask is this: when do things compose something? This is the so-called Special Composition Question, which we will take up in Section 6.1. It is possible to take this question to be a trivial one, with a trivial answer: Always. Those who provide this answer are called "Universalists." Universalists typically take the postulation of inclusive material wholes to be a lightweight matter, requiring no special justification. For example, David M. Armstrong insists that we can enjoy an "ontological free lunch" when adding such composite entities to our ontological inventory (Armstrong 1997: 12–13). We will examine this idea in Section 6.2.

We will then proceed in Section 6.3 to two relatively simpler answers to the Special Composition Question: Never, and Just Once. Those who deny that composition ever happens are the Atomists. According to Atomists, every fundamental thing that exists is mereologically simple, without any parts whatsoever. A diametrically opposing view is that of Monism, according to which there is just one fundamental thing, namely, the entire universe, a thing having every other material thing as one of its parts. Atomism (if proposed as a necessary truth about the fundamental structure of the world) is incompatible with the possible existence of what David K. Lewis called "gunk." A material thing is gunky if it has parts but no atomic (simple) parts. Similarly, Monism is incompatible with the possible existence of junk,

Metaphysics: The Fundamentals, First Edition. Robert C. Koons and Timothy H. Pickavance.
© 2015 Robert C. Koons and Timothy H. Pickavance.
Published 2015 by John Wiley & Sons, Ltd.

where something is junky if it is part of some more inclusive whole, but not part of anything that isn't part of something still larger. Therefore, we will consider the possibility of gunk and junk in Section 6.4.

The last section of the chapter contains a view – Compositional Pluralism – that rejects each of the simple answers (Universalism, Atomism, and Monism). Compositional pluralists believe that some of the world's fundamental things are medium-sized: neither atomic nor cosmic. It is common for compositional pluralists to talk of composite wholes "emerging" from the combination of their parts, so we will investigate in Section 6.5 the possibilities of such emergence. We will lay out possible sources of evidence for emergence, and we will evaluate the prospects for emergent entities of various kinds, including organisms, artifacts, social groups, and natural formations.

6.1   The Special Composition Question

Under what conditions do some material things come to compose a further thing, in such a way that they come to be parts of a more inclusive whole? This is the "Special Composition Question," which Peter van Inwagen introduced into the contemporary discussion in his book, *Material Beings* (1990). The Question arises in the context of the metaphysical theory of parts and wholes, called "mereology" (from the Greek word for "part," *meros*).

There is a simple answer that is popular among metaphysicians: the answer of Universalism. According to Universalists, every set or class of material beings is of such a kind that its members collectively compose some one thing. This simple answer has some surprising and downright odd consequences. It follows, for example, that the left half of Rob Koons and the right half of Tim Pickavance compose a single material being, with a somewhat scattered location (one part in Austin and the other in Los Angeles). Similarly, the bridges of the world collectively form a single, scattered entity, made up partly of a wide variety of materials (steel, wood, rope, and so on). These are entities that neither science nor common sense have ever found need to postulate: Universalism seems to inflate our ontological inventory of the world needlessly.

In addition, Universalism gives rise to the ancient Problem of the Many. Consider a particular dog, Fido. Now consider all the parts of Fido that do not overlap his left ear. According to Universalism, these parts compose something, so let's call it Fido-Minus. Is Fido-Minus a dog? He's certainly something very like a dog, since Fido could himself survive as a dog without his left ear. In fact, there is, if Universalism is true, some huge, even astronomical number of things just like Fido-Minus, each of which is composed by some set containing nearly all of Fido's parts. It seems that we have, not just one dog, but zillions of dogs contained simultaneously in Fido's doghouse!

Universalists have proposed several solutions to the problem of the many. They might insist that Fido-Minus and the other aren't dogs at all, since to be a dog is to be a maximal doggy entity. Or, they might concede (as David K. Lewis recommends in Lewis 1993), that Fido-Minus and the others are real dogs, and that they are really distinct from each other, but insist that, when we count how many dogs are in the doghouse, we count Fido and the multitude of Fido-Minuses as *just one dog*. Still, the fact that Universalism entails that our world is inhabited by zillions of heretofore unnoticed dog-like creatures seems a weighty disadvantage.

Finally, Universalism is difficult to reconcile with the fact that many things (including organisms like you and we) are mereologically inconstant, in the sense that they can gain or lose parts over time. The particles that composed RCK ten years ago no longer compose RCK today. Yet, if mereological Universalism is true, the particles that composed RCK ten years ago still compose something today, call it Ten-Plus. If this *sum* of particles existed ten years ago and also exists today, then it seems that Ten-Plus has a much better claim to being the *same entity* (strictly speaking) that RCK was ten years ago than RCK himself does. Similarly, the particles that compose RCK today also composed something ten years ago. Call this thing Ten-Minus. It would seem that Ten-Minus has a better claim to having been ten years ago the *same entity* (in the strict, metaphysically relevant sense) as RCK is today. Thus, we should say that RCK was really Ten-Minus ten years ago, and that the person who was called "RCK" ten years ago is now Ten-Plus. But Ten-Minus was not a human being ten years ago, and Ten-Plus is not a human being now. Thus, there are *no* truly persistent human beings, and everything is mereologically constant, incapable of gaining or losing parts. These seem to be absurd consequences (van Inwagen 1990: 77–78). We will take this question of persistence up again in Chapter 9.

Peter van Inwagen takes this last objection to Universalism to be decisive. Van Inwagen's proposed answer to the Special Composition Question is this: some things compose something if and only if their joint activity constitutes a life. Thus, only living organisms have parts: everything else is simple (part-less). Van Inwagen's defense of this answer relies on five assumptions:

> (vI1) There is a relatively simple answer to the Special Composition Question.
> (vI2) Any relatively simple answer to the Special Composition Question would involve some combination of the following conditions: (i) being some things whose activity constitutes a life (composing an organism), (ii) being some things that have been put together or function together for some purpose of some user or users (composing an artificial thing or artifact), or (iii) being some things that are bound, glued, or fused together.
> (vI3) Living organisms exist.
> (vI4) Artifacts do not exist.
> (vI5) When a pair of living organisms is bound, glued, or fused together, they do not thereby compose a third thing.

Van Inwagen runs through a series of thought experiments designed to convince us that assumption (vI5) is true. For example, if two people are shaking hands and while shaking, their hands become locked or glued together, it does not seem plausible to say that they together compose some new thing. The situation remains one in which there are two things bound or glued together, not a situation in which a third, composite thing has been generated, having each of the two people as parts. Van Inwagen argues that this is obviously true, even in the case of people who are seamlessly fused together, as happens in the case of Siamese twins.

We will look at some of the arguments against the existence of artifacts, both by van Inwagen and by others, in Section 6.6 below. Van Inwagen supports (vI3), the existence of living organisms, both by a direct appeal to common sense, and by means of René Descartes' *cogito* argument. Descartes (a seventeenth-century French philosopher and rationalist) argued that each of us cannot doubt his or her own existence, since we cannot think anything at all, even by way of doubting something, without existing. Hence, the proposition that I doubt my own existence entails the proposition that I exist. There is something unstable or untenable about denying my own existence. In addition, van Inwagen takes it as obvious that, if I exist, I am a living organism, and so there exists at least one living organism, as required by (vI3).

Van Inwagen's main argument for his answer proceeds by way of a process of elimination. We start by assuming that there is a relatively simple answer to the Special Composition Question (vI1), consisting of one or more sufficient conditions for composition, taken from a short list of possible conditions (vI2). Van Inwagen argues that being bound, glued, or fused together is not a sufficient condition for composing something (vI5), nor is being put together or functioning together for a single purpose (vI4). Consequently, living organisms are the only composite material things.

But why should we assume that the Special Composition Question has a simple, or even a finite, answer? Ned Markosian (1998) has suggested that we take seriously the thesis of Brutal Composition, according to which there is no answer to the Special Composition Question that can be given in a finitely long statement. If we want to respect all of the commitments of common sense, we could embrace a series of partial answers to the SCQ, one for each of the many kinds of entities that we are inclined, as a matter of common sense, to acknowledge:

> The *x*'s compose something if they form a living organism.
> The *x*'s compose something if they form a cup.
> The *x*'s compose something if they form a club or team.
> The *x*'s compose something if they form a mountain.
> And so on, potentially *ad infinitum*.

In order to make any progress toward an interesting and informative answer to the SCQ, we must supplement the appeal to common sense with some further constraint, a constraint that will enable us to reject Markosian's Brutal Composition and a laundry-list approach that simply reflects our initial assumptions about the world. One such constraint is Ockham's Razor, named after the fourteenth-century English philosopher and theologian William of Ockham (or Occam). Ockham's Razor directs us to prefer, when possible, relatively simple theories, theories that minimize the number of basic kinds and categories of things in the world, as well as the number of individual things.

A common-sensical version of Brutal Composition would violate Ockham's Razor twice over, first by insisting that there is a very large, even possibly infinite, number of different *ways* by which composite things are composed, and second by multiplying greatly the number of individual composite things that are consequently acknowledged to exist. Van Inwagen's answer to the Special Composition Question, for example, is to be preferred to the Brutal Composition Theory in both of these ways. According to van Inwagen, there is just one kind of composite thing (organisms), all of which are composed by their parts in the same way (by the activity of their parts' constituting a single life). In addition, the sheer number of composite entities is drastically reduced by van Inwagen's answer, since it denies the existence of any of the non-living composite entities that we might otherwise be inclined to accept, including ships, shoes, mountains, or stars.

In chapters 2 and 3, we introduced the idea of fundamental truths and fundamental kinds of entities. The notion of *metaphysical fundamentality* can be fleshed out in a variety of ways, including one that appeals to truth-makers. A fundamental truth is one that asserts in a simple and direct way the existence of a truthmaker, and the fundamental kinds of things would be the kinds of truthmaker and of components of truthmakers that are needed for a complete account of the truth of our assertions.

With that distinction in hand, we can distinguish between fundamental kinds of things and non-fundamental or *derived* kinds. We can also label individual entities as either "fundamental" or "derived" entities, depending on whether or not they belong to a fundamental kind. We can now ask: does Ockham's Razor apply to derived or non-fundamental entities? It seems that it does not. In building our theory of the world, we should strive to be economical or parsimonious with regard to our theory's fundamental kinds and fundamental entities, but having a large number of derived kinds and derived entities seems to be no problem. In fact, the more derived kinds and things, the better, since these will reflect our theory's power to encompass a wide variety of phenomena.

Some philosophers, following Willard Van Orman Quine, reject the notion of fundamentality altogether. For such Quineans, the task of ontology is simply to determine what exists, period. Quineans who adopt Ockham's Razor must apply it to all kinds of entities.

In effect, there are two versions of the Special Composition Question, one for those who accept fundamentality and another for Quineans. Fundamentalists or Priority Theorists must ask: When do some things compose a fundamental entity? Quineans ask the SCQ in its simpler form, as proposed by van Inwagen: When do some things compose anything at all? However, so long as both groups apply Ockham's Razor to possible answers to these questions, evaluation of various ontological theories will proceed in very similar ways for both groups.

6.2   Ontological Free Lunch?

Some Universalists argue that Ockham's Razor should not apply at all to composite entities. As David M. Armstrong (1997: 12–13) has expressed this idea, composite things should be treated as an "ontological free lunch," in the sense that it should not count at all against a metaphysical theory that it posits a large number of composite things or a large number of kinds of composite things. This could be taken in two ways. The first is to suppose that only simple or atomic things are fundamental, and that all composite things are merely derived entities. This amounts to a position of Priority Atomism, which we will discuss in Section 6.3.

The other way to take Armstrong's suggestion is one that could be embraced by Quineans, who reject the idea of fundamentality, and by those who think that composite entities are just as fundamental as their parts. On this interpretation, even if composite entities are fundamental, they still do not come within the scope of Ockham's Razor, on the grounds that the composite entities and their properties *supervene* on the properties of their parts, in the sense that fixing the properties of the parts fixes both the existence and the properties of the whole. Consequently, a composite thing is no "addition to being," nothing "over and above" the parts and their properties. No substantive addition to the acknowledged matters of fact is involved in recognizing the existence of composite entities.

The Free Lunch Principle

If (i) a theory T_1 entails both the existence of the x's and also the existence of y, while theory T_2 entails only the existence of the x's, and if
(ii) according to T_1, the x's wholly compose y (i.e., nothing overlaps y without overlapping one of the x's),

then the fact that T_1 entails the existence of y does not favor T_2 over T_1 (in respect of the application of any version of Ockham's Razor).

This claim can, in turn, be defended in one of three ways. The first, more radical way, is by means of the theory of Composition as Identity. On this theory, whenever we have a set of two or more things, it is a matter of pure logic that there also exists a whole that contains those things as parts, and nothing separate from those things. The second way depends on controversial assumptions about powers and the natures of properties and property instantiation. It is a way that fits best with Neo-Humeism about powers and Resemblance Nominalism about properties. On this view, the addition of composite entities involves no commitment to irreducibly new facts about the world, and so should be immune to objections based on Ockham's Razor. The third way depends on assuming that only simple things (atoms) are fundamentally real.

6.2.1   Composition as Identity

In order to make clear what the Composition as Identity Theory consists in, it is helpful to make use of the logic of plurals developed by George Boolos (1984). According to Boolos, we need to recognize that language includes both singular and plural terms, including singular and plural variables. Many proper names, for example, are singular terms, like "Austin" or "Julius Caesar," purporting to refer to a single entity. Other names are plural in nature, such as "the St. Louis Cardinals" or "the Beatles." These names refer to many things at once: to the various members of a baseball team or a rock group, for example. We must also recognize singular variables (often expressed by singular pronouns, "he," "she," and "it") and plural variables ("they"). We can also form plural quantifiers, like "some people" or "some nations." For example, we can say things like the following:

1.   If some people play baseball together, they will come to like one another.
2.   There are some nations that recognize only those governments that recognize all of them.

Composition as Identity (Baxter 1988) takes composition to be a form of simple identity. That is, a whole simply is identical to its parts (taken collectively, not distributively). If an encyclopedia is composed of ten volumes, then the encyclopedia simply is the ten volumes, and the ten volumes are the encyclopedia. The cloud is identical to its constituent droplets, and the droplets are identical to the cloud. On this view, the whole is nothing "over and above" its parts.

Composition as Identity doesn't, by itself, entail Universalism, as Kris McDaniel has noted (2010). Baxter's CAI theory could be taken to imply no more than that, if some things do compose a whole, then the whole is identical to its parts. Such a minimal reading of CAI would leave it open whether any plurality of things constituted a single thing or not. Indeed, CAI on this reading is compatible even with Nihilism, the thesis that many things never count as one thing. A CAI-Nihilists would suppose that things never compose a whole, but, if they did, the whole would be identical to its parts.

There is, however, a bolder version of Composition as Identity: one according to which *every* plurality is identical to one thing simply by being identical to themselves. Since the droplets in the sky are identical (collectively) to themselves, there is something (namely, the plurality of droplets) that they compose. This bolder version of Composition as Identity treats plural names and variables as replaceable with singular terms and variables, as a matter of logic. Since it is always the case that the y's are identical to the y's, it would be a matter of logic that there is some one thing (namely, the plurality of the y's, taken as one) that the y's are identical to. This would give us Universalism as a truth of logic.

From the viewpoint of such bold or *Reductive* CAI, a theory that posits the existence of a whole, given any collection of parts, doesn't commit its endorsers to any addition to reality, over and above the parts themselves. If the droplets exist, so does the cloud; if the volumes exist, so does the encyclopedia; and, in general, for any non-empty set S, the members of S jointly form a whole, the whole being nothing more than the parts themselves.

Thus, according to *Reductive* Composition as Identity, a singular term referring to a composite thing is really just a plural term in disguise. To refer to a composite "thing" is really just to refer collectively to its parts. Consequently, whenever we have some things, call them the x's, there will always be some *thing* (namely, the x's themselves, taken collectively) of which they are all parts, and with which nothing overlaps that doesn't overlap with one of the them.

Thus, whenever some x's compose some y, the x's just are identical to y. Consequently, any x's whatsoever will compose something, since the x's will always be identical to the x's. When we refer to the x's collectively, we can call them "y," and it will follow by logic alone that the x's compose y. As a result, Universalism is justified.

Donald Baxter's theory of composition is one way of interpreting the theory of parts and wholes, known as "mereology." The theory of mereology, proposed by the Polish logician Stanislaw Lesniewski (1886–1939) and introduced to the wider world by Goodman and Leonard in a 1940 article in the *Journal of Symbolic Logic* (Leonard and Goodman 1940), provides that vocabulary and such a model. Reductive Composition as Identity (RCAI) theory could include the following definitions of parthood and of composition:[1]

> x is an *RCAI-part* of y if and only if there are some z's, x is one of the z's and y = the z's.
> The x's *RCAI-compose* y if and only if the x's = y.

One objection to Composition by Identity, mentioned by Peter van Inwagen (van Inwagen 1994), is the charge of ungrammaticality. Is it grammatically proper to say that some things (plural) are identical to some one thing (singular)? There is a long tradition in logic, going back to Aristotle, of assuming that strict identity can be expressed only by means of two singular terms: *a* is identical to *b*. We can also understand what it means to assert that some things, the *x*'s, are identical to some other things, the *y*'s. This would mean that every *x* is identical to some *y*, and vice versa. However, can we make sense of saying that some things are identical to some one thing?

In response, the defender of Composition as Identity can either deny that such statements are ungrammatical, or respond that linguistic rules are only an imperfect guide to metaphysical truth.

There is perhaps a still more fundamental objection. A single thing is always one, and some things are always many. Unity or one-ness seems to be contrary to many-ness or plurality. If a single thing is identical, in the strict sense, to many things, that that thing would have to be simultaneously one and many, an apparent contradiction.

Defenders of Composition as Identity could appeal here to an idea of Gottlob Frege's (Frege was a logician and philosopher of mathematics in Germany in the late nineteenth and early twentieth centuries). Frege argued that "one" and "many" and other numerical quantifiers are semantically incomplete expressions (Frege 1950: 58–60, 64–68; orig. pub. 1884). We can always ask, "One what?" or, "Many what?" For instance, the Cardinals could be one team but many players, and the Beatles could be one rock band but many musicians. Consequently, it isn't obvious that unity and plurality are contrary properties.

However, we can legitimately ask whether *RCAI*-parts are really parts, and whether Baxter-composition is real composition. There is a principle of mereology that is widely accepted, the principle of the transitivity of parthood.

Transitivity of Parthood: If *x* is part of *y*, and *y* is part of *z*, then *x* is part of *z*.

There are some apparent exceptions to this. For example, the left thumb of Jeter is a part of Jeter, and Jeter is a part of the Yankees, but we don't suppose that Jeter's left thumb is a part of the Yankees. However, these exceptions can be easily explained away by supposing that there are shifting domains of discourse associated with our statements. Thus, when thinking about the parts of a baseball team, we don't usually include the parts of the players in our domain for the purpose of evaluating our statements. So, let's suppose that, in the strict sense and with the widest possible domain of discourse fixed, transitivity of parthood is a logical truth.

Is *RCAI* parthood transitive? Consider first a concrete example. Let's define *the United States* as the plurality identical to the 50 states, taken collectively (for simplicity's sake, we'll ignore the District of Columbia, Puerto

Rico, and all the territories). Let's also define each state as the plurality of its counties (or parishes, in the case of Louisiana). So, Texas is Harris County, Bexar County, Travis County, etc. Harris County is (by definition) part of Texas, and Texas is part of the United States, but is Travis County part of the United States? There is nothing in reductive CAI that entails this. Let's define *the United States-C* as the plurality of all the counties and parishes of states in the United States. Now, Travis County is a part of the United States-C, but is the United States-C the very same thing as the United States? Reductive CAI does not give us the resources to answer this question.

Let's take an abstract example. Let's suppose that A is an $RCAI$-part of B, and B is an $RCAI$-part of C. According to the definitions of $RCAI$-parts, this means that there are some x's such that $B =$ the x's, and A is one of them, and there are some y's such that $C =$ the y's, and B is one of them. Does it follow that there are some z's such that $C =$ the z's and A is one of the z's? No, it does not follow. To demonstrate this, let's take a simplified version of this example. Let's suppose that $B = (A$ and $D)$, and $C = (B$ and $E)$. In this case, clearly A is a $RCAI$-part of B and B is an $RCAI$-part of C. Is A an $RCAI$-part of C?

We might think that it can be proved that A is a $RCAI$-part of C, once we use the law of identity (Leibniz's law) to re-describe C. Since $C = (B$ and $E)$, and $B = (A$ and $D)$, it follows logically that $C = ((A$ and $D)$ and $E)$. So, shouldn't it follow that A is an $RCAI$-part of C? No, because all we know is that C is identical to the *pair* consisting of E and of A and D (taken as one). We do not know that C is identical to the *triple* consisting of $A, D,$ and E, nor do we know that C is identical to the pair consisting of A and of E and D (taken as one). The laws of logic and the definitions of Reductive CAI alone do not allow us to rearrange the groupings (represented by parentheses) in this way.

We know that A and D together form an $RCAI$-unit (namely B), and we know that B and E taken together form an $RCAI$-unit (namely, C). We also know that the three things $A, D,$ and E together form an $RCAI$-unit, but we do not know from definitions and the logic of identity alone that C is identical to the $RCAI$-unit that the three things $A, D,$ and E form together.

Similarly, the $RCAI$ definitions do not support another basic principle of mereology, known as Strong Supplementation.

> Strong Supplementation: If x is not a part of y, then x has a part, z, that does not overlap y (i.e., that has no parts in common with y).

Strong Supplementation can also be stated this way: if every part of x overlaps y, then x is a part of y. Consider again the State of Texas and the United States-C (which is defined as identical to the counties and parishes in the 50 states). All of the parts of Texas (the various counties in it) overlap the

United States-C; in fact, each of them is a part of the United States-C. Thus, Strong Supplemenation demands that Texas be a part of the United States-C. However, reductive CAI does not support this conclusion.

Let's consider again a simple abstract example. Let's suppose that $F = (G$ and H and $J)$, and let's suppose that $K = (H$ and $J)$. Clearly, K has no parts that are not also parts of F, and so all of its parts overlap F. Strong Supplementation would require that K be a part of F. However, we cannot show that K is a CAI-part of F, since F is identical to a triple $(G, H,$ and $J)$, none of which is identical to K (which is identical to the pair of H and J, taken together).

Consequently, the hypothesis of Reductive Composition as Identity, even if it were true, could not provide, all by itself, an adequate basis for the theory of mereology. The arguments above demonstrate that parthood cannot be reduced to or replaced by RCAI-parthood, nor composition by RCAI-composition. The hypothesis of Reductive Composition as Identity must be supplemented by non-trivial mereological axioms, like transitivity and strong supplementation. The definitions of CAI-part or CAI-composition cannot, by themselves, serve as adequate replacements for true parthood or true composition. Therefore, the bold Composition as Identity proposal cannot make Universalism true by logic or stipulation. The stipulation can make it true that the members of any set *RCAI*-compose something, but it cannot by itself guarantee that the members of any set *really* compose something.

6.2.2   Free Lunch Based on Theories of Property Instantiation

There is a second, more metaphysical route to the conclusion that Universalism doesn't incur any ontological cost. This second route depends on assuming the truth of both Neo-Humeism and Resemblance Nominalism (discussed above in chapters 3 and 4).

Positing a whole or a sum in addition to its parts does not involve any addition to or alteration of the distribution of qualities in space and time, or the pattern of resemblances across space and time. Consequently, such ontological inflation is costless, not a difference in fact but only in our way of representing the facts.

This deflationary picture of the ontological cost of composition depends on Resemblance Nominalism about properties and Neo-Humeism about powers. Powerists must be interested in finding a metaphysical theory that eliminates causal redundancy, as Trenton Merricks has argued (Merricks 2003: 57–58, 66–83). If composite entities exist and are as fundamental as their parts, then they must bear causal powers, powers that would redundantly duplicate the powers of their parts.

Similarly, those Realists who believe in either universals or modifying tropes have good reason to treat the addition of composite entities to our ontological inventory as costly. If composite entities are as fundamental as their parts, then both the composite things and the parts will be equally tied to appropriate universals or modifying tropes. To posit composite things along with their parts as fundamental is to introduce a modificational redundancy into our theory, with more ties of instantiation or modification between particulars and properties than is strictly necessary. Ockham's Razor directs us to minimize the number of such ties.

There is, however, a way to reconcile Realism and Powerism with the Free Lunch Principle. Realists and Powerists can embrace the FLP, so long as the *power* of each whole consists in the powers of the parts, and the *instantiation* of a universal by the whole consists in the instantiation of the universal by the parts. In other words, if we can apply the FLP first to powers, universals, and instantiation-nexuses, then we can go on and apply it to the composite substances themselves. This requires powers, universals, and instantial ties or nexuses (if there are any) to have proper parts that correspond one-to-one to the proper parts of each composite thing.[2]

How this would work out in detail depends on whether we assume a Relational or a Constituent version of Realism. Relational Realists would have to posit composite nexuses that connect composite objects to universals in such a way that the proper parts of each composite particular are connected to the same universal by proper parts of the nexus. Relational Realists who don't posit nexuses can't make use of this solution. Since they treat instantiation facts as primitive, they must reject the Free Lunch Principle.

Constituent Realists would have to posit composite universals, in such a way that, when a composite whole instantiates a universal, there are parts of the universal that are contained in the parts of the particular. Solutions of this sort are going to be available only in special cases. For example, such a solution might work as an account of how composite particulars instantiate spatial-location universals. It is plausible that, if composite body C (consisting of parts A and B) instantiates location universal L (consisting of sub-locations M and N), then A must also instantiate M and B instantiate N (or vice versa). One might argue that C's instantiating L just is A's instantiating M and B's instantiating N. However, this won't work in the case of quantities. For example, suppose the same composite C instantiates the universal of HAVING-4-GRAMS-OF-MASS. It is not at all plausible that this universal can be divided into two equal parts, such that A instantiates one and B the other. This would require there to be two distinct universals of two grams of mass, which is absurd.

Consequently, many Relational Realists and all Constituent Realists will have to reject the Free Lunch Principle.

Even some Ostrich Nominalists may agree with these Powerists and Realists, since they seek to minimize their fundamental vocabulary, eliminating where possible terms that apply only to composite things. Similarly, Natural Class Nominalists must try to avoid positing natural classes that contain only composite things. However, other Ostrich Nominalists and Natural Class Nominalists will disagree, namely, those whose theories employ a uniform vocabulary that applies equally at all scales, applying to composite entities only when they equally to all their parts, no matter how small.

Those who are both Neo-Humeists about powers and Extreme Resemblance Nominalists about properties may also be in the camp of awarding ontological free lunches to composite entities. Positing composite entities doesn't seem to add any new resemblance-facts: the fact that two composite things resemble each other is no fact over and above the facts about the similarity of their parts and the similarities of the relations between two or more of them. This would be true of both Extreme Nominalists (with no tropes at all) and of Modular Trope Nominalists who rely on resemblance as their primitive, since the resemblance of two composite modular tropes would also be wholly reducible to the resemblance of their parts and the resemblance of the relations among those parts. Even this route to the FLP might fail, however, if there are natural *Gestalt* qualities: ways that wholes resemble other wholes that cannot be reduced to facts about the resemblance of the parts and their relations. Some psychologists talk about such "Gestalt" properties of wholes as perceived.

6.2.3   Free Lunch Based on Atomism

There is a third way in which one might try to trivialize the Special Composition Question. Suppose that one thought that all of the world's fundamental things are *atoms* (i.e., metaphysically simple things without proper parts). One could then take all composite entities as derived or reducible to atoms, in such a way that Universalism would be exempt from Ockham's Razor. We don't count it against a theory if it provides a rich ontology of derived entities. In fact, the more, the merrier. This sort of moderate or Universalistic Atomist can also provide a neat account of the nature of the part–whole relation: A is a part of B if and only if (by definition), all of the atoms of A are included among the atoms of B.

However, this approach does not in fact trivialize the Special Composition Question – it merely forces us to focus on the *fundamentalist* version of that question, and it then gives a metaphysically controversial answer to this question. That is, if we ask when do some things compose a *fundamental* thing, the Moderate Atomist answers, Never. This answer requires a justification. We will take up this issue in the next section.

6.3   Atomism and Monism

For the remainder of this chapter, we will assume that the Special Composition Question both requires a non-trivial answer and is subject to Ockham's Razor. We now turn to a very simple and economical answer to the question:

Atomism. Atomists insist that composition never occurs: all entities are mereologically simple, without parts. As we have mentioned above, we can distinguish between Quineans and Priority Theorists. Priority Theorists recognize a distinction between metaphysically fundamental entities and derived entities, while Quineans deny any such distinction.

As a result, we can also distinguish between strict or Quinean Atomists, who deny the existence of any composite entities whatsoever, and Priority Atomists, who insist only that all fundamental things are simple. To keep things relatively simple, we will focus in this section and the next on Priority Atomism. First, let's clearly define what we mean by an "atom" in this context:

Definition of "Atom": x is an *atom* if and only if x has no (proper)[3] parts.

Atomism seems plausible. It relies on a pattern of grounding that is "bottom-up": wholes derive their properties from the universals, tropes, and powers of their atomic parts, together with spatial relations of those parts to one another. This sort of bottom-up determination has become the dominant model of the structure of reality in the last several hundred years, thanks to the success of particle physics and physical chemistry in explaining so much of our familiar macroscopic phenomena. The alternative model, a model of top-down determination, is much less popular, although it has always had a significant cadre of supporters. On the alternative view, at least some parts are determined by the wholes to which they belong: properties and powers flow from wholes to parts, and not always from parts to wholes.

Here's some terminology that will simplify our discussion. Let's say that a composite entity is a "mere heap" of its parts just in case the nature of the composite is grounded in and determined by the natures of its parts and their relations. Let's say that a part is a "mere fragment" of some whole if its nature is grounded in and entirely determined by the nature of that whole.

x is a *mere heap* of the y's if and only if the y's compose x, and every fact about the intrinsic character, location, and motion of x is wholly grounded in the facts about the intrinsic characters, locations, and motions of the y's (taken individually) and the spatial relations of the y's to one another.
x is a *mere fragment* of y if x is a part of y and every fact about the intrinsic character, location, and motion of x is wholly grounded in some facts about the y (considered as a whole).

Atomism is the view that every composite entity is a mere heap of its constituent atoms. There is a view that replaces bottom-up with top-down determination: Priority Monism. According to Priority Monism, the only fundamental material thing is the entire universe, and every other material thing is a mere fragment of the universe.

There are two sorts of objections to Atomism. The first sort includes direct objections to the thesis, based on arguments for the existence of fundamental composite things of various kinds, such as people and other organisms. We will take up this sort of objection in Section 6.6.

The second sort involves appeals to a certain apparently possible sort of things whose existence is forbidden by Atomism: the possibility of *gunk*. "Gunk" is a term that David K. Lewis introduced as a convenient way of referring to a certain possibility (Lewis 1991: 20–21). A material thing is *gunky* or made of *gunk* just in case it has material parts but no atomic parts. This means that a gunk entity can be sub-divided over and over again, without limit. However, such infinite divisibility is not sufficient to be gunky: it must also be the case that *every part* of the gunky thing is also infinitely divisible in this way. There must be no atoms (in our technical sense) that are included as parts of the gunky thing.

Gunk is a problem for Atomism. The existence of gunk is inconsistent with strict or Quinean Atomism, since the Quinean Atomists insist that nothing exists except atoms, while no gunky thing can be atomic (all gunky things are by definition composite). The existence of gunk is also inconsistent with Priority Atomism, if we assume that nothing can exist unless at least one fundamental thing exists. This seems reasonable, since the existence and nature of any derived thing must be dependent on the existence and nature of the fundamental things.

We don't have any empirical evidence that there are in fact any gunky entities. However, such gunk seems *possible*: we can conceive of a world that contains gunk without encountering any obvious contradictions, and conceivability seems to be good evidence for possibility. Now, it seems that the defenders of Atomism will have to claim that Atomism is, if true, a necessary truth. If we know Atomism to be true, we must know it as a metaphysical truth, and all metaphysical truths seem to be necessary truths. Thus, if Atomism is true, gunk must be impossible. So, if gunk is possible, Atomism is false.

Do we have any independent reason for thinking that gunk might be impossible? There is one such argument: the super-cutting argument of Hawthorne and Weatherson (2004), based on a thought-experiment invented by José Benardete (Benardete 1964: 184–185). The Hawthorne–Weatherson argument is not an argument against the possibility of all kinds of gunk, but it does provide an argument against the most plausible kind of gunk, which we will call "spatial gunk."

A material body is *spatially gunky* if and only if it is gunky (i.e., has parts but no atomic parts), and every part of the body occupies a region of space with a finite volume. Every bit of spatial gunk is infinitely divisible – not only into parts with less matter, but also into parts occupying smaller volumes of space. In other words, spatial gunk contains no point-sized parts.

The thought-experiment proceeds as follows: let's suppose that we start out with a cubic meter of gunk, one meter in length on all sides. We then split the block in half along on axis, and then split those halves in half along the same axis, and so on *ad infinitum*. After each splitting, we move the results of the split apart by a distance equal to the length of each new product. Thus, we move the half-meter blocks half a meter apart, the quarter-meter blocks a quarter of a meter apart from each other, and so on. Let's suppose that the first cut takes half of a minute, the second cut takes a quarter of a minute, and so on. The sum of such an infinite series of decreasing periods is exactly one minute: hence, at the end of that minute, the block will have undergone an infinite number of cuttings along the one dimension, resulting in an infinite number of slices or chips, each one meter by one meter square but with absolutely no depth in the dimension along the axis of splitting. Each of these chips therefore has a zero volume. These two-dimensional chips will be spread out over a distance of two meters, with a finite distance between any two chips. We can also repeat this process along the other two dimensions, resulting in a volume of dimensionless points of matter, spread discontinuously throughout eight cubic meters of space. (This part of the argument depends on assuming that matter cannot move discontinuously – in particular, that it cannot jump from one location to another location at a finite distance instantaneously. Otherwise, the matter could all jump at the last moment back into the original cubic meter of space it occupied at the beginning.)

At the end of the super-cutting process, we seem to have annihilated the block of spatial gunk that we started with, assuming that spatial gunk cannot occupy space discontinuously. That is, spatial gunk must by its very nature fill one or more regions of space continuously – it cannot occupy a set of dimensionless, volume-less points, each isolated spatially from the others. Let's call this the principle of Connected Occupation:

> Connected Occupation: If no part of a body is point-sized, then no part of the body occupies an isolated point – i.e., if some part of the body occupies a point P, then there is some region, including P and extended in three dimensions, that is filled by parts of that body.

Given Connected Occupation, we must say that all the spatial gunk has been annihilated by the super-cutting process. However, this seems impossible. Surely it is impossible to annihilate matter simply by moving it. This is a third crucial assumption of the argument – the indestructibility of material bodies by mere motion.

The super-cutting objection relies on one more crucial assumption: the assumption that the structure of time and causation permits the completion of such an infinitary *super-task*. In Chapter 9, we consider arguments against the possibility of such super-tasks. If such arguments succeed, they will provide the defenders of the possibility of gunk with an answer to the super-cutting argument.

The super-cutting objection, therefore, provides some reason to reject the possibility of gunk, but the argument is far from irresistible. Against it has to be laid the fact that gunk seems to be conceivable, and conceivability (as we've said before) provides good evidence for possibility. Consequently, many philosophers are willing to grant, despite the super-cutting thought experiment, that spatial gunk is at least metaphysically possible.

Jonathan Schaffer (2010) has argued that the possibility of gunk provides good grounds for rejecting Atomism in favor of Priority or Cosmic Monism, according to which all determination is top-down. The only fundamental thing is the whole universe. Everything else is a mere fragment of the universe, with no nature of its own. Here is Schaffer's argument:

1. Either Atomism or Monism must be true (because either all determination is bottom-up or it is all top-down).
2. If Atomism is true, it is necessarily true.
3. If Atomism is true, gunk does not exist.
4. Gunk is possible.
5. So, Atomism is possibly false. (3, 4)
6. So, Atomism is false. (5, 2)
7. So, Monism is true. (6, 1)

The weakest links of Schaffer's argument are premises 1 and 2. Against 1: why can't the world contain both top-down and bottom-up determination? What can't there be medium-sized fundamental things, neither mere heaps of their atomic parts nor mere fragments of the world? And, against 2: why can't Atomism be contingently true?

In addition, Schaffer's Monism is vulnerable to a parallel argument: the appeal to the possibility of *junk*. Junk is defined in a way parallel to the definition of gunk. Just as gunk is something with parts but no atomic or indivisible parts, so junk is something that belongs to larger wholes, each of which belongs to still larger wholes. It will be convenient here to have a term for the relation that is the converse of parthood. We will use the term "encompasser" as the converse of part. If x is a proper part of y, then y is an *encompasser* of x. That is, an encompasser of x is a whole that contains x as a proper part.

An atom has no parts, and a universe has no encompasser. A gunky thing is a thing with parts but no atomic parts, and a junky thing is a thing with encompassers but no universal encompasser. Junk seems just as conceivable as gunk, so we have just as good a reason for believing in the possibility of junk as we do the possibility of gunk. However, the possibility of junk provides an argument against Monism, since junk cannot exist if the universe does.

1. If Monism is true, then it is necessarily true.
2. If Monism is true, then junk does not exist.
3. Junk is possible.
4. So, Monism is possibly false. (2, 3)
5. So, Monism is false. (1, 4)

Thus, we have a stalemate between Atomism and Monism. In addition, those who would reject both positions (the compositional pluralists we will discuss in the next section) can use the possibility of both gunk and junk as arguments against both Atomism and Monism.

Schaffer offers two additional arguments for Priority Monism. First, he appeals to modern quantum theory, especially quantum cosmology. Some models of the universe, using the resources of quantum mechanics, suggest that the entire universe is one inseparable and "entangled" system. On this interpretation, all of the facts about local events are merely aspects of the one, indivisible quantum state of the universe. However, there are other interpretations of quantum mechanics, including the so-called *Copenhagen* and other *collapse* interpretations, that do not have this consequence.

Schaffer's other argument appeals to the distinction between entities with sharp or precise boundaries and those with indefinite or vague boundaries. Schaffer argues that all ordinary physical objects have vague boundaries, while only the universe avoids this vagueness, by simply having no boundaries at all, that is, by containing absolutely everything. Schaffer concludes his argument by claiming that no entity with vague boundaries can be a fundamental thing. Hence, the universe is the one and only fundamental thing.

However, both of Schaffer's premises can be challenged. First of all, it is not obvious that all material beings have vague boundaries. If there were atoms, they would have precise boundaries (including themselves and nothing else). More importantly, if there are composite material things with emergent causal powers (of the kind we will investigate in the next section), there might be laws of emergence that determine precisely which bits of matter are or are not included in such things. A widely defended theory of vagueness, epistemicism, entails that there are no entities with intrinsically vague boundaries: vagueness is simply the consequence of our incurable ignorance about where the precise boundaries actually lie.

Second of all, it is not obvious that vague things couldn't be fundamental. Perhaps a certain amount of vagueness is part of the fundamental structure of things (a position defended by Peter van Inwagen, among others).

Finally, the Powerist understanding of science (as we described it in Chapter 3) provides an argument against Monism. Monism is inconsistent with the possibility of real scientific knowledge, understood in accordance with the Powerist model. On Powerism, only a fundamental kind of thing can bear a causal power. Thus, if Monism and Powerism were both true, there would be only one fundamental kind of powerful entities, with only a single member (the whole universe). By definition, we cannot isolate this thing from outside influences and interact with it. We can only observe its autonomous unfolding. We cannot *interact* with the universe, if Monism is true, since we are merely a dependent part of the universe. If the universe has causal powers of its own, there is no way for us to discover them by experimental interaction. If the universe were the only fundamental thing, then all real causal powers would be powers of the universe, conferred upon it by its unique and inimitable nature. We would then be unable to discover the powers of anything.

Given Powerism, science requires ontological pluralism. There must be many things with real causal powers, belonging to a number of different natural kinds. This makes it possible for us to discover those natures and their powers by well-designed experimental interaction with isolated members of each kind.

6.4   Emergence and Compositional Pluralism

Recall our definitions of mere heaps and mere fragments. A composite thing is a mere heap if its nature and existence are wholly grounded in the nature and existence of its parts, and an encompassed thing is a mere fragment if its nature and existence are wholly grounded in the nature and existence of one of its encompassers.

Let's say that a composite thing is *emergent* if it is not a mere heap, and that an encompassed thing is *autonomous* if it is not a mere fragment.

The thesis of Compositional Pluralism is the thesis that there exists at least one emergent and autonomous thing. An autonomous emergent thing is something that has both parts and encompassers and is not a mere heap of its parts nor a mere fragment of its encompassers.

Compositional Pluralism is inconsistent with Atomism, since Atomism denies that there are any emergent things, and it is also inconsistent with Monism, since Monism entails that there are no autonomous things.

Compositional Pluralism seems to entail that there are at least two fundamental things. Suppose that there were only one fundamental thing – then everything else would be either a mere fragment or a mere heap of it. But nothing can be a mere heap of just one thing, because there would be nothing to distinguish it from its one fundamental part. Consequently, everything would have to be a mere fragment of this thing. But then it would have to be the entire universe, in which case it wouldn't be encompassed, and so couldn't be autonomous.

When we talk of a thing being "emergent," we mean emergence in an ontological sense, not an epistemological one: that is, we are referring to how things are in themselves, not to how they are known by us. Ontologically emergent wholes are not mere heaps of their proper parts, and this concerns the lack of a relation of metaphysical grounding between the nature of the whole and that of its parts and their spatial relations. In contrast, a whole is *epistemically emergent* from its parts if there are facts about the whole that could not be deduced *a priori by us* from the set of empirically observable facts about its proper parts and their spatiotemporal relations.

There is a similar distinction between ontological autonomy and epistemic autonomy in relation to a thing's encompassers.

Epistemic emergence is neither necessary nor sufficient for ontological emergence. It is not necessary, since an ontologically emergent whole could mimic the behavior of its constituents, in way that was epistemically indistinguishable from a case of being a mere heap. This would be a case of *disguised emergence*. Epistemic emergence is also not sufficient, since there could be merely computational or conceptual limitations to our ability to derive the nature of the whole from that of its parts. This would be a case of *disguised reduction* to parts or a *disguised heap*.

Nonetheless, epistemic emergence is good *prima facie* evidence for ontological emergence. And, it may be difficult to find good grounds for ontological emergence in the absence of particular cases of epistemic emergence.

We will introduce one more piece of terminology to aid in our discussion, this one drawn from the work of Aristotle and his followers. Aristotle called a fundamental unit of reality an "*ousia*" (in the Greek), which is usually translated "substance" (from the Latin "*substantia*," or underlying thing). We will use the term "Aristotelian substance" or "real substance" in a way that reflects Aristotle's Compositional Pluralism:

> Definition of Substance: An *Aristotelian* (or *real*) *substance* is an autonomous emergent whole.

There can be wholes that are coequal with some of its parts, with partial determination in both directions. The whole is emergent from its parts, although partly determined by them, and the parts are autonomous relative to the whole, although partly determined by it. The intrinsic nature and powers of each depends in part on the other. In this case, we can have real substances that are parts of other real substances.

6.5 Possible Evidence for Compositional Emergence

To establish the existence of real substances, we would have to find evidence that medium-sized objects (larger than atoms but smaller than the entire universe) are both autonomous and emergent. We've already discussed the evidence for autonomy: all of science involves the investigation of the natures of things smaller than the entire universe. It is emergence that poses a greater challenge today, given the remarkable success of bottom-up explanation of phenomena in terms of the natures of fundamental particles and their spatial relationships.

In this section we will examine the shape of possible epistemic emergence. Even if we cannot find absolutely conclusive evidence for ontological emergence, we may be able to find good evidence for it: cases in which real properties and powers seem to be possessed by medium-scale composite objects. The first piece of evidence of emergence we might look for is that of novel causal powers, especially novel active powers. By "novel" powers we mean powers of the whole that cannot (even in principle) be deduced from the powers of the parts and their spatial relations to one another. For example, if the behavior of living organisms could not be deduced from the powers of their microphysical particles and the particles contained in their environment, the unexplained behavior would have to be attributed to novel powers.

However, the discovery of such powers would not be sufficient, all by itself, to provide even a *prima facie* case for ontological emergence. In a classic paper on emergence, Meehl and Sellars (1956) argued that such novel behavior could always be attributed to latent powers of the microparticles involved: powers possessed by the microparticles but only manifested when they are combined spatially in certain ways (such as the way they are combined in living organisms). If that's right, then epistemic emergence has to involve more than just novel powers.

What do we need to add? Here are four possibilities:

1   Essentially unitary properties. These would be properties that cannot be conceived of as being instantiated only by atoms, either individually or jointly. Biology provides many plausible examples of such unitary properties: being alive, eating, growing, fleeing danger, fighting enemies, or reproducing oneself. Each of these properties, if it really exists at all, is a property of a living organism and not of its constituent parts. Being alive is not a property of a relation among a set of particles, because a bearer of life (a living organism) can never be simply identified with a collection of particles. The same organism can be composed of different particles at different times.

Mental properties and properties of consciousness are also good candidates for unitary properties. To be in pain, for example, is a property of a whole organism, and not of its microphysical atoms. Both sets of examples can and have been challenged. There have been many attempts to reduce biological and mental truths to microphysical facts, claiming that there are microphysical truthmakers for all such truths. If such reductions were successful, we would have to deny that there were universals or tropes corresponding to the biological and mental predicates, and so no real biological or mental properties (in the ontological sense of "properties"). However, these reductive programs have not yet succeeded (see, for example, Searle 1992; Chalmers 1996; Kim 2007; Koons and Bealer 2010), and so in the meantime the apparent reality of such properties supports the case for emergent (real) substances.

2   Indeterministic fusion of parts, along with autonomous laws of the persistence of composite wholes. This is a possibility suggested by both Paul Humphreys (1997) and Timothy O'Connor and H. Y. Wong (2005). When atoms combine in suitable ways, ontological fusion (the coming into existence of an emergent whole) does not always take place, but, when it does, the composite entity has a tendency to persist, raising the probability, at each subsequent moment, of the existence of an emergent whole at that moment. For example, suppose that, if fusion has not yet taken place, there is a 10% chance that the particles, arranged as they are, will undergo fusion in the next hour, resulting in an emergent whole. If, in contrast, fusion has taken place, there is an 80% chance that the emergent whole will persist throughout the next hour. If we suppose that whether or not fusion takes place affects present and future causal powers of the entities involved, there is a real difference between cases in which fusion has taken place and those in which it has not, which is not reducible to any difference in the particles themselves (apart from their composing or not composing such a whole). This difference would clearly demark such cases of ontological emergence from cases of merely latent causal powers of the atoms.

3   Hierarchical emergence. Suppose ontological fusion occurs in stages, with intermediate composite entities fusing into still larger wholes, in accordance with some simple, universal laws of fusion. The intermediate composite entities would then be theoretically indispensable, needed to explain the existence of active powers at higher levels of organization. Such hierarchical emergence seems to take place in both biology (molecules into cells, cells into organism) and in the social world (towns into provinces, provinces into nations).

4   Indirect statistical evidence for the disappearance of the individual identity of the parts. One form that ontological fusion could take is that in which the parts lose their individual identities as a result of being incorporated into the whole. This seems to happen in the formation of quantum systems according to modern quantum mechanics. When two electrons become entangled or correlated, a unified system results, one that in some sense contains *two* electrons, and yet in which there is no distinct identity associated with either electron.

This results in the replacement of classical statistics with Einstein–Bose statistics. For example, electrons can be in one of two spin states: either spin *up* or spin *down*. When we have two separated electrons, classical statistics applies, resulting in four possible states (each with an equal, 25% probability): both electrons up, both electrons down, the first electron up and the second down, and the second up and the first down. However, when two electrons fuse into a single, emergent system, the electrons lose their individual identities. As a result, Einstein–Bose statistics apply, with three possible states (each with an equal one-third probability): two electrons up, two electrons down, and one electron in each state. There is no distinction, in the fused case, between two possible ways for one electron to be up and one down. The individuality of each electron has been absorbed into that of the whole, two-electron system.

6.5.1 Prospects for the Justification of Emergence

Let's look at some particular kinds of possible real substances, in light of these possible manifestations of emergence.

Case 1: Molecules and other Quantum Fusions As we mentioned above, the fact that quantum theory applies Einstein–Bose statistics, rather than classical statistics, suggests that fundamental particles undergo a real fusion into an emergent system whenever quantum entanglement occurs. In those cases, it seems that the particles become mere fragments of the whole system, which has certain inseparable properties that are not reducible to the states or interrelationships of the constituent particles.

Quantum chemistry provides an important case of this emergence: the emergent nature of whole molecules (Hendry 2006, 2010; Bishop 2005). Take for example, a water molecule, a molecule of H_2O. Such molecules consist of a quantum system with 18 protons and electrons and (typically) eight neutrons. The quantum equation for such a system of particles is spherically symmetrical in shape. However, we always find water molecules to be asymmetrically organized in a V-shape, with approximately a 106° angle between the two chemical bonds, and the global behavior of water gives us reason to believe that this is so prior to observation (before, that is, the *collapse of the wave packet*). This asymmetric V-shape of the molecule appears to be an emergent property of the whole that has to be determined empirically, not deducible from the physical properties of the particles, even taken collectively (at least, not deducible given our current knowledge of quantum chemistry).

Case 2: People – Consciousness and Free Will At the opposite extreme of the scale, human beings provide a plausible case for emergence. The qualities of consciousness (as in our experience of color and other sensory qualities) and the intrinsic intentionality of thought have so far resisted reduction to microphysical states (see Koons and Bealer 2010). Yet, we know that we exist, since (as René Descartes argued in his famous *cogito* proof) it is incoherent to try to deny one's own existence. If we exist as fundamental entities, then we must be something more than mere heaps of particles.

Human agency, especially that sort of action that we think of as guided by free will, provides more evidence for emergence, as William Hasker has argued (2001). Particles don't decide to act in certain ways, either individually or collectively. It is persons that do so.

If human beings are fundamental, must they be emergent wholes? Some philosophers, including Descartes (1993; orig. pub. 1647) and Roderick Chisholm (1976), have proposed instead that human beings are autonomous atoms, without any parts at all. This could be combined either with the view that human beings are immaterial minds (Descartes) or with the view that we are a peculiar sort of sub-atomic particle located somewhere in the brain (Chisholm, and possibly Gottfried Leibniz).

These views are defensible, but they do suffer from various drawbacks. First, they run counter to our common sense, which supposes that people are medium-sized material beings of a kind, with familiar shapes, sizes, and weights. Second, they raise some difficult questions about how to understand the interaction between the mind and the body. For Cartesians (followers of Descartes) this is especially acute, since it is hard to see how a wholly immaterial mind can interact in a persistent way with a particular organic body. Third, these views don't fully accord with certain ethical truths, since they demand a distinction between human beings and human bodies. My body becomes something like a possession of mine, a mere tool through which I act upon the world. If that is so, then we cannot make a deep and principled moral distinction between abusing a human body (e.g., through torture, mutilation, or rape) and vandalizing other pieces of property.

A better theory would be one that identifies human beings and living human bodies, attributing to these things both physical and mental attributes, as P. F. Strawson detailed in his classic book, *Individuals* (1959).

Case 3: Organisms More Generally If human beings are organisms, and we human beings are fundamental, then we have good grounds for supposing that all organisms are metaphysically fundamental as well. As we've seen, biological properties like growth, flight, and reproduction are plausible candidates for essentially unitary properties. If biology is a genuine science, then these properties must really exist and cannot be merely useful fictions or systematic errors.

Case 4: Inanimate Artifacts What about artifacts – things like tools, books, buildings, and so on? They do resemble living things in certain ways.

They have an overall, unifying organization, and their parts cooperate in fulfilling macroscopic functions, like hammering nails or protecting us from inclement weather. Should these analogies lead us to recognize artifacts as emergent real substances?

The best case for the fundamentality of artifacts is an appeal to hierarchical emergence. Some complicated artifacts, like automobiles, airplanes and engines, are by their very nature composed of other artifacts, such as gears, shafts or pistons. It seems that the existence of the whole machine is grounded in the prior existence of its functional parts in a way that requires those parts to be fundamental entities.

There are, however, several reasons for resisting this extension.

First, artifacts do not seem to possess any novel powers. We do not have a science of artificial things that is comparable to the science of biology. In addition, the very design of artifacts depends on the fact that the behavior of the whole is predictably grounded in the natural behavior of its component parts. It would be disastrous if our tools literally took on a life of their own, as they do in some Disney animations.

Second, whether a real substance exists should, it seems, depend only on that real substance and its parts, not on extrinsic facts. However, it seems that some artifacts exist only because they were produced by human beings in a certain way, and they continue to exist only so long as they are used and maintained, or at least recognized, by human beings. Consider, for example, ancient Neolithic axes. These consisted of single stones that had been chipped into a suitable shape. It is possible that other stones have been chipped into similar shapes by purely natural forces. Whether a particular chipped stone is an axe depends not on its intrinsic nature but on its history.

Consider also a statue that has been cut out from a single stone, like Michelangelo's David. The stone that composes David already existed before Michelangelo's chisel freed it from its environment. The sculpting didn't change the stone – it merely changed its environment from stone to air.

Third, functional organization and use seems to be insufficient to ensure the existence of a fundamental thing with a corresponding nature. For example, it is possible to make a living thing into an artifact. One could, for example, weave a hammock out of a living vine (or, perhaps, even out of a living snake). It's implausible to suppose that such making can destroy the organism and replace it with an artifact, but it is also problematic to suppose that this making changes the fundamental nature of the organism into some sort of organism–artifact hybrid. Finally, it is equally implausible to think that we have two fundamental things, each with its own fundamental nature, since it is doubtful that the nature of a living thing could tolerate its material body's instantiating a different, potentially incompatible nature.

Alexander Pruss has also pointed out (in conversation, 2010) that there are pairs of artifacts in which one member of the pair is a material object and the other is composed entirely of immaterial things. For example, a chess piece is typically a physical object, made of wood or stone, but it would be possible to play chess by means of moving differently shaped holes through some viscous liquid. In that case, the black queen might consist of an octagonally shaped hole, but it is implausible to think that holes can be fundamental entities. Therefore, we have a second case in which artificiality and functionality do not suffice for fundamentality.

Finally, there are problems about the persistence of artifacts through time that raise serious doubts about whether artifacts can be fundamental. We will take up these problems in Chapter 9.

Peter van Inwagen (van Inwagen 1990) is an example of a metaphysician who accepts the existence of composite organisms but rejects that of composite artifacts. Of course, such a position presupposes that there is a principled boundary between the two sets of cases. As van Inwagen puts it, organisms have lives, and artifacts don't. What about robots? Robots seem to be like organisms in various ways: they move about autonomously, they respond to varying environmental conditions, some can even repair themselves or "communicate" with other robots.

One important issue: Is robotics a natural science, in the way that biology is? Do classes of robots constitute natural kinds, in the way that species and genera of organisms do? To talk about something's having a life, it seems that it must have a shareable essence or nature that places it in a real kind which can be scientifically investigated. If we someday create robots that successfully and regularly reproduce themselves, constituting a self-perpetuating species with its own ecological niche, then such robots might well be real organisms. Nothing we have said entails that organisms cannot be products of human art. Thus, we should qualify our negative conclusion: it is *non-living* artifacts whose existence we have reason to doubt.

Why is life of some kind essential to real substances? Only living things have a functional organization that is truly intrinsic, that doesn't depend on the intentions or practices of separate beings. Participation in the cycle of life of a relatively stable species provides an objective basis for such functional character, as Ruth Garrett Millikan has argued (Millikan 1984). In addition, lives are generally proprietary in a mutually exclusive way: no particle can be caught up simultaneously in two separate lives at the same time. Finally, living things do seem to be associated with novel, irreducible powers, like sensation and intentional motion.

Case 5: Social Groups and Institutions   What about social groups and institutions? Are nations or clubs or teams fundamental? Many of the objections to artifacts apply also to social groups. It is unclear whether social groups have any fundamental powers of their own. It seems, rather, that all the causal powers involved are powers of the individual members, acting either individually or collectively. It may be that the members acquire new powers by virtue of their membership – for example, citizens have the power to vote by virtue of the existence of the nation. However, this could be explained as the manifestation of latent powers in an appropriate context, as in Meehl and Sellars (1956).

In addition, the existence of a group is in some cases constituted by external facts. A team might exist, for example, only because it is recognized by the authorities of a league, or a committee might exist by virtue of the action of the whole society. The persistence of groups through time also raises doubts about their real existence (for reasons to be discussed in Chapter 9).

Case 6: Natural Formations: Grains of Sand to Galaxy Clusters   Finally, what should we say about various natural formations – things that are neither alive nor made, and that do not constitute unified and isolated quantum systems? There are a wide variety of such things, from grains of sand, pebbles, raindrops, and motes of dust, to rivers and lakes, mountains and mountain ranges, and on to planets, stars, galaxies, and galaxy clusters. Are any of these emergent wholes or are they all mere heaps of particles or molecules?

Like statues, the existence of natural formations is not an intrinsic matter. When a pebble breaks off from a larger rock, there need be no intrinsic change to the rock that makes up the pebble.

There are few good candidates for essentially unitary properties of natural formations. Whenever we describe the state of one of these things, we seem to be stating nothing more than how the constituent parts are arranged and how they are interacting.

6.6   Conclusion

There seem to be two leading competitors for the correct answer to the Special Composition Question: Universalism and Compositional Pluralism. Universalists are on the strongest ground when they can claim that their postulation of a vast class of composite entities is an "ontological free lunch," exempt from the strictures of Ockham's Razor. This claim, in turn, is most plausible if we have already embraced both Neo-Humeism about powers and Extreme Resemblance Nominalism about powers, since these commitments will ensure that composite entities require no new facts in order to exist. They will be nothing over and above their parts, even if we count them as fundamental entities.

In contrast, those who are attracted to Powerism or to Realism about universals or modifying tropes are best served by embracing either Atomism or Compositional Pluralism. In this case, composite entities have to earn their status as fundamental or emergent entities by virtue of possessing both novel powers and unitary real properties. Molecules and living organisms provide reasonably strong grounds for such an elevated status, while artifacts, groups, and natural formations stand on much weaker ground.

Notes

1 Thanks to Richard Lawton Davis (2014) for suggesting this version of Composition as Identity Theory.
2 Thanks to Richard Lawton Davis (in conversation) for this point.
3 Mereologists find it convenient to define "part" in such a way that everything is a part of itself (just as every number is less-than-or-equal to itself, and every set is a subset of itself). They use the phrase "proper part" to signify something that is a "part" in a more colloquial sense: i.e., *part but not identical to*.

7

Modality

Some truths have to do with the way the world in fact is. From the earliest stages of this book, we've occupied ourselves especially with atomic sentences, and these have mostly concerned the way the world in fact is. We have been interested in the metaphysical grounds for these truths and in the nature and metaphysical structure of the things that are part of those metaphysical grounds. Therefore, we have explored the natures of properties and substances. We have, though, already seen that some sentences cause a bit more trouble for theories interested in supplying a metaphysical ground for truth. In particular, we explored the connection between conditionals, which don't slot easily into a theory in which there is truthmaking, and powers. These conditional claims have to do with what might or would be, given the presence of certain conditions. Still other claims have to do with the way the world could have been but isn't, the way the world must be, and so on. In this chapter, we will explore in a general fashion the nature of modality. To study the nature of modality is to study the nature of possibility and necessity.

In order to circumscribe our subject matter more precisely, consider the following claims:

(1) THP had yogurt and granola for breakfast but might have had oatmeal instead.
(2) Had THP's wife not made granola yesterday, he would've had oatmeal instead of yogurt for breakfast.
(3) It is impossible for a human to travel to the sun and back in half an hour.
(4) Charlie Strong's new offensive system will probably improve Texas's offensive output, but it might not.
(5) Necessarily, two plus two is four.

Metaphysics: The Fundamentals, First Edition. Robert C. Koons and Timothy H. Pickavance.
© 2015 Robert C. Koons and Timothy H. Pickavance.
Published 2015 by John Wiley & Sons, Ltd.

Each of (1–5) makes a claim about what might, would, can't, or must be. Words like "might," "would," "can't," "must," "will," "possible," "necessary," and so on are *modal* words. They signal that one is making a claim that is true or false depending on what might or would or can or can't be. For example, THP did in fact have granola for breakfast on that day of this writing. But he might have had oatmeal. (In other words, (1) is true.) Consider the latter claim: THP might have had oatmeal for breakfast. This claim is true not because of what THP in fact had for breakfast. After all, THP had yogurt and granola! Why is it that this claim is true? It's pretty clear that "THP had yogurt and granola for breakfast" is true because of THP's activities on the morning of the writing of these paragraphs, and the relation of those activities to certain quantities of yogurt and granola. But it is equally clear that nothing about THP's *actual* activities or *actual* quantities of oatmeal can explain the truth of "THP might have had oatmeal." But then, what *does* explain the truth of this sentence? Similarly, if we say, "The dog wags its tail," we are saying something that has to do with the dog and a tail wagging. But suppose the dog isn't wagging its tail, and we say, "The dog might have been wagging its tail." It appears that we're saying something about the dog, but it's not entirely clear how this sentence is meant to come out true, since we have supposed that the dog is not, in fact, wagging its tail. When we study modality, we are investigating the metaphysics of these sorts of truths.

There are a number of interrelated varieties of modality. For example, there are uses of "might" and "could" that have to do with knowledge. One might say, for example, "The book might (could) be on my desk (but I'm not sure)." Here, one is saying that, for all one knows, the book is on one's desk. Other bits of modal vocabulary have an epistemic sense as well. There are also uses of modal vocabulary that have to do with moral obligation. For example, one might say, "Societies must help their poor," or "Sometimes, one can break one's promises." Here, one is saying that a society is morally obligated to help the poor by deploying the modal word, "must," or one is saying that it is sometimes morally permissible to break one's promises by deploying the modal word "can." Other bits of modal vocabulary have a deontic sense as well. There are uses of modal vocabulary beyond even these, indeed, our modal vocabulary is quite flexible, and can be used to express a number of different ideas. We are interested in focusing on a particular type of modality, what philosophers have called "metaphysical" modality. The sentences (1), (2), and (5), on their most natural readings, are claims about metaphysical modality. The most natural reading of (3), on which the "might" is taken *not* to be epistemic, also expresses metaphysical modality. (4), on the other hand, may involve metaphysical modality, if it is taken to express the claim that it's not metaphysically possible, given current technology (or something of that sort), to travel to the sun and back in half an hour.[1] Most importantly, it is very unnatural to read any of (1–5) except (3) as involving epistemic modality, and it is unnatural to read any of (1–5) as involving deontic modality. The kind of modality that is naturally expressed is metaphysical, or closely connected with metaphysical modality.

Modality of this metaphysical variety is important if only because of its connection to our practical reasoning, our reasoning about how to conduct our lives. If there are no alternative possibilities, no facts about what could or might be, then our deliberations about which choices we ought to make are either irrational or unfounded. For example, when one considers whether and what to have for breakfast in the morning, one might reason in this way: if I don't eat, then I will underperform at my studies, and will be therefore less likely to succeed in my coursework; and if all I eat is a donut, then I'm likely to crash well before lunch, and will be in similar danger; therefore, I ought to have oatmeal for breakfast, since that will allow me to concentrate and study well. When one reasons in this way, one is considering alternative possibilities, one without any breakfast, one with a donut breakfast, and one with an oatmeal breakfast. By using one's knowledge of facts about one's own nutritional needs, one can then make predictions about how those possibilities would unfold, and make a wise, or at least more informed, decision about which possibility to bring about. If there are no such possibilities, then this sort of practical reasoning is irrational. It is, therefore, worth inquiring as to whether we can supply a metaphysical foundation for modal truths.

Philosophers have traditionally distinguished between modality *de dicto* and modality *de re*. Modality *de dicto* is modality concerning the meanings of the things we say. That is, modality *de dicto* has to do with what propositions or sentences are necessary, possible, impossible, contingent, and the like. Modality *de re* is modality concerning things. That is, modality *de re* has to do with the essential and accidental features of objects. Consider the sentence,

(6) Necessarily, the President of the United States is the President of the United States.

Read one way, (6) says that the proposition expressed by "The President of the United States is the President of the United States" is necessarily true. And there is something we might mean by "The President of the United States is the President of the United States" that is, in fact, necessarily true. For how could the president not be the president? To have a president that is not the president is contradictory. So the meaning of "The President of the United States is the President of the United States" is necessarily true. At any rate, to read (6) in this way is to read it as expressing *de dicto* modality. On the other hand, suppose one reads (6) a different way, according to which (6) expresses a proposition that is true just in case the President of the United States, namely Barack Obama, must be the president. Read in this way, it is clear that (6) is false, since Barack Obama might not be the president. Indeed, in early 2017, he will in fact no longer be the president. Thus, to say that he must be the president is to say something false. In other words, this second, *de re* reading of (6) demands that a certain thing, namely, Barack Obama, necessarily has a certain feature, namely, the property of being *the POTUS*. This chapter divides into two sections which respectively examine *de dicto* and *de re* modality.

7.1   Possible Worlds: Concretism versus Abstractionism

Since Leibniz, philosophers have found the idea of a *possible world* useful when thinking about modality. But what is a possible world? A possible world is a maximal way the world might be. A way the world might be is a situation or scenario that could occur or could have occurred (in the metaphysical sense of "could"). THP could have had oatmeal for breakfast, RCK might have worn a green shirt yesterday, Lyle could have colored with crayons rather than markers; these are ways the world might be. But *two plus two's being five, substance S's being both human and non-human*, and *that ball's being both red and blue all over at the same time*, these are ways the world could not be. They are *ways*, but not ways the world might be. They are not *possible* ways. A way the world might be is maximal if and only if every proposition is either true or false according to it. Consider a possibility like *THP's having oatmeal for breakfast*. This possibility represents THP's having oatmeal for breakfast, but represents nothing about the color of RCK's shirt yesterday. A possibility like *THP's having oatmeal for breakfast and RCK's wearing a green shirt yesterday*, on the other hand, represents THP's breakfast and RCK's shirt yesterday. It is, we might say, more representationally rich. A maximal possibility is one that is maximally representationally rich. One cannot pick a proposition that a maximal possibility represents nothing about. A maximal possibility represents THP's breakfast choice, the color of RCK's shirt yesterday, the facts of math, the existence of God, and so on. Maximal possibilities, maximal ways the world might be, are possible worlds.

The vast majority of these maximal possibilities somehow misrepresent the world. Indeed, all but one must do so.[2] One maximal possibility represents THP's having oatmeal for breakfast, one that he had yogurt, one that he had an egg sandwich, and so on. Only one of these possibilities matches the actual state of the world. This special maximal possible way the world might be, this special possible world, is the *actual* world.

Possible worlds can be used to clarify *de dicto* possibility, necessity, impossibility, and contingency. A proposition is possibly true if and only if there is some possible world according to which that proposition is true. For example, the proposition expressed by the sentence "THP has oatmeal for breakfast" is possibly true if and only if there is some possible world according to which THP has oatmeal for breakfast. The proposition expressed by the sentences "THP could have had oatmeal for breakfast" and "Possibly, THP has oatmeal for breakfast" are true under those same conditions. A proposition is necessarily true if and only if the proposition is true according to every possible world, that is, if and only if there is no possible world according to which the sentence is false. So the proposition expressed by "$2+2=4$" is necessarily true, and the proposition expressed by "Necessarily, $2+2=4$" is true, since the proposition expressed by "$2+2=4$" is true according to every possible world, that is, since there is no possible world according to which the proposition expressed by "$2+2=4$" is false. A proposition is impossible, or not possibly true, if and only if there is no possible world according to which the proposition is true, and a proposition is contingent if and only if there is a possible world according to which the proposition is true and a possible world according to which the proposition is false.

This connection between possible worlds and these modal notions only takes us so far, and we are left with important metaphysical questions. First, there are questions about the exact nature of possible worlds and about the way that possible worlds represent. These questions have to do with what possible worlds are. Second, there is the question whether modal facts are reducible to facts about possible worlds. As it turns out, one's answers to these questions are interrelated. We will move toward the most prominent answers to them by considering two broad views about the nature of possible worlds, namely Concretism and Abstractionism.

As their respective names suggest, Concretism and Abstractionism differ fundamentally over whether possible worlds are concrete or abstract. The Concretist maintains that possible worlds are concrete, while the Abstractionist maintains that possible worlds are abstract. The distinction between abstract and concrete objects isn't easy to characterize, but there are at least two features that helpfully distinguish concrete from abstract objects. First, concrete objects, but not abstract objects, typically have a definite location in space and time.[3] Concrete objects, at least in typical cases, are not wholly located at more than one spatiotemporal location. Abstract objects, on the other hand, tend to have no spatiotemporal location at all, or are at least capable of being wholly in many spatiotemporal locations. Second, concrete objects, but not abstract objects, have active and passive powers. Concrete objects can change other concrete objects, and are able to undergo change themselves. Abstract objects do neither of these. So Concretism is roughly the view that possible worlds are like parallel universes, universes like our own, populated with donkeys and buildings and people and stars and so on. (We will construct a more careful definition below.) Abstractionism is roughly the view that possible worlds are maximal possible propositions, propositions like those we considered in Chapter 2. As we will see, these differences manifest in still further, possibly more fundamental disagreements between Concretists and Abstractionists.

7.1.1   Concretism

Concretism insists that every way that some world could be is a way that some world is.[4] Concretism takes very seriously the talk of *ways*. Suppose our world is just the universe. (We don't mean to commit to this, but the supposition will help the reader catch the idea.) Our actual universe is a certain way, and there are many ways our universe is. For example, grass is green rather than black, and so grass's being green is a way our universe is. But grass might have been black, and so grass's being black is a way the world might have been. It is tempting to think that these ways that the universe is are just facts of various sorts. The fact that grass is green is a way the universe is. So it is also tempting to think that the actual world, the maximal way the world in fact is, is just the universe (where that is taken as including even non-physical things, if such there be). But if ways are just facts, and the actual world is just our universe, then possible ways must be facts as well, and so other possible worlds must be other universes. For the facts of our world are constituted by objects and properties and relations, and so merely possible facts must be constituted by objects and properties and relations as well. Otherwise, they are not facts at all. The possibility that grass is purple must be a fact, constituted by some grass and the property of *being purple*. But then other possible worlds are just like our universe, the actual world, in being populated with objects with various properties and standing in various relations. This is the sense in which Concretism is the view that possible worlds are parallel universes. Counterintuitively, there is purple grass, there are humans that can fly without mechanical aid, and there are objects unaffected by gravity. It's just that none of these things are a part of our world. They are possible, though, and so they exist in other worlds, other parallel universes.

It is important to forestall a common confusion at this point. The Concretist does *not* say that there is actually existing purple grass. The Concretist simply says that there is purple grass, purple grass that really does exist. But this grass is non-actual. It is merely possible. The difference between actual and merely possible objects, however, does not consist in a special way that the merely possible things exist. Rather, it is a matter of proximity. In particular, it is a matter of proximity to *you and us*. What it is to be actual, according to Concretism, is to be a part of our world.

Things that are parts of our world are actual, whereas things that are parts of world that are not ours are merely possible. Just as important, the designations of "actual" and "merely possible" are *indexical*, not absolute. Things are actual *with respect to* other things, and merely possible *with respect to* other things. Think about a word like "here." THP might say, "THP's computer is here." And what he says would be true. But truly calling that particular computer "here" does not require that the computer have a special property of *hereness*. All it requires is that it bear a certain (contextually determined) proximity[5] to THP. To see this, consider the fact that RCK might simultaneously say, "THP's computer is not here," and not contradict what THP said. This might happen if THP makes his utterance in Fullerton, California, while RCK makes his in Austin, Texas. Concretists maintain that "actual" is like "here" in this way. We can truly say, "There is no actual purple grass," while someone in some other world can truly say, "There is actual purple grass." No contradiction is involved because "actual" is indexical, like "here," and so the first saying says that there is no purple grass in one world, while the second saying says that there is purple grass in some different world. No contradiction there. Since actuality is indexical according to Concretism, merely possible objects are not actual, though they do exist. The view is not that all possible things are actual, but that all possible things exist. Which is to say, all possible things exist, just not in our world!

One virtue of Concretism is that it has a very natural understanding of what it is for a proposition to be true *according to* a world, and therefore, it has a straightforward way of accommodating the account of modal truth in terms of possible worlds highlighted earlier. Whatever it takes for a non-modal proposition to be true in the actual world, that is what it is for that proposition to be true according to the actual world. And whatever it is for a proposition to be true according to the actual world, that is what it is for a proposition to be true according to some merely possible world. In other words, the Concretist can piggyback on whatever view of truth one adopts for actual truth, and say that that view works equally well for other possible worlds. (This will require some modification to accommodate *de re* modality; we take this up below.) Suppose, for example, that one opted for Atomic Truthmaker Theory. Then "Lyle is sweet" is true in the actual world in virtue of the existence of some truthmaker, which truthmaker is a part of the universe, that is, the actual world. Propositions are true according to other worlds in just this way: in virtue of the existence of truthmakers in those worlds, or by supervenience on them. To be clear, the Concretist needn't adopt Atomic Truthmaker Theory. This is just meant to be an example. The idea is that one can simply import whatever view of truth one adopts for non-modal claims in our world and apply it straightforwardly to what it is for a non-modal claim to be true according to other possible worlds. Truth according to a world w is just like truth in the actual world, except that one restricts one's attention to what exists in w. (As we will see, matters are a bit more complicated for Abstractionism.) Concretism can then supply an account of modal truth in just the way outlined above. Suppose sentence s expresses proposition p. Then "Necessarily, s" is true if and only if p is true according to every world. "Possibly, s" is true if and only if p is true according to at least one world. And so on.

This account of modal truth is reductionistic, in the sense that there need be no fundamental modal truths in the theory. All modal truths are cashed as truths about other possible worlds, and there is nothing modal in the Concretist's account of what it is to be a possible world, since possible worlds are just parallel universes. (Whether the Concretist can maintain a non-modal understanding of what it is to be a possible world is a question we will take up when we consider the "Problem of Isolation," below.) If this is right, then the Concretist has an advantage in terms of qualitative economy over any view of modality for which there are fundamental modal truths. In particular, we will discover below that Abstractionism is unsuited to supply a reductionistic picture of modality. This is one of, if not *the*, major advantage of Concretism over against Abstractionism.

This advantage in qualitative simplicity, however, exacts a steep quantitative cost. On top of all the green grass that exists in our world, the Concretist must commit to the existence of all the possible purple, pink, and magenta grass inhabiting other worlds. The Concretist's metaphysic includes not just actual humans, but all the merely possible ones as well; not just any actual extraterrestrial persons, but all possible extraterrestrial persons; not just the actual coffee beans, but all the possible ones as well. This is not to mention the objects whose kinds we have never even conceived, the true "aliens." If something is even possible, according to Concretism, it exists. The Abstractionist does not have to commit to all this grass and coffee, or all these humans and people.[6] When it comes to theoretical economy, the Concretist gains in terms of qualitative economy but loses in terms of quantitative economy.

The issue of theoretical economy is difficult to judge, and so we will turn now to problems for Concretism. We will consider four such problems: the Problem of Irrelevance, the Problem of Ethical Fatalism, the Problem of Non-Indexical Uses of "Actual," and the Problem of Isolation.

Problem 1: The Problem of Ethical Fatalism   Concretism seems to entail a number of ethical absurdities. In particular, it seems to entail ethical fatalism, the idea that our choices cannot make a moral difference. If what is necessary, possible, and impossible is settled once and for all, then there can be no changes in the nature of possible worlds. Since the Concretist thinks that all possibilities exist, then the total collection of what exists doesn't change. If THP actually chooses to wear a green shirt rather than a white shirt, then in some other world THP (or one of his counterparts; see Section 7.2.2 below) chooses to wear a white shirt rather than a green shirt. Both choices are made, and nothing that we actually choose can change this fact. But if this is true for shirt choices, it's also true for morally salient choices. If THP actually chooses to help an elderly person cross the street rather than stand idly by and watch him stumble and fall, then there is some other parallel universe in which THP (or one of his counterparts) chooses to stand idly by. The total amount of good and bad, pleasure and pain, virtue and vice is simply fixed once and for all, since what is possible, and therefore what exists, cannot change if Concretism is true. We can push this a bit further.[7] Suppose one has come to believe that Concretism is true, and one is concerned about all the parallel universes in which there is lots of evil. Then, bizarrely, one can perform morally heroic actions by actually choosing what is evil, because thereby one will have prevented someone in a different possible world from doing evil by ensuring that they do the good. By actually choosing to stand idly by while the elderly man stumbles and falls while crossing the street, THP can guarantee that another world involves someone's lending a helping hand to an elderly person in need. By choosing what is evil in our world, we can save others from doing evil in their own.

The Concretist will reply to this Problem of Ethical Fatalism by insisting that morality is a *local* matter, or that we should adopt an *agent-centered* morality. The idea is that we don't have any obligations to reduce or minimize the overall amount of suffering or pain that exists, or to increase or maximize the overall amount of goodness or pleasure. We are only obligated to minimize the suffering and pain and maximize the goodness and pleasure that there is in our world.

Problem 2: The Problem of Non-Indexical Uses of "Actual"   There seem to be uses of the word "actual" that are not indexical in nature, contrary to Concretism. Consider, for example:

(7) The actual world might not have been actual.

The word "actual" occurs in this sentence twice. The first occurrence does seem indexical, but the second cannot be. If the second were indexical, then (7) could not be true. Call the actual world, "Alpha." If the second use of "actual" in (7) were indexical, then (7) would be equivalent to (8):

(8) Alpha might not have been Alpha.

But (8) is necessarily false. On the other hand, consider (9):

(9) Alpha might not have been actual.

(9) seems true, and also seems to express the same proposition as (7), a proposition that is not expressed by (8). So the second use of "actual" in (7) is not indexical.

The most promising reply on behalf of Concretism is to insist that the second use of "actual" in (7) ought to flagged with scare quotes:

(7a) The actual world might not have been "actual."

The idea is that the first use of "actual" in (7a) is used indexically in our world, and so picks out the actual world, Alpha. The second, scare-quoted use of "actual" is meant to be *transported*, so to speak, to a different world in order to refer to a world that is not Alpha. Think of it this way: (7a) expresses the proposition that there are worlds in which one could truly utter the English sentence, "Alpha is not actual," where "actual" is used indexically to refer to one of those other worlds. This is, no doubt, true. Consider a world, Beta, that is not Alpha, but where there are English speakers. If an English speaker in Beta uttered "Alpha is not actual" she would express the proposition that Alpha is not Beta. And this, by hypothesis, is true: Alpha is not Beta.

Problem 3: The Problem of Irrelevance   Suppose there are myriad universes other than our own, as the Concretist insists. Why should one think this has anything whatever to do with the facts of modality? It is unclear why one would think that the existence of universes other than our own makes it the case that things could have been other than they are. The distinction between local and non-local facts doesn't seem to match the distinction between actual and merely possible scenarios. To appeal to facts about parallel universes in order to ground modal truths would be like appealing to something's shape to ground a claim about its color. Color facts just aren't the same thing as shape facts, and so the latter are ill-suited to ground the truth of claims about the former. In a similar way, whether or not there is a plurality of universes seems to be irrelevant to the truth of modal claims; this is the "Problem of Irrelevance." Concretists, on the other hand, think that nothing could matter *more* to the modal facts than what is going on in other parallel universes. They say that the modal facts *just are* facts about the plurality of universes, or that modal truths *just are* truths about the plurality of universes. The fact that almost everyone accepts a connection between possible worlds and modal facts is a help to the Concretist at this point. This is because parallel universes just are possible worlds, if Concretism is true, so the connection between parallel universes and modal facts should not be controversial if one has granted already that possible worlds can be parallel universes. The Problem of Irrelevance, then, must turn on whether it is plausible to think of possible worlds as parallel universes. If the objection is just insisting that this cannot be so, then it is question begging.

Maybe the Problem of Irrelevance is attractive for a different reason. We mentioned earlier that we are not meant to think of the Concretist's universes as *actual* (other than our world, the actual world, of course), only as *existing*. But if one is tempted by the thought that universes other than our own are actual, then the Problem of Irrelevance is particularly troubling. For if everything in the Concretist's plurality of universes is actual, then there are no merely possible objects, and Concretism thereby gets the modal facts wrong. If we are being charitable to the Concretist, though, we cannot simply insist that these other universes are actual. However, there is a different way to approach this problem, a way that is importantly different from the Problem of Irrelevance but that captures some of its spirit. This other problem is concerned to show that Concretists cannot *isolate* worlds from one another and that, therefore, there is really just one world. While this will not show the irrelevance of *other* worlds to modality, it would show something equally damaging.

Problem 4: The Problem of Isolation   We noted above that it is crucial to the Concretist's reductionistic view of modality that they can offer a non-modal account of possible worlds. For if they cannot, then they cannot carry out their reduction of the facts of modality to non-modal facts about possible worlds. One would simply trade one type of modal fact for another, and that is not the sort of reduction the Concretist is targeting. Given that the qualitative advantage gained by this reduction is crucial to the plausibility of accepting the quantitative expansion, it would be well nigh devastating to the Concretist to not supply a non-modal account of possible worlds.

The issue here can be approached by considering the following question: what makes it the case that something is a world on its own, rather than being a part of some bigger world? It is tempting to think, given the existence of all these so-called worlds, that there is just One Really Big World of which all the possible worlds are parts. If this is right, then there aren't really any possible worlds after all. Actuality is just bigger than we thought it was. We might call this Concretism's Problem of Isolation, as it calls for the Concretist to explain how the possible worlds are isolated from one another. In order to overcome the Problem of Isolation, the Concretist needs to say what it takes for two things to be parts of the same world, to be *worldmates*.

Concretists have offered three views of the worldmate relation. First, one might say that two things are worldmates if and only if they are causally interrelated. On this view, causal interrelatedness is what unites worlds; two universes are separate worlds rather than one giant world because no part of one universe is causally related to any part of the other.[8] Second, one might say that two things are worldmates if and only if they are spatiotemporally interrelated. On this view, spatiotemporal interrelatedness is what unites worlds; two universes are separate worlds rather than one giant world because no part of one universe is spatiotemporally related to any part of the other. These two views of the worldmate relation are problematic because it seems possible for there to be, as part of one and the same world, two spatiotemporally and causally disconnected universes. Indeed, take any two worlds w_1 and w_2; there would seem to be a possibility according to which duplicates of w_1 and w_2 are combined together into a single world with parallel universes.[9] If there were such parallel universes, though, these views of the worldmate relation would force the Concretist to count them as separate worlds, rather than parallel universes that are part of just one world.

The only plausible alternative view of the worldmate relation, the third view of the three, is that the worldmate relation is fundamental. On this view, what makes two things separate worlds rather than parts of one bigger world is just that no part of one stands in the metaphysically fundamental worldmate relation to any of the parts of the other. This allows the Concretist to admit the possibility of parallel universes within the same world. However, it upsets the ability of the Concretist to supply a reductive account of modality. For the worldmate relation is a modal relation, and so the view that it is metaphysically fundamental introduces a fundamental modal relation into the Concretist's view. This is deeply problematic for Concretism; if it cannot achieve the qualitative simplicity that comes with a reductive view of modality, then there is no payoff for accepting the quantitative profligacy that Concretism requires.

7.1.2   Abstractionism

In light of the above problems for Concretism, and maybe just because Concretism is so implausible from the start, one may want to give Abstractionism a test run. Abstractionism does not require a commitment to the existence of concrete worlds populated with non-actual donkeys and tanks and trees and so on. Possible worlds, according to Abstractionism, are abstract objects. What sort of abstract object is a matter of intramural dispute among Abstractionists. Some Abstractionists take possible worlds to be maximal possible states of affairs.[10] States of affairs are abstract objects that represent the world in various ways, and that either obtain or fail to obtain. For example, *grass's being green*, *2 + 2's being 4*, and *THP's having had yogurt and granola for breakfast* are all states of affairs. When grass is green, the state of affairs *grass's being green* obtains. Had grass been pink, that state of affairs would have failed to obtain. A possible state of affairs is a state of affairs that could obtain. The three states of affairs listed above are possible, whereas *2 + 2's being 5* is not. And a state of affairs *s* is maximal if and only if, for any state of affairs *s'*, *s* either includes *s'* or precludes *s'*. *s* includes s' if and only if s could not obtain if s' did not obtain as well, and s precludes s' if and only if s could not obtain if s' obtained as well. The conjunctive state of affairs *grass's being green & 2 + 2's being 4* includes the state of affairs *grass's being green* and precludes the state of affairs *2 + 2's being 5*. Maximal possible states of affairs, then, are in a sense complete descriptions of the way the world is. For a maximal possible state of affairs to obtain, the world must be a particular way, and nothing could change without changing which maximal possible state of affairs obtains. In this sense, maximal possible states of affairs are possible worlds. Other Abstractionists take possible worlds to be maximal possible propositions.[11] Instead of talking in terms of obtaining and failing to obtain, these Abstractionists talk of truth and falsity. Maximality is characterized in terms of entailment, rather than inclusion and preclusion. A proposition p is maximal if and only if for any proposition q, either p entails q or p entails the not-q. Still other Abstractionists take possible worlds to be maximal possible properties, properties that could be exemplified only by a maximal object. There are a number of other Abstractionist views as well, but the distinctions among these views won't matter to our discussion of Abstractionism; to simplify our discussion, we will talk as if Abstractionists adopt the view that possible worlds are maximal possible propositions.

Because Abstractionists think of worlds as maximal possible propositions, they cannot offer a reductive account of modality. Entailment is a modal notion, and it is not clear how the Abstractionist could give a reductive account of it. Proposition p entails proposition q if and only if *necessarily* it is the case that q is true whenever p is true. The "necessarily" there is ineliminable. The only hope for eliminating it goes like so: p entails q if and only if q is true in every world where p is true. But we were trying to characterize what a world is! We need the notion of entailment to say what a world is, so we cannot give a reductive account of entailment in terms of worlds. That is to go around a circle. Such circles are fine if illumination is all that one is after, but not okay for supplying reductions of one thing to another. Insofar as entailment is modal and needed to say what a world is, Abstractionism cannot reduce modal facts to facts about worlds. This is a qualitative cost relative to Concretism, but allows the Abstractionist to avoid commitment to the zoo of objects needed by the Concretist.

At any rate, our focus in what follows will be on the way an Abstractionist might understand what it is for something to be true *according to* a possible world. The views we have canvassed so far do not speak to this question. What is needed is an account of what it is for a possible world to represent that so-and-so. This is a species of a more general question concerning the way that states of affairs and propositions represent that so-and-so. (Thus we return to the question put off in Section 2.1, on propositions.) There are three Abstractionist views of representation. The more general application is not far to seek, so we leave that to the interested reader. David K. Lewis (1986: 136–141) has called the three Abstractionist views of representation Magical, Linguistic, and Pictorial, respectively. The Magical Abstractionist thinks there is no informative answer to the question of how it is that possible worlds represent. The Linguistic Abstractionist thinks that possible worlds represent like language represents. And the Pictorial Abstractionist thinks that possible worlds represent like pictures represent. Presently, we will consider each of these views in more detail.

View 1: Magical Abstractionism   If Magical Abstractionism is true, then possible worlds are abstract objects that represent that so-and-so in a primitive way. All we can say about representation is that a possible world *w* represents that *p* if and only if necessarily, if *w* were actual, then *p* would be true. Consider the actual world, Alpha, for example. (Importantly, the actual world, Alpha, is not the universe! It's an easy mistake to think it is, but Alpha has no people or dogs or mountains or stars as parts. It is an abstract thing, along with all the other possible worlds.) Since Alpha is actual, it must represent that THP had yogurt and granola for breakfast. But all there is to say about this is that Alpha is such that, necessarily, if Alpha is actual, then the proposition that THP had yogurt and granola for breakfast is true. Worlds just represent what they do, and that's all there is to that. Importantly, and in contrast to Linguistic and Pictorial Abstractionism, Magical Abstractionism denies that worlds represent in virtue of some sort of metaphysical structure. If possible worlds have parts, then those parts and their interrelations are irrelevant to what the world represents.

As a result of his commitment to primitive representation, the Magical Abstractionist cannot offer a reductive account of modality. (This is a reason in addition to that highlighted above, for Abstractionist views generally.) The representational facts about possible worlds are modal facts, for they are facts about what is necessarily the case. Alpha represents that THP had yogurt and granola for breakfast because *necessarily*, if Alpha is actual then the proposition that THP had yogurt and granola for breakfast is true. Likewise, Beta, a non-actual world according to which THP had oatmeal for breakfast, represents that THP had oatmeal for breakfast because *necessarily*, if Beta is actual, then the proposition that THP had oatmeal for breakfast is true. The modal language is ineliminable, since there is no deeper account to give of these representational facts. This is a decidedly non-reductionist view of the representational features of possible worlds, and thus Magical Abstractionism cannot give a reductive account of modality.

David K. Lewis (1986: 176–187) complained that Magical Abstractionism is subject to a dilemma. If propositions represent ways that things are, then the way things are selects for certain propositions. The proposition that grass is green represents that grass is green, and since grass really is green, the way things are (which includes the fact that grass is green) selects the proposition that grass is green. The way things are, in its totality, uniquely selects a possible world. In the case of the way things are around us, the actual world, Alpha, is selected. Had things been different, a different world would have been selected. Thus, which world is selected seems to be a function of the intrinsic character of the way things are. Given that things are the way that they are, the only world that could be selected is Alpha. Lewis thought that there was a dilemma concerning the selection relation: selection must be either internal or external, and either way is problematic. An internal relation between two things A and B is a relation that must obtain between A and B given the intrinsic character of A and B, that is, given the way A and B are in themselves. For example, the relation of *being more massive than* is internal. Mass is an intrinsic feature of things, it is had by things in virtue of the way they are in themselves, not in virtue of their relation to other things. Suppose A is ten kilograms, while B is one kilogram. These mass features are intrinsic features of A and B, and given that A and B have those features, A must be more massive than B. A and B couldn't but stand in the relation of *being more massive than*. An external relation, on the other hand, is not internal. It is a relation that is not guaranteed to obtain given certain intrinsic features of its relata. Spatial relations are extrinsic. One can keep A and B intrinsically just as they are while moving them around relative to one another. Just because A is ten kilograms and B is one kilogram does not guarantee that they will be some distance from one another. Maybe they are five meters apart, but they could become ten meters apart without affecting their intrinsic nature.

On to Lewis's dilemma. Suppose that selection is an external relation, that it is not a function of the intrinsic features of the way things are and of possible worlds. Lewis thinks that, if this is right, then the selection relation must be magical. What did he mean by this? Everyone agrees that worlds, and propositions more generally, have their representational features essentially. Alpha could not represent things as being a different way than it in fact represents them as being any more than the proposition that grass is green could fail to represent that grass is green. This point is almost too obvious to state. It would be strange indeed to think of the proposition that grass is green representing that grass is blue, or worse, that there are exactly 17 electrons in the universe. One would be right to wonder what a person meant by "represent" if they were to make such a suggestion! So, what a world represents is essential to it. But selection is just the dual of representation; the two go hand in hand. Worlds are selected if and only if what they represent in fact occurs. Thus, selection must be a relation that *must* obtain, given that things are a certain way, and given the representational features of worlds. But every uncontroversially external relation is contingent. Consider again spatial relations. Just given the fact that two things stand in a certain spatial relation does not *guarantee* that they stand in that spatial relation. A necessary connection that isn't anchored in the intrinsic natures of the two relata would be a brute, inexplicable necessity. This is something that, at the very least, metaphysicians should try to keep to a minimum.[12] Therefore, Lewis thinks, if selection is necessary while being external, the selection relation is magical. In other words, no relation can be both external and necessary, in the above way.

Suppose, then, that selection is internal. And it seems that selection is an internal relation. Indeed, that is how we introduced it. Given the way things are, given the intrinsic character of the universe (that is, us and all our surroundings, including any immaterial things), Alpha could not fail to be selected. And had the universe been different, Alpha couldn't have been selected. We might think of it this way. Given that worlds must represent what they in fact represent, selection must be an internal relation. But if selection is internal, then it's a relation that holds in virtue of the intrinsic characteristics of worlds and the intrinsic characteristics of the universe. So worlds must exemplify a rich variety of intrinsic features. Presumably, these intrinsic features are just the representational features of worlds. To simplify, consider any world in which grass is green. This world represents that grass is green, which is to say, it has the representational property of *representing that grass is green*. In virtue of this representational feature, this world is selected if and only if grass is green. Magical Abstractionists, given that they say nothing more about these representational features, have here "danced around a tiny circle," according to Lewis (1986: 178). We thought we were getting an account of the selection relation, and the Magical Abstractionist has offered us representational features. But in order to understand what these representational features are, the Magical Abstractionist points us back to selection. We cannot, therefore, come to understand what these representational properties are without understanding the selection relation, and we cannot understand the selection relation without understanding what these representational features are. Thus, we have no way to truly understand the selection relation. If we are able to grasp it, says Lewis, *we* must have magical powers. Whether the selection relation is internal or external, Magical Abstractionism involves magic. And philosophical views oughtn't to involve magic.

Maybe things aren't so bad as Lewis thinks, though. Lewis seems to be presupposing that we have to come to an understanding of either the representational features of worlds (and propositions more generally) or of the selection relation. But it is not clear why this would have to be so. Maybe we can understand what the representational features of worlds are independently of our grasp on the selection relation, or vice versa. We certainly do not sensorily experience the representational features of propositions, but, plausibly, there are other sources of knowledge than sensory experience.

Many philosophers maintain that we have what might be called "intellectual" experience. Our knowledge of mathematics and pure sets and other abstract objects, for example, does not plausibly stem from sensory experience. Our knowledge of propositions is plausibly of this purely intellectual sort, and so we might come to know about the representational features of propositions via intellectual experience. Since worlds are just special propositions, namely the maximal possible propositions, we can come to understand the representational features of worlds on the basis of intellectual experience. And thus, we can come to understand the selection relation by virtue of our understanding of representation.

View 2: Linguistic Abstractionism   If Linguistic Abstractionism is true, then possible worlds are abstract objects that represent that so-and-so in the way that language does. According to Linguistic Abstractionism, possible worlds are like exceptionally detailed stories or exceedingly long sentences. Consider a sentence like, "Gretchen is impish." This sentence represents that Gretchen is impish. A plausible view of how this representation works goes like this. The sentence "Gretchen is impish" contains words that stand for certain worldly items, and puts those words together in a certain grammatically appropriate way. In particular, the name "Gretchen" picks out the three-year-old person, Gretchen Pickavance, while the predicate "is impish" designates the property of *being impish*. It also concatenates, respectively, the name and the predicate, and there exist grammatical conventions in our language community that guarantee that when one concatenates, respectively, a name and a predicate, the resulting sentence says of the thing named that it exemplifies the property designated by the predicate. All that to say, sentences represent by having parts that refer to or designate worldly items, together with conventions governing the way that those parts are combined together to produce something that represents a state of the world. According to Linguistic Abstractionism, propositions, and thus worlds, represent similarly. They are *built up*, as it were, from more basic items that refer to or designate worldly items. These more basic parts are arranged in accordance with a kind of propositional grammar. Consider, then, the proposition that Gretchen is impish. It will be built up from a propositional element that picks out Gretchen (the analogue of the name "Gretchen" in the sentence, "Gretchen is impish") and a propositional element that designates the property of *being impish* (the analogue of the predicate "is impish"), and these two parts are arranged in a propositional grammar in the way needed for the proposition to represent that Gretchen is impish. (Importantly, one doesn't have to buy the story we just told about language. *Absolutely everyone*, not just Linguistic Abstractionists, has to say something about how words and phrases and grammars contribute to the meanings of sentences, and the Linguistic Abstractionist simply wants to say that the way that the things that combine together to make propositions contribute to the representational features of propositions need be no different from one's favored view of linguistic representation.)

There is an obvious and important contrast between Linguistic Abstractionism and Magical Abstractionism. Magical Abstractionism is *silent* about how worlds represent, whereas Linguistic Abstractionism tries to give an account of how worlds represent. It tries to do more than say that a world w represents that p if and only if necessarily, if w is actual then the proposition that p is true. Further, it is the *metaphysical structure* of worlds that determine what it is they represent. That is, worlds have metaphysical parts, or constituents, and these constituents, together with their arrangements, determine the representational features of worlds. Linguistic Abstractionism says that the relevant structure is much like linguistic structure. Below, we will consider Pictorial Abstractionism, and this view is committed as well to structural representation. The difference between Linguistic and Pictorial Abstractionism concerns the kind of structure that determines worlds' representational features. Linguistic Abstractionists think that worlds represent in the way outlined above for propositions more generally. Obviously, though, worlds will have a much more complicated structure than the proposition that Gretchen is impish, for worlds must represent in a maximally specific way everything there is to say about the way things are. The representational structure of worlds would be the same in kind, but more rich in variety and detail.

The Problem of Alien Possibilities is a trouble for Linguistic Abstractionists. In order to see the problem, we need to first highlight an important feature of Linguistic Abstractionism, and to give a bit more flesh to the nature of the propositional elements that constitute propositions. First, the important feature: Linguistic Abstractionism is a version of *Actualism*. Actualism is the view that there are no non-actual things. Everything that exists, according to Actualism, is a part of the actual world. This stands in sharp contrast to the Concretist, who maintains that there exist non-actual things, even non-actual donkeys and stars and electrons and so on. Concretism is, in this sense, a *Possibilist* view. Possibilism is just the denial of Actualism, so Possibilists maintain that there exist non-actual things. More generally, Abstractionist views tend to be Actualist, while Concretism is Possibilist. At any rate, because of Linguistic Abstractionism's commitment to Actualism, propositional elements must be actual entities, not merely possible entities. We will return to this point below. Second, the flesh on the nature of propositional elements: one plausible account of the nature of the propositional elements is to say, more or less, that the elements are just the objects they represent. On this view, the propositional element that picks out Gretchen is just Gretchen herself, and the propositional element that designates the property of *being impish* is just the property of *being impish* itself.

The proposition that Gretchen is impish is, therefore, constituted by Gretchen and the property of *being impish* (in a certain propositional grammatical arrangement, which we can ignore at this point). More generally, objects serve as their own propositional names, and properties serve as their own propositional predicates. Following David K. Lewis (1986: 145), and with his nod to Swift's *Gulliver's Travels*, we can call this sort of propositional language, where things refer to themselves, a "Lagadonian" language.

We are now in a position to develop the Problem of Alien Possibilities. Given Actualism, no merely possible thing exists. This follows directly from the claim that the only things that exist are actual. Given that there is no actual thing Pegasus, Pegasus simply does not exist. Pegasus, being an "alien" to our world, a possible but non-actual thing, simply does not exist. But given the Lagadonian view of the propositional language, there cannot be a proposition that represents that Pegasus has wings. A commitment to the Lagadonian propositional language requires that objects serve as their own names, and so if there is a proposition that represents that Pegasus is a certain way, it must involve Pegasus itself. But again, given Actualism, there is no Pegasus. So no proposition can represent that Pegasus is any way at all, much less as having wings. More specifically to Linguistic Abstractionism, no *world* can represent that Pegasus has wings, since there is no Pegasus to serve as its own name. This problem will apply to any object that is alien to our world, that is, to any merely possible thing. This is the Problem of Alien Possibilities.

There are at least two ways to overcome this problem. First, one might reject Actualism in favor of Possibilism. This solves the Problem of Alien Possibilities because one would then have merely possible objects like Pegasus in one's ontology, and therefore available to serve as their own names in the propositional language. We do not have the space to delve deeply into the issues here, but one important concern for non-Concretist versions of Possibilism is that it is not entirely clear what merely possible objects are meant to be like. Merely possible horses, for example, are not meant to exemplify the property of being a horse, for if they did, they would be concrete things with a particular shape, color, size, mass. Such a horse, then, would seem to be either actual or a part of some other world. If it is actual, then one is back to Actualism, and if it is part of some other world, then one is just a Concretist. So it's not entirely clear how to consistently embrace both Linguistic Abstractionism, with its denial of Concretism, and Possibilism.

Second, one might reject the Lagadonian view of the propositional language. Probably the most plausible strategy for replacing the Lagadonian view is to deploy the haecceities of objects, in place of the objects themselves, as the propositional elements that designate objects. (Those who skipped, or who have maybe just forgotten, the discussion of haecceities in Chapter 5, may want to read or review before moving on.) For example, instead of Gretchen being herself a propositional element, Gretchen's haecceity functions in that capacity. If haecceities exist and are necessarily existing objects, then the haecceity of every possible object is an actually existing thing, and there would thereby be enough resources in one's ontology to have a propositional element uniquely paired with every possible object. Here again, we don't have the space to go into this issue in detail, but here are two hurdles that a theory of haecceities must overcome. First, many philosophers deny that all properties are necessarily existing. David M. Armstrong (1997: 38–43), for example, argues that properties only exist if they are instantiated. If he is right, then the haecceities of merely possible objects do not exist. But further, it raises a more general problem. Suppose, for example, that there were no yellow things. Then, according to Armstrong, there would be no property of *being yellow*. Thus, the property of *being yellow* could not serve as a propositional constituent in, for example, the proposition that sunflowers are yellow. Merely possible *properties*, not just merely possible substances or particulars, raise the Problem of Alien Possibilities. If some properties are merely contingent, then the haecceity strategy would require haecceities not just for merely possible substances and other particulars, but for merely possible properties as well. And the idea that properties have haecceities may be too much for some. Further, Robert M. Adams (1981) complains that haecceities, if they can go uninstantiated, are creatures of darkness. A haecceity is just the property of *being so-and-so*, for some so-and-so, but we don't really know what it is to be the property of *being so-and-so* if there is no so-and-so to be identical to (that is, if the haecceity is uninstantiated)! Adams, then, thinks that haecceities, if they exist at all, must be *object-dependent*: they only exist if the object that instantiates them exists. There is another kind of trouble as well. On a view that deploys haecceities as propositional elements that refer to objects, the proposition that Gretchen is impish is just the proposition that Gretchen's haecceity is co-instantiated with the property of *being impish*. More generally, the proposition that *o* is *F* is just the proposition that the haecceity of *o* is co-instantiated with the property of *being F*. But this doesn't seem to be true, in general. Consider, for example:

(10) Whatever instantiates Gretchen's haecceity necessarily is (identical to) Gretchen.

(11) Whatever instantiates Gretchen's haecceity necessarily instantiates Gretchen's haecceity.

On the view we are considering, (10) and (11) express the same proposition. But (10) seems to be a substantive metaphysical claim, while (11) is trivially true. The solution that rejects the Lagadonian picture may exact a steep price. One might wonder whether a different Abstractionist view with structural representation fares better.

View 3: Pictorial Abstractionism   Pictorial Abstractionism is another such view. If Pictorial Abstractionism is true, then possible worlds are abstract objects that represent that so-and-so in the way that pictures do. Worlds, on this view, are like maps or realist paintings or photographs. Pictures represent, to once again borrow from Lewis (1986: 166), by iso-morphism. That is, pictures represent by having parts that are *literally similar* to the things they represent. (Or anyway, this is part of the story with pictures, and the *whole* story, as we will see, for Pictorial Abstractionism.) Consider a photograph of Lyle and Nana The Grandma. (There are many such photographs.) A photograph of this sort represents Lyle by having a part that *looks like* Lyle. It has a head-shaped part, two blue-eye-colored parts, is likely to have a dinosaur shaped part, or a book-shaped part, and so on. It also has another two blue-eye-colored parts, another, slightly larger head-shaped part, and so on, parts that *look like* Nana The Grandma. This is how the picture of Lyle and Nana The Grandma represents Lyle and Nana The Grandma. According to Pictorial Abstractionism, worlds (and propositions more generally) represent by having parts that are literally similar to the things they represent. Pictorial Abstractionism also goes for structural representation, but instead of having quasi-linguistic elements that represent as language does, the Pictorial Abstractionist claims that worlds are built up from elements that represent by having features that are just those features that ordinary objects have.

Being an Actualist view, Pictorial Abstractionism faces the Problem of Alien Possibilities no less than does Linguistic Abstractionism. (We leave it to the reader to work out why this is so.) But Pictorial Abstractionism also faces the Problem of Representational Detail. Worlds must be maximally specific, maximally thorough representations, and must be able to distin-guish every possibility from one another. It is clear that ordinary pictures don't do this. Consider again a picture of Lyle and Nana The Grandma. No actually existing picture of them represents everything about them. (You'll have to take our word for it!) For example, one cannot work out, even if given all the time in the world, how many hairs are on Lyle's head by considering a picture of him. There will always be some that are hidden in some way or another, not to mention the technological problem of having a sufficiently fine-grained image to distinguish one hair from another. So we need maximally fine-grained images, images that are four-dimensional and include representations of every cross-section of everything that has, does, or will exist. Consider a three-dimensional cross-section of this four-dimensional image. To represent that Lyle is 48 inches tall, the natural thing to say is that the image will have a 48-inch tall part, with an eye-shaped part that has as a part a blue-iris-shaped part. It will also have ten finger-shaped, peach-colored parts; ten toe-shaped, peach-colored parts; around a hundred thousand hair-shaped, blonde-colored parts; and on and on. It's beginning to look as though, in order to do its job, the Pictorial Abstractionist's world is going to have to include something that is just like Lyle but for being concrete. That is, there is just going to be an abstract avatar of Lyle. In such a case, it's not really clear what the difference is between Pictorial Abstractionism and Concretism. A huge, maximally specific four-dimensional object full of things that have properties literally identical to the properties had by things in our spatiotemporal surroundings is just a Concretist-style world. That is the Problem of Representational Detail (from Lewis 1986: 171–174).

The Pictorial Abstractionist will insist that these representational objects are abstract rather than concrete. But it's not clear what we can make of that difference at this point. The representation of Lyle, for example, is going to have to stand in various causal relations, or relations that look an awful lot like causal relations, to other objects in the picture. And Lyle is going to have a definite location in the (representation of?) time and space of the picture. These were the paradigmatic sorts of features had by concrete but not abstract objects. The representations of the Pictorial Abstractionist are simply not plausibly abstract.

Each of our Abstractionist views has faced trouble. None are reductive. The Magical Abstractionist faces Lewis's dilemma about the selection relation. Both Linguistic Abstractionism and Pictorial Abstractionism face the Problem of Alien Possibilities, and the latter faces the Problem of Representational Detail as well. Concretism's quantitatively bloated ontology, on the other hand, is radically implausible from the get-go, and is plagued as well by the problems of Ethical Fatalism, Non-Indexical Uses of "Actual," Irrelevance, and Isolation.

7.2   Modality *De Re*: Transworld Identity versus Counterpart Theory

Maybe, though, we can make further progress by considering modality *de re*. As we will see, Concretism and Abstractionism each strongly suggest a view about modality *de re*, and it might be that the choice between the two views will be easier to make once we consider the plausibility of those *de re* modal views. Modality *de re* contrasts with modality *de dicto*, as we saw above. Modality *de re* concerns the essential and accidental features of objects, whereas modality *de dicto* concerns the modal status of propositions or sentences, whether they are possible, necessary, impossible, or contingent. We are presently turning our attention directly to modality *de re*. This is an important issue, for it seems substances, among other things, have certain features essentially and others accidentally. A property *F* is essential to an object *o* if and only if necessarily, if *o* exists then *o* is *F*, but a property *F* is accidental to an object *o* if and only if possibly *o* is *F*, and possibly *o* is not-*F*. Consider Lyle. He is a human essentially, but sweet only accidentally. It would be possible for him to exist and be cruel, but impossible for him to exist and be a dog. Up to this point, though, we have been concerned with modality *de dicto*, with how possible worlds might help us make sense of the truth or falsity of modal propositions, propositions that say that such-and-such must be the case, or that so-and-so might be the case, and so on. Our discussion centered on the two interrelated questions, whether possible worlds are concrete or abstract, and how it is that possible worlds represent that something is the case. These reflections, and the views that emerged, do supply some insight into how we might understand modality *de re*. We might say, for example, that Lyle is essentially human if and only if every world that represents Lyle represents that he is human. And Lyle is accidentally sweet if and only if there is at least one world that represents Lyle as sweet and at least one other world that represents him as cruel (supposing sweetness and cruelty are incompatible). This seems right so far as it goes.

The question that has dominated discussions of modality *de re* in recent philosophical work is whether one and the same object can exist in many possible worlds. Those who think that objects can exist in many possible worlds believe in Transworld Identity. Those who deny Transworld Identity, who think that objects exist in only one world, are *worldbound*, must find a way to recapture the intuitive account modality *de re* given a few sentences ago. The most common such view is Counterpart Theory. Roughly, Counterpart Theory says that worlds represent an object *o* not by involving *o* itself, but by involving one of *o*'s *counterparts*, something that is very much like *o* but which is not, strictly speaking, identical to *o*. As will emerge, though, metaphysicians even dispute what it is for a single object to exist in many possible worlds. The differences to do with modality *de re* are driven in large measure by differences about the nature of possible worlds more generally, which drive differences in what it is for something to be *in* a world, or, alternatively, differences in what it is for a world to *involve* some thing. In particular, Abstractionists tend to go for Transworld Identity, while Concretists tend to go for Counterpart Theory. We will examine each of these views in turn, and will display how a commitment to Abstractionism naturally drives one toward Transworld Identity, while a commitment to Concretism naturally drives one toward Counterpart Theory.

7.2.1   Transworld Identity

Abstractionism naturally drives one toward Transworld Identity. To see that this is so, let's consider a natural Abstractionist characterization of modality *de re*. Consider again, the claim that Lyle is essentially human. This claim is true if and only if Lyle has the property of *being essentially human*. Being a modal claim, there is a connection between its truth and facts about possible worlds, even if the connection is not a reductive one. So, despite being anti-reductionist about modality, Abstractionists can agree that Lyle has the property of *being essentially human* if and only if every possible world that represents Lyle at all represents him as having the property of *being human*. But what is it for a possible world to represent Lyle as being a certain way? We considered three Abstractionist views of representation above, but there is something that they have in common in this area: almost every Abstractionist view agrees that, however Lyle gets represented, a world does *not* represent him by having him as a part.[13] Lyle is a part of no possible world (not even the actual one), in a strict sense. The only sense in which Lyle is part of a world is that he is represented by it. Lyle is literally part of the actual world if Concretism is true, but he is not literally a part of any world if Abstractionism is true. He is simply represented. The actual world represents him as he is; the others as he could have been.

There are differences, though, in *how* the Abstractionist views represent Lyle as being some way or other. If Magical Abstractionism is true, we can't say anything meaningful at all about how this happens. However, it will be the case that the worlds that represent Lyle have certain representational features in common. For example, every world that represents Lyle has the property of *representing Lyle*. (Uninformative, but that's to be expected!) If Linguistic Abstractionism is true, then worlds represent Lyle by having a "name" of him as a constituent. Maybe, for example, a world represents Lyle by having his haecceity as a part. If Pictorial Abstractionism is true, then worlds represent Lyle by having a highly detailed, four-dimensional, abstract simulacrum of Lyle as a part.

Notice, though, that on all three of these Abstractionist views, Lyle is represented by two worlds w_1 and w_2 if and only if w_1 and w_2 literally have something in common. In the case of Magical Abstractionism, there is sharing of a property; in the case of Linguistic and Pictorial Abstractionism, there is sharing of a part, whether a "name" or an abstract simulacrum. Because of this, it is right to say that, had a world representing Lyle been actual, Lyle himself would have existed. That is, he would have been part of our spatiotemporal surroundings. In this sense, these views are committed to, or at least are compatible with, Transworld Identity, the claim that it is possible that actual objects would have existed even if a different world had been actual. One way to express the idea of Transworld Identity is as the thought that a single object can exist *in* many worlds. Given that the word "in" can be understood either representationally or mereologically, we must be careful to say to what exactly Abstractionists are committed. Everyone, Concretists no less than Abstractionists, agrees that a single individual can be *represented in* many worlds. The distinctive commitment of Transworld Identity is the claim that it is possible for some actually existing thing to be a mereological part of the concrete universe even were a different world actual. The view may crystallize by considering its chief rival, Counterpart Theory.

7.2.2   Counterpart Theory

Recall that Concretists take possible worlds to be like parallel universes. If this is right, then it would be very odd to say that a single thing could exist in multiple worlds, where "in" is understood to mean "be a part of." For if one thing was a part of many worlds, then possible worlds would overlap. Lyle, for example, would be a part of many worlds, because he could be many different ways. But where two things have a common part, they overlap. Thus, every world which has Lyle as a part overlaps. This leads to certain difficulties, however. For example, Lyle is sweet but might have been impish. Thus, there is a world according to which Lyle is sweet and a different world according to which Lyle is impish. Concretists, however, cash "according to" in a reductive way. What it is for Lyle to be sweet according to a world w_1 is for him to be a part of w_1 and literally have the property of *being sweet*. What it is for him to be impish according to a world w_2 is for him to be a part of w_2 and literally have the property of *being impish*. But if we think w_1 and w_2 represent Lyle as existing simply by having him as a part, such that they overlap, then the very same thing, namely Lyle, has both the property of *being sweet* and the property of *being impish*. Assuming these properties contradict one another, we have a problem.[14] It seems that Concretism with overlapping worlds is problematic if there are things that might have had different intrinsic properties than those they in fact have. And there do seem to be such properties. Lyle is sweet but might have been impish, 48 inches tall but possibly 45, blue-eyed but possibly brown, and so on.

Thus, Concretists ought to deny that worlds overlap, that things literally can be a part of multiple worlds. However, Concretists must be careful to maintain the idea that a single thing can be represented by more than one world. Otherwise, they won't be able to make sense of the idea that Lyle might have been impish. For they think that Lyle might have been impish if and only if there is a possible world that *represents him* as impish. And that world cannot be the actual world, since according to the actual world, he is sweet. What to do?

Counterpart theory, if workable, solves this problem. The idea is that individuals have *counterparts* that exist in possible worlds other than their own. In typical cases, some thing *s*'s counterpart in some world *w* is the thing in *w* that most resembles *s*. Lyle, on this view, only exists in one world, the actual world. Other worlds do not literally contain Lyle as a part, but they contain other children with biographies very much like his. Maybe they are named "Lyle," have philosopher fathers, live in cities called "Fullerton," and so on. These other children are Lyle's counterparts in these worlds, and it is because they have certain features that Lyle himself has the modal features that he in fact does. For example, Lyle might have been impish because he has a counterpart who really is impish. He might have been 45 inches tall because he has a counterpart who really is 45 inches tall. And so on. In general, to say that an individual might have had some feature *F* is to say that that individual has a counterpart who really does have *F*. It should be clear that, if Counterpart Theory is true, things are only *in* one world in the mereological sense, but are *in* many worlds in the representational sense.

The "Humphrey Objection"   Famously, Abstractionists have objected that Counterpart Theory detaches *de re* modal facts from the things that those facts are supposed to be about. For example, it's Lyle who might have been impish, but Counterpart Theory seems to say that this has to do with someone other than Lyle himself, that is, it has to do with his counterparts. What happens to a thing's counterparts just seems irrelevant to what is true about a thing itself. They are just distinct objects, and where they exist in distinct worlds, they in principle cannot interact in any way. If we don't take seriously the idea that what is possible and not for Lyle is affected by what is actually true of Gretchen or Barack Obama, how much less seriously ought we to take the idea that what is possible for Lyle is affected by other-worldly individuals! Saul Kripke puts the point this way:

> [According to Counterpart Theory] if we say "[Hubert] Humphrey might have won the [1968 United States presidential] election" ..., we are not talking about something that might have happened to *Humphrey* but to someone else, a "counterpart". Probably, however, Humphrey could not care less whether someone *else*, no matter how much resembling him, would have been victorious in another possible world. (Kripke 1980: 45)

Thus this objection has come to be called the "Humphrey Objection."

In response to this worry, the Counterpart Theorist should say that Humphrey *himself* really does have the property of *possibly having won*, that Lyle really does have the property of *possibly being impish*. It's just that Humphrey and Lyle have these features, respectively, in virtue of standing in counterpart relations to other things that have other properties. To put the point differently, what goes on with one's counterparts has *everything* to do with what *modal* properties one has. It's just *what it is* to possibly win that one has a counterpart that wins. And, most importantly, *you yourself* wind up exemplifying the relevant modal features. It's not your counterparts who have the *modal* properties; they just have the non-modal properties relevantly associated with the modal properties you yourself have.

In response, Abstractionists can insist that our understanding of what we mean by predicating modal properties is so clear that we can just see that the intrinsic properties of counterparts cannot possibly be the ground of modal truths about actual individuals. Metaphysical theories must treat such intuitions with due respect, or else we would have to take seriously theories that proposed that Humphrey's potentiality for winning the election is really grounded in some properties of numbers or of the empty set.

We should note, however, that this response is available only to Magical Abstractionists and to Lagadonian Linguistic Abstractionists. According to non-Lagadonian Linguistic Abstractionists and Pictorial Abstractionists, possible worlds represent Lyle by having a "name" (Linguistic Abstractionism) or a simulacrum (Pictorial Abstractionism) among their parts. Such Abstractionists must agree, therefore, that the exemplification of modal properties implicates something other than the things that have the modal properties. It's not clear, *pace* the Humphrey Objection, why it's worse to have these other things be concrete objects, rather than abstract representations.

Notes

1 To be clear, we doubt that this is the right way to read (4), but it is one way to do so, and it is closely related to a better, more semantically subtle reading. Here, unfortunately, is not the place to enter into the details.

2 There is an implicit assumption: we must suppose that distinct possibilities must have distinct representational features in order to guarantee that there is only one maximal possibility that accurately represents the world.

3 God, angels, and Cartesian souls may be exceptions.

4 This is the way that David K. Lewis, the most prominent defender of Concretism and one of the most influential metaphysicians of the last hundred years, put the view in his *On the Plurality of Worlds* (1986: 1–2). Anyone who is familiar with Lewis's work on modality will sense the tremendous debt our discussion owes to him.

   Importantly, we are now using the word "way" a bit differently than we did back in Chapter 4. We take it that the English word is flexible enough to accommodate this shift, but one must mark the shift.

5 The talk of "proximity" here shouldn't be taken too literally. It's not as if other worlds were far away from us: they don't stand in any spatial or temporal relation to us at all. By "proximate," we just mean at *some* distance from us.

6   We will examine this in more detail below.

7   Cf. Pruss (2011: 100–107).

8   This view of the worldmate relation couples poorly with Neo-Humeism, the view of causation advocated by David Lewis, Concretism's chief advocate. This is not a principled objection to the view, but rather just to the package of views advocated by Lewis. We will not pursue it further.

9   Given this possibility of parallel universes within the same world, it should be clear that describing Concretism as the view that worlds are parallel universes is a bit misleading. Worlds, according to Concretism, are *like* parallel universes, in that they are populated with objects in just the way that our world is, but they are not, strictly speaking, parallel universes.

10 Cf. Plantinga's extensive work on the metaphysics of modality, esp. his *The Nature of Necessity* (1974).

11 Cf. Adams (1974).

12 There is a principle, known as "Hume's Dictum," which dictates that we should never posit necessary connections between "separate" beings. See Wilson (2010) for a discussion of the merits of the dictum. Wilson concludes that, while there is no direct evidence for the dictum, it is useful methodologically.

13 The exception is the Lagadonian take on Linguistic Abstractionism, according to which things serve as their own "names." It will turn out that this nicety won't matter for what we're about below, and anyway, the contrast here is between how things are parts of Concretist worlds versus how they are represented by Abstractionist worlds. Such a contrast exists even on the Lagadonian Linguistic Abstractionist view.

14 The assumption that they do contradict doesn't do any real work here. We could have picked a different pair of properties, like those of *being 48 inches tall* and *being 45 inches tall*. These *do* contradict, and are both possible for him to exemplify.

8

The Passage of Time

Time is simple and unproblematic, until we start thinking about it (as Augustine of Hippo noted in his *Confessions* in the 4th century AD). Although time is something that we are all intimately familiar with, its true nature poses some of the most enduring mysteries of philosophy. In this chapter, we will focus on just one of those mysteries: does time really pass? Do times really change from being future, to being present, and finally to being forever past?

8.1 The A Theory and the B Theory

The Cambridge metaphysician J. M. E. McTaggart (1866–1925) introduced a useful distinction between two kinds of temporal series: the A and B series. These two series consist in two different kinds of temporal relations. When we compare two events in terms of how far they lie in the past or future, we are comparing them with respect to the A Theory. In contrast, when we compare them in terms of which is earlier or later in time, we are referring to the B Theory. Consider, for example, the following propositions:

> (1) Julius Caesar lived over 2000 years ago, while Napoleon Bonaparte was alive just 200 years ago.
> (2) The election of the first female US president is just three years in the future, while the first US colony on Mars is at least 30 years in the future.
> (3) The election of the first black US president is in the past, while the election of the first female US president is in the future.
> (4) Julius Caesar lived 1800 years earlier than Napoleon Bonaparte did.

Metaphysics: The Fundamentals, First Edition. Robert C. Koons and Timothy H. Pickavance.
© 2015 Robert C. Koons and Timothy H. Pickavance.
Published 2015 by John Wiley & Sons, Ltd.

(5) The election of the first female US president is at least 27 years earlier than the first US colony on Mars.

(6) The first black US president was elected before the first female US president.

Propositions (1) through (3) refer to positions in the A series, while propositions (4) through (6) refer to the B series. We shall call propositions like (1) through (3) "A-propositions" and those like (4) through (6) "B-propositions." There is a crucial distinction between the two classes of propositions. B-propositions never change their truth-value: once true or false, the proposition keeps the same value forever. In contrast, A-propositions can change their truth-value over time. Proposition (1) was false until 1943 (since before then, Caesar had not yet been dead for 2000 years), and it will become false again in 2021 (since after then, Napoleon will have been dead for more than 200 years). In contrast, proposition (4) has always been true and always will be true.

We can extend this distinction between A-propositions and B-propositions to propositions that refer to single events. Consider, for example, (7) and (8):

(7) Julius Caesar lived over 2000 years ago.

(8) Julius Caesar lived before 14 AD.

Proposition (7) is an A-proposition, since it was false before 1943 AD, at which time it became true. Proposition (8), in contrast, has always been true, assuming that we can take the conventional Christian dating system as referring to relative positions in the B series.

We can use these distinctions to formulate two competing theories of time: the A Theory and the B Theory. According to A Theorists, A-propositions like (1) through (3) and (7) correspond to real, objective facts about the world. B Theorists, in contrast, hold that only B-propositions express objective, observer-independent facts about the world, while A-propositions are made true at different times by appropriate B-facts, that is, facts about how the relevant events stand in the B series. Thus, the present truth of proposition (7) is wholly grounded in the truth of proposition (8). There is no further fact in the world – no fundamental degree of pastness that is exemplified by the life of Julius Caesar. What makes it true that Caesar's life is now in the past is simply the B-relation between our thoughts now and the life of Caesar.

We could put this distinction by saying that, according to B Theorists, only the B-truths are fundamental, with all A-truths wholly grounded in B-truths. A Theorists, in contrast, insist that A-truths are also fundamental. Similarly, A Theorists insist on the fundamentality of A-properties, like pastness, presentness, and futurity, while B Theorists claim that only the B-relations, like earlier than, simultaneous with, and later than, are truly fundamental.

There is, however, a complication in this case: according to B Theorists, a single A-truth is grounded in different B-truths at different times. The truth of proposition (7) is now grounded in the truth of proposition (8), but in 2015, it will be grounded instead in the truth of (9):

(9) Julius Caesar lived before 15 AD.

This fact of variable grounding means that B Theorists cannot claim that A-propositions can be translated into equivalent B-propositions. For example, if we tried to translate sentence (7) into a purely B-language (a language referring only to the B series), we would fail, since any B-proposition is either eternally true or eternally false, while (7) must change from false to true in 1943.

Some early B Theorists (defenders of what is now known as the "Old B Theory") tried to translate sentences like (7) into a purely B-language by means of self-reference. For example, one might try to translate (7) into (7*):

(7*) Julius Caesar lived at least 2000 years before the utterance of this very sentence.

If sentence (7*) is uttered in 2014, then it expressed the same B-proposition as that expressed by sentence (7). If (7*) were not uttered until 2015, then it would express the B-proposition expressed by (9). However, this attempt clearly fails, since one who utters (7) is talking only about the temporal location of the life of Julius Caesar. It is just implausible to suppose that a sentence like (7) is covertly or implicitly referring to itself, or to some particular utterance of itself.

Arthur Prior (1959) criticized the Old B Theory in a very vivid way. Suppose that I have been dreading an unpleasant visit to the dentist. The day of the appointment finally comes, and the unpleasant procedure is completed. Afterwards, I exclaim, "Thank goodness that's over." I am happy about the truth of the following proposition:

(10) My unpleasant visit to the dentist is in the past.

It is obvious that I am not happy about the truth of the following sentence:

(11) My unpleasant visit to the dentist occurred before the utterance of (10).

Suppose I do utter sentence (10) after my visit to the dentist. Then proposition (11) has always been true: it was true before the dental visit began. Clearly, I am not pleased about the eternal B-relation between my visit to the dentist and the utterance of (10): what I am happy about is that the visit to the dentist is in the past.

The New B Theory accounts for the truth of A-propositions by making use of the linguistic concept of *indexicality*. A type of sentence is indexical when the truth-value of particular uses of that sentence-type (their truth or falsity) depends upon facts about the context of utterance. Some familiar expressions that introduce indexicality are "I" and "here." Consider the following sentence-types:

(12) I am a philosopher.
(13) The climate here is sub-tropical.

When a sentence of type (12) is uttered, its truth or falsity depends on who is doing the uttering. It is true when uttered by Saul Kripke but false when uttered by Tom Cruise. Similarly, whether a particular utterance of (13) is true depends on where it is uttered: true when uttered in Houston, Texas, false when uttered in Nome, Alaska. B Theorists propose that the tenses (past, present, and future) and temporal adverbs (like "now" or "in the past") are indexical devices. We don't have to posit real properties of pastness or futurity in our metaphysical theories: we just have to pay close attention to when such sentences are uttered. The temporal location of the utterance determines which facts about the B series are the truthmakers (or falsity-makers) for the statement or expressed proposition.

8.2   Varieties of A Theories

A Theorists believe that there are fundamental properties of pastness, presentness, or futurity. Strictly speaking, they need just one of these properties to be metaphysically fundamental. Suppose, for example, that temporal presence is fundamental. We could then define the property of being past as the property of being earlier than the present.

There is a variety of theories about what being temporally present consists in, giving rise to a variety of A Theories. First, there is Minimal A Theory. According to Minimal A Theory, being temporally present is a simple and indefinable fundamental property. This property is always instantiated by a single, unique moment of time, and which moment of time instantiates presentness is constantly changing. The minimal theory is sometimes called the "moving spotlight theory": think of the moment that instantiates presentness as illuminated by a spotlight. As time passes, the spotlight of presentness moves to successively later moments.

A second version of the A Theory focuses on the difference between the openness of the future and the fixity of the past. At any point in time, there are a number of different, alternate futures, all of which are possible. Which future is realized depends on how existing things exercise their powers.

If human beings have free will, for example, they select among possible futures by actualizing their powers and capacities in specific ways. In contrast, the past is fixed and inexorable. As Aristotle put it, it makes no sense to deliberate about the past. On this theory, the present can be defined as the latest moment at which all earlier events are fixed and necessary. This has been called the "falling branches theory": there are always multiple branches stretching into the future, but only one trunk stretching into the past (McCall 1976, 1984, 1994). As time progresses, possible branches disappear, as the events they represent change from being possible futures to being impossible might-have-beens.

On some versions of the falling branches theory, future contingent propositions are neither true nor false. For example, if there is one possible future in which the Houston Astros win the pennant in 2020 and another in which they do not, it is now neither true nor false that they will do so. Other versions embrace the law of bivalence, insisting that one or the other future contingent proposition is now true, although both are still possibly true (in the relevant sense). Even if it is now true that the Astros will not win the pennant in 2020, that fact is not yet inevitable or necessary.

A third version of the A Theory focuses instead on the nature of predication. On this view, the present tense corresponds to simple predication or instantiation. If A is now F, then A is F simpliciter. That is, A instantiates the universal of F-ness or contains or is modified by an F-trope (depending on our theory of predication). In contrast, the past and future tenses involve some indirect or higher-order relation between a thing and a property. If A was F, then A now stands in the *having-been* relation to the property of F-ness. This *having-been* relation connects concrete particulars to universals; it is a relation other than simple instantiation or exemplification. It is a real and not merely a logical relation, in the sense that we can posit a *having-been* universal without running into any danger of an infinite regress. The logical relation of instantiation relates the *having-been* universal to pairs of concrete particulars and other universals. A version of this theory has been defended by John Bigelow (1996).

For example, the city of Houston now has a population of more than two million, but it once had a population of fewer than one million. Consequently, it now stands in the *having-been* relation to the property of having a population of fewer than one million, while it simply instantiates the property of having a population of more than two million.

This third, predicational version of the A Theory privileges the present moment: how things are in the present is how they are, period. In contrast, things are alienated to a degree from the ways they were in the past or will be in the future. This alienation is crucial, if we are to accommodate the phenomenon of intrinsic change. Consider the example of McTaggart's iron bar, which was cold in the past and is now hot. Coldness and heat are two contrary properties and yet both are somehow intrinsic to the rod. The Predicational A Theorist solves this problem by affirming that the rod is hot simpliciter and not cold simpliciter, but it does have a certain relation to coldness, namely, the once-having-been relation. In the past, the rod had coldness simpliciter and stood in the eventually-will-be relation to heat.

These last two versions of the A Theory are compatible and could be combined into a single theory. The predicational theory could be used to define the present moment, and the falling-branches picture could then be used to distinguish the future from the past.

There is a fourth version of the A Theory, one according to which the present moment encompasses all of reality. There is nothing real that exists merely in the past or merely in the future. It is true that there *once were* dinosaurs or that someday there *will be* human colonies on Mars, but dinosaurs and Mars colonies do not fall within the scope of existence. Presentists need not deny the existence of past and future times or the real flow of time, but the things belonging entirely to the past or to the future are in some sense unreal. This fourth version is called "Presentism."

The articulation and evaluation of Presentism involves some subtle issues about the nature of existence and non-existence, the possibility of tenseless truths, and the role of truthmakers, issues that would take us too far afield. For example, in order to formulate Presentism precisely, we would have to ask whether everything exists. If some things don't exist (as possibilists and followers of Alexius Meinong believe), then Presentism would have to be stated as the view that everything *that exists* exists in the present. Actualists, who believe that everything exists, will prefer to use the starker formulation, according to which absolutely everything exists in the present – that is, absolutely nothing exists in the past or the future, except for those things that also exist in the present.

If Presentists are possibilists, believing that some things don't exist, then they will also have to affirm that there is such a thing as a *tenseless predication* of existence. On this view, when we say that there is a prime number between three and five, we are not saying that such a number exists *now*, but rather that it exists simpliciter, in a way that is entirely free of temporality. If there is such a tenseless sense of existence, possibilistic Presentism could be stated as the view according to which everything *that exists tenselessly* exists in the present. If there is no such tenseless predication of existence, then possibilism renders Presentism vacuous and trivial, since it would be a mere tautology to say that everything that exists in the present exists in the present, and it would be false to say that everything that existed in the past exists in the present.

Actualists, in contrast, can be Presentists by denying that there is tenseless predication of existence. Actualists can express Presentism by simply stating that *absolutely everything* exists in the present. The quantifier "everything" has no tense, for the Actualist; it simply includes the whole domain of quantification, in the widest, most unrestricted interpretation of the terms of language or thought.

In order to avoid these complexities, we will set aside Presentism and focus instead on the three simpler versions of the A Theory. Fortunately, the predicational form of the A Theory privileges the present moment, in a way very similar to the way that Presentism does, so little of consequence will be omitted.

8.3   Arguments for the B Theory

8.3.1   A Simpler Account of the Semantics of Tense

B Theorists can appeal to Ockham's Razor: why add real and objective properties of presentness, pastness, and futurity to our theory of the world, when the linguistic hypothesis of indexicality enables the B Theory to provide an adequate semantic account of the tenses and temporal adverbs? The B Theory has a leaner ontology, with fewer basic properties than most versions of the A Theory.

This is certainly true if we compare the B Theory with the Minimal A Theory. The Minimal Theory simply adds a new primitive, a basic property of presentness, to the machinery of the B Theory. When comparing the B Theory with other versions of the A Theory, the issue is more complicated. If B Theorists try to respect the fact that what is possible varies with time, gradually becoming narrower as opportunities for alternative branchings are passed by, they will have to introduce a kind of relativized possibility: *possible at time t*, while the A Theorist can get by with just one property of absolute possibility, which changes its scope over time. In this case, the advantage might go to the falling-branches A Theorist.

In addition, the B Theorist will need fundamental relations of temporal distance between events, while the Predicational A Theorist will have fundamental relations between particulars and properties corresponding to different degrees of pastness or futurity. This looks like a tie, since the Predicational A Theorist can define the B-relation of temporal distance in terms of distance in the A series.

The B Theorists can respond by arguing that the B theoretic account of temporal modalities forms part of a simpler and more unified account of the semantics of our natural languages. We already need the theory of indexicals to make sense of expressions like "I" and "here." It seems natural to extend that theory to the case of "now" and "later," treating these as similarly context-dependent.

Consider how odd it would be to defend the counterpart of the Minimal A Theory for the semantics of "I" or "here." We would have to suppose that, for each person, there was a primitive property of me-ness, and for each location in space a primitive property of here-ness. If I say that I am a philosopher, I would be saying that the unique property of me-ness that belongs to me and the property of being a philosopher are instantiated by the same thing, and if you say that you are a philosopher, you would be saying that the unique property of me-ness that belongs to you and the property of being a philosopher are co-instantiated. Surely it would be much simpler to suppose that, when each of us uses the word "I," we simply refer directly to ourselves, without needing any special property to be the vehicle for the reference.

The counterpart to the Predicational A Theory would be even weirder, since it would mean that each of us, when using the sentence "I am a philosopher, and so are you," was supposing that he or she was the uniquely privileged individual to whom the property of being a philosopher can be attributed, while the other person, the one being addressed as "you," would instead have some sort of alienating you-relation to that property, a relation that does not entail really being a philosopher at all. If we tried to construct the counterpart to Presentism, the result would be weirder still. We would have to embrace solipsism as the implicit theory of the users of "I," each of whom would have to be represented as believing that only he or she really existed.

8.3.2 The Special Theory of Relativity

A second crucial argument for the B Theory appeals to the results of modern science – in particular, to Einstein's theory of relativity. The most natural and straightforward interpretation of special relativity entails that there is no objective relation of absolute simultaneity. Instead, we can meaningfully speak of one event as simultaneous (or earlier or later) than another event only relative to some frame of reference. When two objects A and B are moving relative to each other, they belong to different frames of reference. When objects belong to different frames of reference, different events will count as simultaneous to each other.

If we represent the history of the world in four dimensions (three for space and one for time), then for each frame of reference, there is a set of hyper-planes of simultaneity. Different frames of reference correspond to different ways of slicing the four-dimensional block of history into such planes. Here's an illustration in which we have used just one dimension for space and one for time (Figure 8.1). The solid lines represent the planes of simultaneity for frame of reference A and the dotted lines for frame of reference B. Note that, according to frame of reference A, events 1 and 2 are simultaneous, and 3 occurs later than both of them. But, according to frame of reference B, events 2 and 3 are simultaneous and 1 occurs earlier than

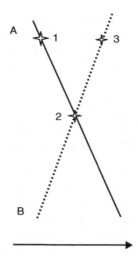

Figure 8.1

either of them. This sort of situation is possible so long as none of these events occur in the "light cones" of the other two – that is, so long as they are far enough apart in space and close enough in time that it would not have been possible for a light signal to reach one event from another. (This is called "spacelike separation.")

If the A Theory were true (in any of its forms), all present events would stand in a relation of absolute simultaneity, as would all events that are a fixed number of units of time in the past or the future. Thus, A Theory seems to stand in direct contradiction to this fundamental principle of relativity theory.

It is possible for A Theorists to suppose that existence itself is frame-relative: what exists for me, in my frame of reference, may be different than what exists for you, in your frame of reference, even if we are both now looking at reality from the same spacetime point. This is a fairly radical form of metaphysical relativism, calling into question whether observers in different inertial frames can be said to be occupying the same reality at all. Better to look elsewhere.

The best response for A Theorists would be to insist upon a non-standard interpretation of relativity theory, one that does not deny the existence of a metaphysically privileged, absolute simultaneity relation. A Theorists can plausibly argue that all that physicists can claim is that they do not need to postulate a relation of absolute simultaneity in giving physical explanations of phenomena. However, the absence of postulation is not the same thing as the postulation of absence.

Physicists can rightly point out that no physical observation or experiment can settle the question of which spacelike-separated events are really simultaneous and which are not. However, to make the further inference that there is therefore no such thing as absolute simultaneity is to assume the truth of the thesis of *verificationism*. Verificationists claim that no proposition can be true unless it can be scientifically verified. However, there is little reason to believe that verificationism is true, and many reasons for doubting it. Most crucially, verificationism seems to be self-refuting, since there is no scientific way to verify verificationism itself.

Nonetheless, there remain two weighty reasons for preferring the B Theory. First, it is clear that in this case Ockham's Razor favors the B Theory: the B Theory's account of the physical world doesn't require as much information as does the A Theory, and the additional information added by the A Theory does no additional work within physics.

Second, the A Theory faces the conspiracy of silence problem. The A Theory entails that there is an empirically undetectable relation of absolute simultaneity: a relation that manages somehow to elude discovery. The B Theory has a simple and plausible explanation of why we cannot detect absolute simultaneity: the relation simply does not exist. A Theorists must suppose that the relation exists, and yet there is a conspiracy of physical transformations that conceal the relation from detection.

8.3.3   If Time Passes, How Fast Does It Move?

One way of expressing the difference between the A and B Theories of time focuses on the question, does time move? According to the A Theory, the present moment (that is, the moment that uniquely instantiates the property of presentness) is constantly in motion relative to the B series, moving from earlier to later moments. The Australian philosopher J. J. C. Smart (1949) has used this fact as the basis for a further objection to the A Theory. If time is indeed moving, it seems that we should be able to ask, how fast is it moving? What is its rate of motion?

There seem to be only two possible answers. Either time moves necessarily at the rate of one second per second (comparing its motion to its own measure), or time moves at some rate of x seconds per *meta-second*, where a *meta-second* is some (to us unknown) unit of meta-time. Meta-time would have to be some kind of new series or pair of series – a second A and B series, by which we can measure the rate of change of the first, familiar A series. The problem with the proposal of meta-time is that it seems to lead immediately to an infinite regress. We can always ask, how fast does meta-time pass? Answering this question would seem to require meta-meta-time, and so on *ad infinitum*.

However, what is wrong with the simpler answer that time passes at one second per second? This is an odd sort of speed, but the motion of time is a unique kind of motion. Here's an objection to the simple answer. If something moves at a certain rate, it should be possible (at least metaphysically speaking) for it to move at a slightly slower or faster rate. However, in this case, it makes no sense to say that time is passing at the rate of 1.1 seconds per second. Here is the argument:

1. If time passes, it is in motion.
2. If time is in motion, it is necessarily moving at the rate of one second per second.
3. There is no possible motion that must, as a matter of metaphysical necessity, occur at a single, fixed rate.
    Therefore, it is impossible that time is in motion.
    So, time does not pass.

There are two possible responses to this objection. First, as Ned Markosian (1993) has pointed out, we could use various physical processes in time as a way of measuring the rate at which time passes. Just as it is legitimate to say that the earth revolves at the rate of one revolution per sidereal day, so it is equally proper to say that time passes at the rate of one sidereal day per revolution of the earth. So measured, time could pass more quickly, if the earth's rate of revolution were to slow down.

Alternatively, we could just bite the bullet, and stipulate that the passage of time is unique in that it has a fixed and metaphysically necessary rate of passage (i.e., one second per second).[1]

8.4   Arguments for the A Theory

8.4.1   The Reality of Change

J. M. E. McTaggart, who introduced the distinction between the A and B series (McTaggart 1908), provides contemporary philosophy with an argument against the B Theory's account of tense.[2] Tense involves time, and time is impossible without change. McTaggart's charge against the B Theory is that it entails a perfectly static world, a world in which nothing really changes.

McTaggart (1927: 2.14–15) asks us to consider an iron poker that begins cold at 9 a.m. and gradually changes to a red-hot state at noon. B Theorists can account for this change in either of two ways. According to the B Theory, both the cold poker and the hot poker are equally real, and the predicational tie between the poker and the two contrary properties is equally direct and immediate. In order to avoid the self-contradictory result that the poker is both cold and not-cold, B Theorists must either suppose that being cold is really a relation between the poker and some moment in time, or they must suppose that the poker has two different *temporal parts*, one of which is located within the earlier span of time and is cold, and the other of which is located within the later span and is hot.

However, in both cases nothing really changes. On the relational view, the poker is eternally in the cold relation to 9 a.m. and in the hot relation to noon. These two relational facts are fixed and unchanging. On the alternative, temporal-parts picture, the early part of the poker is always cold and the later part of the poker is always hot. Again, nothing really changes. Defenders of the A Theory can reasonably claim that the B Theory's account of temporal semantics is a non-starter, since we know *a priori* that our temporal sentences cannot be verified in an unchanging world.

In response, B Theorists argue that their account does include real change. Change is simply a matter of having one property at one time and a contrary property at a different time, and this occurs on both the relational and the temporal-parts model. However, A Theorists are unlikely to find this response persuasive, since there is no denying that, in some sense, the fixed *block universe* of the B Theory is eternally unchanging.

8.4.2   Recalcitrant Linguistic Data

In addition, A Theorists can challenge the claim that a B-theoretic indexical semantic theory is adequate for all of our uses of temporal language. Consider, for example, statement (14):

(14) The present year was once future and will someday be in the past.

It's easy to interpret (14) in a way that seems obviously true. The present year (2014) was once in the future – that is, in 1999, it still lay 15 years in the future. Someday, say 2020, it will lie in the past. However, the indexical theory cannot provide us with such an interpretation. Statement (14) clearly entails (15):

(15) The present year was once not the present year and someday will no longer be the present year.

On the indexical theory, the truth of (15), when uttered in the year 2014, would have to be grounded in the truth of the following obviously false proposition:

(16) The year 2014 was once not the year 2014 and someday will no longer be the year 2014.

What we are really trying to say with (15) is something like the following, a proposition that cannot be given a B-theoretic interpretation.

(16) The year 2014 was once not metaphysically present, and someday will no longer be metaphysically present.

Here's another example of a truth that is problematic for B-theoretic semantics:

(17) If the present year were the year 1954, Milton Berle might be live on television right now.

Again, this seems obviously true, and yet the antecedent of the conditional would represent a logical impossibility on the B-theoretic account, and the consequent would be obviously impossible.

(18) If the year 2014 were identical to the year 1954, then Milton Berle might be live on television in the year 2014.

On standard accounts of the semantics of conditionals, this would make the conditional (18) false, despite the truth of the corresponding (17).

8.4.3   Our Experience of the Flow of Time

Another set of arguments for the A Theory appeals to our experience of the passage or flow of time. This temporal experience can be considered in two ways: atomistically (at a moment), and holistically (through a succession of moments).

Experience Considered Atomistically   As Augustine observed in Book 11 of his *Confessions* (orig. pub. 398; Augustine 1991), we experience each moment as fleeting, as being about to pass away. Every experience in time has an ephemeral and tenuous quality. According to the B Theory, this is just an illusion. All moments and all events and facts associated with any moment exist eternally.

B Theorists might explain this experience of fleetingness as the perception of the *brevity* of the present moment. I perceive each moment as having a short duration, and so I also perceive those events occurring in the moment as taking up only a short span of time.

The American philosopher and psychologist William James (1842–1910) introduced the concept of the *specious present*: a finite interval of time that is experienced as a whole, in a single act of consciousness (James 1893: 609). The speciousness of the experienced present moment explains why we are able to perceive change and motion directly. The B Theorist could explain our sense of the fleetingness of time as just the perception of the brevity of the specious present, that is, of its being only a few seconds long.

The length of the specious present is variable, depending on our circumstances and our mental condition. During cataclysmic accidents, the specious present can shrink to a tiny fraction of a second. During periods of inactivity and rest, the specious present can expand to several seconds, when we observe some slow-moving object. We can imagine a sentient being whose specious present was thousands of years long. However, the length of the specious present seems to have no effect on our experience of the fleetingness of the present. No matter how long the specious present is, we still experience it as being on the verge of passing away. B Theorists must treat this residual sense of passage as mere illusion (see, for example, Paul 2010).

As a matter of good methodology, we should treat with suspicion any metaphysical theory that assigns common and normal perceptual beliefs to the category of the erroneous.

Other things being equal, such attributions of error should be minimized.

Experience Considered Holistically   Our experience of time includes our awareness of the inexorability of the succession of moments. We experience time as having an intrinsic, categorical, and irreversible order – an order that must be distinguished from a mere direction or asymmetry. For example, the order of the words in a textbook has an intrinsic direction, from beginning to end. Yet we can read the book from back to front, or in any other order, if we so choose. Time is not like that: our experience of time must, as a matter of metaphysical necessity, occur in the fixed order of earlier to later times. The A Theory can explain this fact, since our experience occurs always in the present, and the present is unalterably moving in the direction of the future. On the B Theory, in contrast, there is no reason why the order of experience shouldn't deviate from the order of time.

This argument is especially cogent in the case of our awareness of the succession of our own mental states. It makes no sense to suppose that we could experience our mental states in any order other than the temporal order in which they actually occur.

A Theorists claim that we experience a unique sort of succession in the succession of the moments of time. All other kinds of *order* on this view involve a kind of metaphorical or indirect reference to temporal succession. Without the real succession of times in the A series, we would have no concept of earlier or later than, of causally prior or posterior. As McTaggart argued, the very idea of an intelligible B order presupposes the reality of the A series.

8.4.4   The Metaphysical Impossibility of Time Travel

Time travel provides one more argument for the A Theory:

1. If the B Theory of time is true, then time travel (travel into the past) is metaphysically possible.
2. Travel into the past is metaphysically impossible.
   So, the B Theory is false.

Let's consider each of the premises in turn. Why does B Theory entail the metaphysical possibility of time travel? According to the B Theory, all times are equally real, with no metaphysically distinguished present moment and no absolute distinction between past, present, and future. To talk about time travel is to imagine a chain of events and processes that connect states at some later time with states at an earlier time in the way that earlier states of a human being are ordinarily connected with later states of that same human being. There are many ways of imagining this happening. For example, we can describe a universe in which time is circular – if one could live long enough, one could survive until one returns to one's own past. The great mathematician Kurt Gödel proved that the equations of Einstein's theory of general relativity permit the existence of such closed time curves.

In contrast, time travel is impossible for the A Theorist, especially if we consider the versions of A Theory that contrast the openness of the future with the fixity of the past (the *falling-branches* model). Since the past is now necessary, it is impossible to return to those past events in such a way that they are once again merely contingent. (This argument assumes the validity of axiom 4 of modal logic: that what is necessary is necessarily necessary.)

Why Is Time Travel Impossible? The Grandfather Paradox   Here is a well-known argument for the impossibility of time travel: the grandfather paradox.

1. If time travel were possible, it would be possible for someone (Mr. X Jr.) to travel back in time and kill his own paternal grandfather before Mr. X's father (Mr. X Sr.) was conceived.
2. It is impossible for Mr. X Jr. to exist if his paternal grandfather died before his father was conceived.
3. It is impossible for Mr. X Jr. to do anything, including travel back in time, if he doesn't exist.
4. Hence, it is impossible for Mr. X Jr. to travel back in time and kill his own paternal grandfather before Mr. X's father was conceived. (From 2, 3)
5. Hence, time travel is impossible. (From 1, 4)

The argument for step 4 is airtight, so the defender of time travel must object to premise 1. Why should the possibility of time travel entail the possibility of Mr. X's killing his own grandfather?

David K. Lewis (1976), in defense of time travel, has challenged premise 1 on the ground that all the grandfather paradox proves is that certain time-travel scenarios are impossible. It doesn't prove that all of them are impossible. It doesn't show, for example, that one couldn't go back in time and meet one's own grandfather as a child, so long as one does nothing to prevent one's own conception. Once we've excluded the logically impossible stories, like the grandfather paradox, there remain plenty of logically possible time travel stories, and each of them is sufficient to vindicate the possibility of time travel.

The problem with this response is that it ignores the issue of the powers that the time traveler brings with him. It seems reasonable to suppose that, if time travel is possible at all, it is possible for the time traveler to arrive in the past possessing all of his or her intrinsic powers and capacities. We can easily suppose that Mr. X possesses, as, sadly, do most of us, the natural capacity to kill another human being at will. When Mr. X arrives in the past, he will find plenty of implements with the natural capacity of ending his grandfather's life prematurely. If we suppose that such causal powers and capacities are intrinsic to the traveler and his immediate environment (which we should do if we are either Powerists or Nomists[3]), then we have to acknowledge the possibility of their exercise, and so the possibility of Mr. X's successful killing of his grandfather. Since we know this to be impossible, we can refute (by *reductio ad absurdum*) the hypothesis that time travel is possible.

This rejoinder to Lewis can be turned aside if we embrace Neo-Humeism about causal powers (a view we discussed in Chapter 3). According to Neo-Humeism, whether or not a certain thing has a causal power is not intrinsic to that thing but depends instead on the whole pattern of states and changes throughout the history of the world. On this view, it would not be problematic or surprising to suppose that Mr. X loses certain lethal capacities when traveling backward in time, since there is no consistent history in which he does succeed in ending his grandfather's life in childhood.

Alternatively, the Neo-Humeist could suppose that Mr. X retains all of his lethal powers when traveling back in time, given his intrinsic qualities and the cosmic patterns involving those qualities, but deny that it is possible for Mr. X to exercise those capacities on his grandfather in this case. For Neo-Humeists, it is the powers and their possible exercise that are grounded in the possibilities, and not the possibilities that are grounded in the powers.

In contrast, Powerists and Nomists have no such option, and they should concede that time travel is metaphysically impossible, providing an important piece of evidence in favor of the A Theory.

8.5   Conclusion

The indexical theory of tense and temporal adverbs has made the B Theory a serious contender, and the theory of relativity adds considerable additional support to it. It is possible to insist that there is a metaphysically real and absolute relation of simultaneity that is physically undetectable, but such an additional postulate comes at a high cost in terms of theoretical simplicity.

In response, A Theorists can maintain that the cost is well worth paying, given the fact that the static "block universe" of the B Theory cannot be made consistent with the obvious fact of real change. In addition, B Theorists must treat our sense of the fleetingness of time and the uniquely mandatory and categorical succession of moments as illusory. Finally, Powerists should find the argument for the impossibility of time travel compelling, providing further evidence for the A Theory.

The choice comes down to a judgment about the relative importance of deference to physics and respect for Ockham's Razor, on the one side, and conformity to the dictates of *a priori* reason and the richness of ordinary human experience, on the other. This choice is complicated by the issue of the relative importance of theoretical physics on the one hand and the special and experimental sciences on the other. Neo-Humeists will side with theoretical physics and lean toward the B Theory, while those who value the special sciences will embrace Powerism. The consequent impossibility of time travel for Powerists tilts the balance to the A Theory.

Notes

1   This at least is not affected by the theory of relativity, since time still flows at one second per second in each frame of reference, even if the physical processes in other frames are retarded.
2   McTaggart himself rejected both A and B Theories, preferring instead to conclude that time itself is unreal.
3   This is true by definition for Powerism. For Nomists, the power of a particular is intrinsic to that particular, taken together with the actual causal laws. The causal laws of a world cannot change from place to place or time to time, so the causal capacities of the time traveler cannot depend on what goes on in distant places and times.

9

Continuity and Persistence

We turn again in this chapter to the problem of time. In Chapter 8 we considered the question of whether time itself is in motion (the A vs. the B Theory). In this chapter, we look to the question of things that are located in and that persist through time. We will begin (in Section 9.1) by looking at the relation between causation and time. How can causal influences be transmitted through time? How can earlier states affect later events? In order to answer these questions, we will examine the nature and unity of *causal processes*.

Next, we will consider briefly a crucial question about the structure of time itself. In particular, we will ask, which are fundamental – instants of time or extended intervals? We will seek an answer to this question by considering the possibility or impossibility of certain infinitely complex tasks (or *super-tasks*), which we take up in Section 9.3.

We then turn in Section 9.4 to the question of the persistence of particular things – things that persist through time and change. It is natural to think that the vast majority of the objects of our everyday experience persist through time and change. Indeed, we ourselves seem to do so; you existed yesterday no less than you exist today, despite that you are no doubt different today than you were yesterday, both physically and mentally. Other important things also persist: our homes, the institutions in which we work and study, our family members, and our most prized possessions. But what metaphysical facts undergird these persistence facts?

There are two possible accounts. The first account, Perdurantism, holds that the fundamental entities are instantaneous. Its alternative, Endurantism, holds that some persisting things are fundamental. Perdurantism comes in

Metaphysics: The Fundamentals, First Edition. Robert C. Koons and Timothy H. Pickavance.
© 2015 Robert C. Koons and Timothy H. Pickavance.
Published 2015 by John Wiley & Sons, Ltd.

two forms: Extreme, which denies the existence of persisting things altogether, and Reductive, which takes the persistence of things to be grounded in the Neo-Humeist mosaic of instantaneous points, together with their intrinsic qualities and spatiotemporal relations. The second account, Endurantism, comes in three forms, depending on whether it assumes the truth of fundamental intervals and processes and whether it holds that the persistence facts are fixed by facts about the Neo-Humeist mosaic. We consider two objections to the claim that persistence facts are fixed by facts about that mosaic. The first objection concerns the possibility of the intrinsic motion of simple entities (9.5), and the second concerns failures of the transitivity of identity for composite entities (9.6). In Section 9.7, we evaluate Extreme or Eliminative Perdurantism. Why must we believe in persisting things at all?

In our final section, we describe two packages of metaphysical theses, one exemplified by Aristotle and the other by David K. Lewis, that have emerged in the course of our investigations through this chapter and its predecessors.

9.1   Discrete and Continuous Causation

Philosophers generally agree that, if there is such a thing as causation at all, causal influences are generally transmitted from earlier events to later ones. If we want to explain the fall of the Western Roman Empire in 476 AD, for example, we will tend to look at the processes and conditions of the empire and its surroundings in the years leading up to that fateful date.

However, there is a problem in accounting for this fact, since there seems to be good reason to deny that causation or action can occur across a temporal gap. If agent A acts on patient P, it seems that the time at which A exercises its active power must be exactly the same as the time at which P undergoes the appropriate transformation. This is especially clear if we embrace the A Theory, since on that account, if the change in P is occurring at the present, then it cannot be explained by the exercise of any power of A's in the past, since A must be alienated from its past properties in order to secure the uniqueness of the present. Agent A's having had some causal power in the past must be irrelevant: what's necessary is for A to have that power now. Consequently, it seems that all cause–effect transactions must be instantaneous.

The answer to this puzzle lies in the notion of a temporally extended *process*. Suppose, for example, that agent A exercises the power of moving P. What occurs at the moment t of action? The agent A exercises its power at t, and in that very moment the patient P begins a process of motion. However, the process necessarily extends into the future, unless and until it is interrupted by some further action. The earlier stages of this process transmit the causal influence of A on P into its later stages. This transmission is continuous and dense rather than discrete, since between any later stage of the process and any earlier stage there are an infinite number of instantaneous stages, each causally prior to the one and causally posterior to the other.

How are we to think about continuous causation? How can there be an infinite number of intermediaries between a cause and its effect? Wouldn't such an infinity of intermediaries involve the existence of infinite causal regresses? It seems, after all, that if E_1 causes E_2, and there is an intermediate cause E_3 such that E_1 causes E_3 and E_3 causes E_2, then the causal link between E_1 and E_2 should *depend upon* the two links between E_1 and E_3 and E_3 and E_2. If there were further intermediate links between E_1 and E_3, and between E_3 and E_2, then those two links would depend on those further intermediate links, and so on *ad infinitum*. We seem to have an infinite regress of causal dependency relations.

The error in this way of thinking about continuous causation is that it tries to understand continuous causation in terms of discrete causal links, as though continuous causation simply consists in an infinite chain of binary causal connections. We should instead take seriously the idea that continuous causation involves an undivided continuum of events. In the basic case, two events are connected by continuous causation when they are both parts of a single process. A real process is a temporally extended whole that is more metaphysically fundamental than any of its unextended, instantaneous parts. Later parts of the process are dependent on earlier parts because both are parts of the same process, not because there is some discrete connection or chain of discrete connections between the two.

Doesn't this solution still involve a problematic infinite regress of dependency? We can find an infinite series of events, each earlier than its predecessor in the series. Consequently, each event in the series would *depend* in some sense on its successor, *ad infinitum*. Isn't this an objectionable kind of infinite regress? How does the metaphysical primacy of the whole process help?

What's needed here is a distinction between a *grounded* and an *ungrounded* infinite regress. We think that it's reasonable to believe in an infinite regress, in which event 1 depends on event 2, event 2 on event 3, and so on, so long as all of these dependency relations are themselves grounded in a common source, one that is independent of all the members and that does not itself give rise to a further regress. The problem with the Bradley regress in Chapter 4 was that were was no way there of introducing such an ultimate ground of the instantiation relation without simply falling into another regress.

More specifically, when each new event emerges as the process unfolds, the new event E_1 is *immediately* dependent on the whole process up to that point and, therefore, on each prior event within the process. This dependency is modal or counterfactual: if the whole process had not unfolded as it did up to the occurrence of E_1, E_1 could not have occurred. Thus, if E_1, E_2, and E_3 all belong to the same process, with E_3 the earliest and E_1 the latest, then E_1 depends immediately on both E_2 and E_3, through its dependence on the whole process, even if it is also true (for similar reasons) that E_2 depends on E_3. E_1 is not dependent on E_3 *via* its dependency on the intermediate E_2. We can find a fundamental ground for each dependency relation in the process itself, and no Bradley-like regress threatens.

9.2   Instants versus Intervals: Which Are Fundamental?

Just as space contains both points and extended regions, so too does time have parts of two kinds: instants and intervals. An instant has no temporal duration, no before or after. An interval, in contrast, has a duration with a finite measure. Each interval can be further divided into shorter intervals.

The linguist Zeno Vendler (1957) introduced a crucial three-way distinction between verbal expressions that signify states and those that signify occurrences (activities, achievements, and accomplishments). Both Alexander Mourelatos (1978) and Anthony Kenny (1963) argued that this linguistic distinction corresponds to a real ontological one. To be in a *state* at an instant t is to exemplify a property that is intrinsic to that instant. In contrast, to be a participant in an *occurrence* is to exemplify a temporally extrinsic property. For example, to be triangular or to weigh exactly 20 kilograms are to be in certain states, since a thing can be triangular or weigh 20 kilograms at t without that fact entailing anything about its shape or weight at other instants. In contrast, to be walking or to be growing hotter are to participate in certain processes, since nothing can be walking for just an instant or growing hotter for just an instant. If I am walking at t, it follows logically and not just causally or physically that I must also be walking at other times sufficiently close to t.

We might suppose that each process has instantaneous parts that are states. For example, if I am walking between my house and the corner store from noon and 12:30 p.m., then at every instant in that interval, I will be in some state corresponding to a location between my house and the corner store. Let's call these states the "stages" of the process. In addition, such a process of walking will have temporally extended processes that take place during sub-intervals, such as walking between noon and 12:15 p.m. or between 12:15 p.m. and 12:30 p.m.

Given these distinctions, we can ask about the relative fundamentality of these temporal entities. Are instants more fundamental than intervals, or vice versa? Similarly, are instantaneous stages and other states more fundamental than temporally extended processes and occurrences, or vice versa? Or are both kinds of things equally fundamental in both cases? We will assume a *principle of correspondence* between times and temporal entities: instants are more fundamental than intervals if and only if instantaneous stages are more fundamental than processes, and processes are more fundamental than stages if and only if intervals are more fundamental than instants.

There is some reason to think that, in each case, one is more fundamental than the other, since we can easily identify intervals with heaps of instants, and we can also easily identify instants with fragments of intervals. Alfred North Whitehead and Bertrand Russell (Whitehead 1919; Russell 1956: 345–364; Jozsa 1986) showed us how to use the tools of modern mathematics to reduce intervals to instants or instants to intervals. That is, we can provide a complete description of the temporal features of the world using the resources of either an instants-only or an intervals-only theory, given the additional resources of modern set theory. The method they employed is known as "logical construction."

Reducing intervals to instants is pretty straightforward. Whenever we want to say something about an extended interval, we can just refer instead to a certain set of instants, a set that is closed under the temporal-betweenness relation – that is, a set that contains every instant that is between any two of its members.

Whitehead called the opposite transformation the method of "extensive abstraction." We can identify points with sets of finite intervals. There are a number of ways of doing this. Here is Russell's suggestion:

> Reduction of instants to intervals (Russell 1936): a set S of intervals is an *instant* if and only if (i) any two members of S overlap in time, and (ii) no interval that is not a member of S overlaps with every member of S.

Using this definition, we can define all of the usual properties of instants in terms of properties of intervals. For example, we can say that one *instant* is earlier than another just in case some member of the first set is wholly earlier than some member of the second set. We can define the temporal distance D between two instants t and t^* this way: D is the least distance such that the gap between a member of t and a member of t^* is always less than D.

Let's call the theory according to which instants are more fundamental than intervals "Instantism," and the theory according to which intervals are more fundamental "Intervalism." There is a third option, according to which each of these categories are equally fundamental. This third view was developed most fully by the Austrian philosopher Franz Brentano (1838–1917). On Brentano's view, intervals are not composed of instants, but only of smaller intervals (Brentano 1988). Instants are not parts of intervals, but neither are they sets of intervals (as in Whitehead and Russell's construction). Instead, instants are dependent *boundaries* of intervals. Each instant is, by its very nature, either an initial or a final boundary of some specific interval. Consequently, there are an infinite number of coincident instants – instants that are distinct and yet occur at exactly the same time. If we'd like, we could define "moments" on Brentano's view as equivalence classes of coincident instants.

Where can we look for evidence for or against these three views of the structure of time? We will have to look carefully at the logical consequences of the three theories. For simplicity's sake, we will examine the case for and against Instantism – we will lump together Intervalism and Brentano's theory. We will also assume that Instantism takes both instants and instantaneous stages of processes to be more metaphysically fundamental than either instants or instantaneous stages, in accord with our correspondence principle.

Both common sense and modern science assume that the series of instants is *dense*,[1] that is, that between any two instants there is always a third instant. This implies that any finite interval of time contains an infinite number of instants. Consequently, Instantism entails that the metaphysical foundation of any interval whatsoever is infinitary, composed of an infinite number of fundamental elements. The Anti-Instantist Theories have no such implication. It is compatible with Anti-Instantism to assume that the metaphysical foundations of any finite interval are finite in number.

One crucial argument against Instantism closely parallels a debate we've already encountered in Chapter 6, the debate over the possibility of gunk. In this context, it is the possibility of *gunky time* that is relevant. A gunky period of time is one all of whose parts are further divisible in time: a period that contains no durationless instants at all. If such gunky time were possible, this would count decisively in favor of Intervalism. However, our intuitions of possibility here are somewhat less convincing than in the case of material gunk.

This difference in assumptions about the fundamental structure of time entails other profound differences in judgments about what is metaphysically possible. This entailment depends on a principle of modal metaphysics introduced by David K. Lewis that has come to be labeled "the Patchwork Principle" (Lewis 1986: 87–92). Here is a simple statement of the principle:

Patchwork Principle: Different recombinations of fundamental elements are equally possible.

The Patchwork Principle implies that if we start with a non-empty set of possibilities, and we recombine elements from these possibilities into a structure or arrangement that is itself found realized among those possibilities, then the resulting recombination is itself a possibility. The *patchwork quilt* metaphor works in this way: the elements of the given possibilities are the patches, the realized structure is the frame, and the new quilt that we produce is the new possibility whose existence we can infer.

Since Instantism and its rivals differ about what is fundamental, they also differ about what is possible (given the Patchwork Principle). Since instants are finer-grained than intervals, Instantism is much more liberal about what is possible: there are more states that result from rearranging instants and instantaneous stages than there are that result from rearranging whole intervals and processes. Both Intervalism and Brentano's theory take temporally extended processes to be fundamental: consequently, if no actual finite process is actually divided into infinitely many sub-processes, defenders of the Anti-Instantist Theories are not compelled by the Patchwork Principle to accept that such an infinite division of a finite process is metaphysically possible, since there is no realized structure (no frame) with infinite internal complexity.

In particular, Instantism entails that an infinitely complex series of changes in a finite period of time should be really possible, so long as each change is individually possible, and so long as the entire series can be squeezed into that finite period. We will call such series "super-tasks." Instantism entails that all super-tasks are possible, while Intervalism and Brentano's theory have no such implication. Thus, if we find some super-tasks are impossible, this will provide decisive evidence against Instantism. In contrast, if we find that all super-tasks are possible, this will provide some positive support for Instantism.

9.2.1 Are Fundamental Processes Compatible with the A Theory?

Is it possible to combine the A Theory of the passage of time (discussed in Chapter 8) with Anti-Instantism? There is a *prima facie* difficulty in combining Intervalism or Brentano's theory, given their commitment to temporally extended processes as metaphysically fundamental, with Presentism, that version of the A Theory that insists that everything that exists at all exists only in the present moment. How can temporally extended processes exist only in the present moment, if the present moment is a durationless instant?

The first thing to note is that there are other versions of the A Theory than Presentism. The falling branches model, for example, in which what is possible or impossible changes as time passes, poses no problem for fundamental processes. The predicational version of the A Theory insists that only present-tense predications are simple or direct in nature. A predicational A Theorist who affirms the fundamentality of processes should focus on process-related predications that refer to the A series. For example, the property of *having been in motion for the past 10 minutes* is a present-tense property that would connect its bearer to a temporally extended process, in contrast to a tenseless, B-theoretic property like *being in motion between noon and 12:10 p.m.*

Even in the case of Presentism, the situation is a little more complicated than it might appear at first. Presentists could deny that processes are the sort of thing that exist at all. Instead, processes occur or take place over time. Processes could be thought of as properties or as states of affairs, rather than as a kind of material entity. Process-theoretic Presentists could suppose that the fundamental properties of currently existing things are temporally extended properties, like *being in a state of motion* or *being in the process of being heated.* They could affirm that all fundamental properties are present-tense properties but deny that all fundamental properties are intrinsic to the present moment, like location in space or qualitative state. On this view, being part of a temporally extended process could be a property of a thing that wholly exists in the present.

9.3   Possible and Impossible Super-Tasks

9.3.1   Zeno's Paradoxes of Motion

The first philosopher to discuss super-tasks was Zeno of Elea, a fifth-century-BC philosopher and follower of Parmenides. Zeno attempted to prove that, contrary to all appearances, motion is impossible. Two of his arguments (usually called "paradoxes" by those who believe in the reality of motion) involved the claim that any motion would require the completion of an infinitary super-task, a task that cannot be completed without completing an infinite number of sub-tasks. These paradoxes were the paradox of Achilles and the tortoise and the dichotomy paradox. We'll focus here on a variant of the second one, which is discussed in Book 6 of Aristotle's *Physics.* Let's suppose that Homer is seeking to walk across a stadium field. In order to cross the field, he must first reach the halfway point. In order to reach that halfway point, he must first reach a point midway between that point and his starting point (i.e., a point one-quarter of the way across). To reach that point, he must cross a point one-eighth of the way across, and so on *ad infinitum.* But no one can complete such an infinitely complex task in a finite period of time, so motion is impossible.

In this context, we will turn Zeno's argument upside-down, assuming that such motion is possible. If so, Zeno's argument demonstrates that some super-tasks can be completed. In response, Aristotle (who defends an Anti-Instantist theory that is a precursor of Brentano's) argues that this isn't really a super-task at all. Homer's walk across the stadium consisted of a single, undivided process (or, at most, a finite number of such undivided processes). The infinitely segmented series of processes described in Zeno's argument did not in fact exist, although it is true that the actual process of walking could have been stopped or interrupted at any of the intermediate points mentioned: halfway across, a quarter of the way across, and so on. The process was potentially divisible into any of these segments but not actually divided. There are an infinite number of possible processes, each with different end-points but there is no possible situation in which an infinite number of distinct processes actually occur.

In response to Aristotle, Adolf Grünbaum (1967) has offered the thought-experiment of the staccato walk. In this case, Homer pauses briefly at each of the intermediate points and only resumes his walking after having come to rest. This results in a jerky or "staccato" walk across the stadium. The pauses ensure that we have an infinite number of distinct processes of movement, each separated from its predecessor and successor by an interval of rest. The staccato walk can be described in such a way that the whole series can be fit into a finite period of time, by stipulating that each period of rest takes an exponentially shorter period of time as the intervals approach the starting point. For example, Homer could take $\frac{1}{2}^n$ hour to cover $\frac{1}{2}^n$ of the stadium and then rest for an equal period of time: half an hour to cover the last half of the stadium, a quarter of an hour to cover the preceding quarter of the stadium followed by a quarter of an hour of rest, one eighth of an hour to cover the preceding eighth of the stadium followed by an eighth of an hour of rest, and so on. The whole journey would take one and a half hours (one hour total of walking, half an hour total of rest).

The staccato walk eliminates Aristotle's covering explanation, since it is clear that Homer is not engaged in a single, seamless process. Instead, he really will have completed an infinite number of discrete walking tasks, each separated from the others by periods of rest. This really is a super-task. However, there is a crucial difference between the normal walk across the stadium and the staccato walk: we know that the first is possible, because it is the sort of thing that happens all the time. In contrast, we have the option of denying that the staccato walk is metaphysically possible, since there are no actual examples of such infinitely jerky motion.

Defenders of the staccato walk can appeal to the role of imagination as a means of verifying what is possible. We can imagine (at least, roughly) a situation of the kind Grünbaum describes, and no obvious contradiction or incoherency forces itself on our minds in doing so. This is at least good evidence for metaphysical possibility. However, it is not absolutely conclusive evidence: it's possible that we can imagine or think we are imagining things that are not really possible.

9.3.2 Thompson's Super-Lamp

Let's turn to a second example of a super-task: the lamp of James Thompson (1954). In this case, the pattern of changes is the mirror image of Zeno's dichotomy. We imagine a lamp with a single On–Off switch. The switch starts in the Off position. We switch it on. One-half second later, we switch it off, then a quarter of a second after that, on again. And so on, after an eighth of a second, one sixteenth of a second, etcetera. After a full second has passed, the switch has been switched an infinite number of times. The question is this: at the end of the full second, is the lamp on or off?

The description of the super-process doesn't yield any answer to this question, so it seems that we can assume either that the lamp will be on or that it will be off. There is, however, a reason to think that the scenario is impossible, a reason having to do with the nature of causation. If we assume two things about causation, we can derive a contradiction from Thompson's description of the lamp: the necessity of a cause of any new state, and the necessary propinquity of every part of a cause with its effect. Whether the lamp is on or off at the end of the full second, it has clearly entered into a new state at that point of time: a state that does not in any way predate the end of the second of motion. If all new states must be caused, we can infer that the new state of the lamp must have a cause.

Further, the cause of the lamp's final state must be some event or process involving the lamp and its switch. Given the principle of propinquity, every part of this cause must endure until the end of the second of motion or, more precisely, it must exist at every time prior to the end of that period. However, the description of the super-task ensures that there is no process or state that endures throughout that period: every process of switching is followed by a still later process, and every state of the lamp and its switch followed by some still later state before the end of the period of motion. Thus, there is nothing that could possibly cause the final state of the lamp.

The defenders of super-tasks must either deny one of these two assumptions about causation or else find some other feature in Thompson's scenario that is responsible for its impossibility. There is one other feature that might raise suspicions. In order to move the switch back and forth in shorter and shorter periods, the velocity of the switch must increase without limit. We know that in the actual world no physical system can move faster than the velocity of light, and we might suppose that in every possible world there is some maximum velocity. But in the case of this lamp, the intervals occurring toward the end of the second will have to involve velocities approaching infinity; at some point, the maximum velocity will have to be exceeded, which is impossible.

In response, we might try modifying the description of the lamp in order to eliminate the faster-than-light velocities. Suppose, for example, that the switch consisted of a single, point-sized particle, and the On position of the switch consisted of the particle's being located on a certain plane, and the Off position consisted of the particle's not being located on that plane. In this case, we could move the particle a shorter and shorter distance as we approach closer and closer to the end of the second. Now, however, the paradox disappears, because we can deduce where the particle will be at the end of the second (assuming that it cannot jump instantaneously through a finite distance): it must be located on the plane, and the lamp must be On. This follows so long as we assume that no discontinuous jump in location can occur at the very last moment. As we approach the end of the second, the particle's location converges on the plane. Thus, the defenders of super-tasks seem to have a plausible answer to this paradox.

9.3.3   Forrest's Super-Urn

Here is a third puzzle, which closes the gap in Thompson's lamp: Peter Forrest's Super-Urn (Forrest 1999). We start with an infinite number of particles in an urn, labeled from 1 to infinity. They are lined up within the urn in the order of their numbers. In addition, there is another particle, particle 0, initially outside the urn. The particles are like bosons or photons, in the sense that two of them can occupy exactly the same place at the same time. We now move particles in and out of the urn, in a way analogous to the switching of Thompson's lamp: one particle is moved in and one moved out in the first half second, then a second particle moved in and a second particle moved out in the next quarter second, and so on *ad infinitum*. At the end of the full second, particles have been moved in and out of the urn an infinite number of times. At the end of the full period, is there a particle outside the urn?

To create a paradox, we must add some further detail. There are two alternative procedures that can be followed. In procedure *A*, particle 0 is moved in and out again in each sub-period. In the first sub-period it is moved to a position that coincides with particle 1 and then moved out, in the second sub-period it is moved so as to coincide with particle 2 and then moved out, and so on. At the end of the full period, using procedure *A* results in particle 0 being outside the urn. In procedure *B*, particle 0 is moved in and made to coincide with particle 1, and then particle 0 is left inside the urn and particle 1 is moved outside. In the next sub-period, particle 1 is moved in and made to coincide with particle 2 and then particle 2 is moved outside, and so on. At the end of the full period, every particle is inside the urn: each particle n occupying the original position of particle n + 1. Thus, procedure *A* and *B* have different results.

However, the only difference between *A* and *B* concerns the identities of the particles that are moved. The two procedures are qualitatively identical.

It seems incredible that a mere difference in the identity (the labeling) of the individual particles could make a substantive causal difference: a difference in whether a particle is left outside the urn at the end of the full period. If so, then we have a good reason to believe that this super-task is impossible. (Importantly, it is possible to fill in the stories of the A and B procedures without using velocities that exceed the speed of light.)

9.3.4 Bernadete's Grim Reaper

Finally, we will consider a super-task that has a structure parallel to Zeno's stadium paradox: the Grim Reaper paradox of José Benardete (Benardete 1964: 259–260; Hawthorne 2000). Let's imagine that we have a victim, Fred, and an infinite number of death-dealing machines, the Grim Reapers, numbered from zero to infinity. Grim Reaper 0 is set to execute Fred at exactly one minute after noon, if no other Reaper has already done so; otherwise, Grim Reaper 0 does nothing. Grim Reaper 1 is set to do the same thing at half a minute after noon, on the condition that no earlier Reaper has executed Fred. Reaper 2 is set to do the same thing under similar conditions at a quarter of a minute after noon. In general, each Reaper number n is set to execute Fred at exactly $\frac{1}{2}^n$ minutes after noon, if no earlier Reaper has already done so. There is no *temporally* first Reaper, since for any Reaper, there will be a Reaper set to execute Fred at an *earlier* moment, but there is a last Reaper in time, namely Reaper 0. (Remember: the larger the Reaper's number, the earlier it is set to operate!)

It is clear that Fred cannot survive until 12:01, since for him to do so would be to contradict the stipulated nature of an infinite number of Grim Reapers. However, it is also easily proved that no particular Reaper can be the one to kill him. In order for Fred to be killed by Grim Reaper n, he must have already somehow survived Reapers $n+1$, $n+2$, $n+3$, and so on. For example, in order for Fred to be killed by Grim Reaper 5, he must have survived Reapers 6, 7, 8, and so on to infinity.

Once again, the proof of the impossibility of this super-task depends on the Patchwork Principle. We can see that each segment of the Grim Reaper story is possible, in isolation. There is no reason why a Reaper could not be designed to function according to the designated rule. If Instantism is true, then we should be able to arrange an infinite number of Reaper sub-processes within a single minute. This can be done without violating the prohibition on velocities greater than the speed of light simply by making the earlier Reapers smaller and smaller at an exponential rate, without limit (i.e., each Reaper needs to be eight times smaller than its successor). Since the result is in fact impossible, we can conclude that Instantism must be false.

Applying the Patchwork Principle to the Grim Reaper story requires that features of the story are metaphysically fundamental. The story does not say what each Reaper does, but only what each is disposed to do. That is, we have specified not the Reapers' actual behavior but their causal powers (both active and passive). Thus, the Grim Reaper argument against Instantism depends on the truth of Powerism. Neo-Humeists reject the fundamentality of powers and dispositions, and, consequently, they can argue that the Patchwork Principle does not apply. Thus, Powerists have good reason to reject Instantism, but this reason will not move Neo-Humeists.

9.4 Persistence: Fundamental or Non-Fundamental, Supervenient or Anti-Supervenient?

We will now turn to the metaphysical questions involving the persistence of material things through time. First, let's introduce a distinction between those facts that are *persistence-free* and those that are *persistence-entailing*. A persistence-free fact is a fact that entails no fact about whether anything ever persists for more than an instant. Some examples of persistence-free facts would be facts about what sorts of things exist at each moment of time, where these sorts refer only to the temporally intrinsic properties of those things, that is, only to properties about how those things are at that moment. These could include facts about the locations, sizes, shapes, quantities of rest mass or other physical attribute, and other qualitative features of things. Persistence-free facts can also describe the spatial and spatiotemporal relations among things of these kinds. For example, to assert that a certain region of space is continuously occupied for ten minutes by a mass of gold would be to assert a persistence-free fact, since we have not asserted that there is a single golden object that occupies that space throughout that period.

We can think of persistence-free facts as filling in the four-dimensional, spacetime framework with instantaneous qualities and quantities. The result is what we called (in Chapter 3) "the Neo-Humeist mosaic." Such a mosaic is consistent with any set of hypotheses about which objects occupying part of spacetime are to be identified with objects occupying other parts of spacetime. It is consistent even with denying that anything persists for longer than a single instant.

The first metaphysical issue to consider is this: are there any metaphysically fundamental facts about the persistence of material objects? Is the Neo-Humeist mosaic the totality of all fundamental facts, or does it omit some? We will call the view that there are metaphysically fundamental persistence-facts "Endurantism." Endurantists affirm that some things really persist or endure through time. The contrary position shall be labeled "Perdurantism."

> Endurantism: Some facts about the persistence of fundamental material particulars are themselves fundamental.
> Perdurantism: All fundamental facts are captured by the Neo-Humeist mosaic and concern the existence and spatiotemporal relations of instantaneous things.

In many cases in the philosophical literature, the distinction between Endurantism and Perdurantism is drawn in a different way. Endurantists are said to believe that persisting objects are "wholly present" in each moment in which they exist, while Perdurantists believe that persisting objects have many "temporal parts," having disjoint temporal parts corresponding to disjoint sub-intervals of their lifespans. It is difficult to define exactly what "wholly present" should mean in this context, and it isn't clear that Endurantists must deny the existence of temporal parts.

In any case, Perdurantists believe that persisting things persist by virtue of having different parts located at different times. The parts and their temporal locations are more fundamental than the persistence of the whole. Hence, persistence is not a fundamental fact for Perdurantists. In contrast, Endurantists believe that persisting material things persist simply by exemplifying properties or being included in states of affairs as a whole at different times. For Endurantists, persistence is not grounded in facts about other things.

There are two versions of Perdurantism: Extreme (Eliminative) and Reductive. Eliminative Perdurantists deny that anything truly persists. Everything, whether fundamental or not, exists only for an instant. Reductive Perdurantists, in contrast, believe that certain non-fundamental things do persist through time, but only by virtue of certain facts involving only instantaneous things.

The fundamentality of processes and extended occurrences (i.e., Anti-Instantism) entails Endurantism. The reason is simple: processes are temporally extended states of affairs or tropes, and the participants or bearers of such processes must be fundamentally persistent.[2] One form of Endurantism is the form that follows from these two views; we call this process-based or Anti-Instantist Endurantism, or p-Endurantism. But there is another form of Endurantism that accepts Instantism, namely Instantist Endurantism, or i-Endurantism. We will focus in this section on i-Endurantism and on Reductive Perdurantism.

Is Instantism consistent with any form of Endurantism? Given the correspondence principle, Instantism entails that only instantaneous states and stages of processes are fundamental, while Endurantism entails that some material objects persist for more than an instant. We will take Instantism to restrict the set of fundamental properties and states of affairs to instantaneous ones, but to leave open the possibility that some fundamental *material objects* persist through time by having properties and being a part of states of affairs at different moments of time. (Similarly, we will take Instantism to be consistent with the thesis that there are fundamental *regions of space* that endure through time.)

The next key issue to consider is whether the facts about persistence are fixed by the persistence-free facts. In other words, do the facts about persistence (both positive and negative) *supervene* on the persistence-free facts? Supervenience is a notion that was introduced into analytic philosophy by the British philosopher G. E. Moore, who argued that the moral facts supervene on the non-moral or "natural" facts. There are a variety of notions of supervenience. For our purposes here, we can make use of the simplest one, the relation of weak supervenience:[3]

> Definition of Weak Supervenience: A set of propositions A *weakly supervenes* on a set B (its *supervenience basis*) if and only if any two possible worlds that differ with respect to the truth-value of one or more members of A also differ with respect to one or more member of B.

To fix the truth-values of the supervenience basis is also to fix the truth-values of all of the supervening propositions. It is impossible for the truth-value of a supervening proposition to vary independently of any variation in the truth-values of the propositions of the basis. In the present case, we are interested in the question of whether the propositions about persistence supervene on the persistence-free propositions, the propositions describing the Neo-Humeist mosaic.

This question does not even arise for Extreme Perdurantists because they hold that all simple persistence propositions are false, whatever may be the case with the spacetime mosaic. Thus, the persistence facts trivially supervene on any facts whatsoever, on that view.

It is clear that Reductive Perdurantists will embrace the supervenience of persistence facts, since they believe that all persistence facts are derived facts. Derivation should entail supervenience.

In contrast, it is clear that all p-Endurantists will reject supervenience, since the persistence-free facts will not include any facts about temporally extended processes. The existence of a temporally extended process will typically entail (we may suppose) the persistence of its participants, since things that participate in processes do so over some finite interval of time and so must persist over that time. Since facts about processes are metaphysically fundamental for p-Endurantists, it would defeat the whole point of their theory to suppose that these facts supervene on the persistence-free facts.

What shall we say about the i-Endurantists, who affirm both Instantism and the existence of fundamental persistence facts? This combination is a somewhat odd one, since i-Endurantists must suppose that the only fundamental facts that are not instantaneous are those facts that concern the identities of persisting objects in successive situations. If one believes in fundamental persistence facts, why not suppose that extended processes are also fundamental? Nonetheless, the combination does not involve any logical inconsistency, and there are a number of philosophers who seem to embrace the two theses.

On the question of supervenience, i-Endurantists can go either way. Thus, we should recognize Supervenient i-Endurantists, who believe that the persistence facts, although metaphysically fundamental, supervene on the persistence-free facts. In addition, there are Anti-Supervenient i-Endurantists, who insist that the persistence facts do not supervene on the persistence-free facts. The Anti-Supervenient i-Endurantists believe that persistence facts are not fixed by fixing the persistence-free facts. We have thus five distinct positions on persistence:

1. Extreme Perdurantism
2. Reductive Perdurantism
3. Supervenient i-Endurantism (Endurantism plus Instantism)
4. Anti-Supervenient i-Endurantism (Endurantism plus Instantism)
5. P-Endurantism (Endurantism with fundamental processes)

There are several serious problems with Anti-Supervenient i-Endurantism (or AIE). This theory involves the postulation of a large number of brute or inexplicable persistence facts. These facts are not metaphysically grounded in the persistence-free facts (an implication of Endurantism), nor are there any other sort of metaphysically sufficient conditions for their obtaining (an implication of the failure of supervenience). The first problem with AIE is that it is hard to distinguish it clearly from p-Endurantism. What possible reason could one have for affirming the existence of fundamental and non-supervenient persistence facts and yet deny the fundamentality of temporally extended processes? At the minimum, wouldn't the persistence of a particular thing be a kind of fundamental process on this view?

In addition, the persistence facts would be causally inert if i-Endurantism were true, in either form (Supervenient or Anti-Supervenient). All the facts about causal powers seem to be persistence-free facts, since (as we argued in the case of Forrest's Super-Urn) facts about bare identity are causally irrelevant. Thus, pure differences in persistence facts would make no difference to the distribution of causal powers, and thus no difference to the observed sequence of events. If the persistence facts are fundamental and causally inert, how do we come to know them? There is a real threat here of persistence skepticism, a well-founded doubt about whether our ordinary beliefs about the persistence of things can count as knowledge.

It is also hard to see why one would prefer Supervenient i-Endurantism (SIE) to Reductive Perdurantism. If the persistence facts supervene on the persistence-free facts, why think that they are fundamental at all? Why not take only the persistence-free facts to be fundamental and treat the persistence facts as metaphysically derivable?

If we can rule out the two forms of i-Endurantism, this leaves us with three possible positions; Extreme Perdurantism, Reductive Perdurantism, and p-Endurantism. Reductive Perdurantism combines Persistence Supervenience with Instantism (as does SIE). In the next two sections, we will look at a series of objections to that combination of theses. If these objections are successful, we are left with just two options: Extreme Perdurantism and p-Endurantism (Anti-Instantism).

9.5   The Persistence of Simple Things: The Problem of Intrinsic Motion

We will begin by looking at an objection to Reductive Perdurantism that applies to simple persisting things. John Hawthorne, in an essay entitled "Motion and Plenitude" (Hawthorne 2006: 111–144), called this the "collapse problem," because Reductive Perdurantism forces us to collapse together possibilities that seem obviously distinct. Here is a simple example of the collapse problem. Let's suppose that we have two simple, point-sized particles, A and B, both of the same kind K. When two particles of type K meet, the laws of nature permit two possible results: they may simply pass right through each other without effect (case 1), or they may collide rigidly and bounce off one another, changing each particle's direction (case 2). Assuming that the particles are of the same mass and perfectly rigid and that Newton's laws of motion apply, the two results would look indistinguishable from each other. In the case 2 collision, the resulting trajectories of the two particles will be exactly the same as the unaltered trajectories of the two particles in case 1. The only difference will lie in the relative location of each particle. Suppose that A arrives at the collision point from the northeast, and B arrives from the northwest. In case 1, A continues to move toward the southwest and B continues to move toward the southeast. In case 2, it is A that moves (after the collision) toward the southeast, and B that moves toward the southwest. The post-collision positions of A and B are switched between the two cases, but otherwise everything is exactly the same.

We seem to have described two distinct and real possibilities, and yet the persistence-free facts are exactly the same in each case. If we ask where are there K particles at each moment in time, the two cases will give us the same two locations. This contradicts the supposed superveni-ence of the persistence facts on the persistence-free facts. Reductive Perdurantists must deny that there really are two distinct possibilities here. They must insist that there are just two different ways of describing one and the same situation, an unintuitive result. P-Endurantists avoid this result, since they can recognize a real difference between the two cases. In case 1, the two processes of motion continue without interrup-tion at the point of meeting. In case 2, the two processes of motion end at the collision, and two new processes are initiated, taking the particles along interchanged paths.

Another example of Hawthorne's collapse problem can be found in cases of thought-experiments involving motion in absolutely continuous and homogeneous substances. Examples of this sort have been offered by C. D. Broad (Broad 1925: 36), Saul Kripke (unpublished lectures in 1977 and 1978), and David M. Armstrong (Armstrong 1980). We could imagine, to use Broad's example, an infinitely long river of homogeneous stuff. Suppose that we've reduced friction to zero, and the river is not undulating or pulsat-ing in any way. We can't tell whether the river is moving at all, or how fast it is moving or in which direction, simply by looking at the changes in quali-ties at various spatial locations, since there are no qualitative changes of this kind. A similar thought-experiment (proposed by Saul Kripke and David Armstrong) involves a sphere of homogeneous stuff that is spinning. Again, its spinning in a certain direction doesn't correspond to any pattern of quali-tative or quantitative change. The sphere maintains its shape and position, and its interior remains homogeneous in quality, density, and chemical com-position. In both cases, the persistence-free facts are utterly unchanging, and yet it seems that there is a multitude of distinct possibilities with reference to motion and rest. The supervenience of persistence would force us to col-lapse all of these possibilities into one. In contrast, p-Endurantists can sup-pose that each bit of homogeneous matter participates in some fundamental process of motion, processes that can differ intrinsically from one possible case to another.

Theodore Sider (2001: 230–234) has argued that Reductive Perdurantists can distinguish multiple possibilities in such cases, so long as they can refer to other, more remote facts. Sider relies upon the Mill-Ramsey-Lewis account of the laws of nature that we discussed in Chapter 3. On this view, the laws of nature are the axioms of the *best* (simplest, most comprehensive and least violated) scientific theory of nature. The MRL account is a version of Neo-Humeism, and as a result the nomic facts supervene on the persistence-free facts about the Neo-Humeist mosaic. Sider points out that Reductive Perdurantists can appeal to the causal laws of nature (so understood) to dis-tinguish cases in which the uniform disk is spinning in one direction from cases in which it is spinning in the other direction, or not moving at all. For example, if the disk has been constructed from material bits that were not (before their composition) moving relative to each other, then the law of inertia will entail that they remain at rest once the disk has been formed. Alternatively, if the disk is struck a glancing blow by some moving body, the laws of motion will ensure that it begins rotating in the direction of the blow, at a rate commensurate with the disk's mass at the amount of energy expended.

Of course, as Dean Zimmerman (1999) has pointed out and as Sider has conceded (Sider 2001: 234), this response won't be available in the case of hypothetical "small worlds." If we imagine a world in which the disk has always existed in its present form and always will exist in that form, and in which there are no other moving bodies or forces at work, then the simplest set of laws will be one in which everything is necessarily always at rest. This will force the Siderian Perdurantist to deny the metaphysical possibility of motion in homogeneous substances in such small worlds.

9.6   The Persistence of Composite Things: Paradoxes of Intransitivity

In this section, we will consider objections based on the persistence of composite things. These objections depend on the fact of mereological inconstancy, that is, the fact that many composite things can persist despite losing or gaining parts. Some philosophers, like Roderick Chisholm (1989: 65–82), have denied the phenomenon of mereological inconstancy, insisting on identifying each composite thing with a fixed inventory of parts, parts that must remain unchanged for as long as it exists. However, many of the most plausible examples of fundamental composite things, including both organisms and artifacts, are obviously inconstant. Organisms, in particular, are constantly taking in new bits of matter and expelling old bits.

The relation of identity is transitive: if A is identical to B, and B is identical to C, then A is identical to C. This simple fact creates some real problems for the thesis of Persistence Supervenience, given some assumptions about spatiotemporal symmetry and the intrinsicality of persistence. If we assume, for example, that whether a persisting thing exists in one place or another at some future time cannot depend on reversible facts about direction or orientation in space nor about facts concerning conditions extrinsic to its history, then we can find possible examples of conflict between supervenience and the transitivity of identity.

9.6.1   Chisholm's Paradox: Extreme Longevity

The first set of examples involves long-lived entities. Roderick Chisholm (1967) constructed a paradox in which one man (Adam) is gradually transformed into the duplicate of another (Noah). In the spirit of Chisholm's paradox, let's imagine a case in which Methusaleh (named after the man who lived 996 years, according to the book of Genesis) lives for hundreds of years, gradually changing from one sort of person to a radically different sort of person, with entirely different features, memories, values, and character traits. Chisholm argues that the original person, alive during the initial 70 years (Methusaleh-0) cannot be said to have persisted until the very end as Methusaleh-1000. However, any successive pair of Methusalehs do provide examples of the sort of persistence-free conditions that are sufficient to ensure the persistence of a single person.

If the differences between M-0 and M-1000 as we have described them are not sufficient to ensure non-persistence, we could make them more radical still. Imagine that M-0 is changed, molecule by molecule, until at the end of the process we have a cockroach or even a virus (M-1000). It seems obvious that no human being could survive in the form of a virus.

To simplify our discussion, let's suppose that Methusaleh-0 would persist as Methusaleh-500, if his lifespan had ended there. Symmetrically, Methusaleh-500 would have persisted as Methusaleh-1000, if his lifespan had begun with M-500. However, it is impossible that Methusaleh-1 has persisted until Methusaleh-1000: these two persons cannot be identical. Then we have a conflict between intrinsicality and transitivity. Given transitivity and the non-identity of M-0 and M-1000, either M-0 is not identical to M-500, or M-500 is not identical to M-1000. However, in the absence of the extrinsic facts about the later history, M-0 would be identical to M-500, and in the absence of the extrinsic facts about the earlier history, M-500 would be identical to M-1000.

9.6.2   Symmetrical Fission and Fusion

Another pair of thought-experiments involves fission and fusion of organisms or other inconstant entities. The basis for these thought-experiments is the fact that many organisms and artifacts are capable of persisting while losing more than half of their material substance, or when more than doubling in size (through grafts and transplants). Suppose, for example, that a human being could survive (given imaginable medical breakthroughs) with just the left side of her brain and body, or with just the right side. If this were possible, then it should be possible to perform a successful fission: divide the person into two halves along the left–right midplane, and then reconstruct each half into a complete and fully operational human being. Let's call the original human being O, the human being resulting from the reconstruction of the left side L, and the one resulting from the right side R. We are supposing that if O were reduced to her left side by an accident, she could survive in a form that would be intrinsically indistinguishable in its history from L. By reason of symmetry, we can assume that the same thing is true with respect to R. Thus, the intrinsicality of persistence forces us to identify O with L and with R. However, L and R are obviously not identical, and so we have a violation of the transitivity of identity.

Similar considerations suggest that fusion is possible. Suppose that we start with two human identical twins (L^* and R^*), each of whom survives with less than half her body, one with a left side only and the other with a right side only. Each could survive the subsequent doubling of her body through the addition of appropriate transplants and grafts. Suppose that we simply graft the two halves together, resulting in a single human being, O^*. Intrinsicality forces us to say that L^* is identical to O^* and that R^* is also identical to O^*. However, we began with the assumption that L^* and R^* were distinct. Again, we have a contradiction with transitivity of identity.

9.6.3 A Supervenient Solution: Coincident Objects

There is one obvious solution that the defender of Persistence Supervenience can offer to both kinds of paradox: the possibility of coincident objects. Two objects are coincident at an instant when they have exactly the same material parts at that instant. Using the idea of coincident objects, we can say that there are actually two coincident organisms at the stage of Methuselah-500, 500A and 500B, with 500A identical to M-0 and not to M-1000, and 500B identical to M-1000 and not M-0. In the case of fission, we would say that there were actually two coincident human beings at every instant prior to the division. In the case of fusion, we can say that both twins persist after the fusion, having become coincident thereafter.

Coincident objects are not an entirely *ad hoc* solution to the puzzles of intransitivity. They have also been proposed to handle other difficulties for the Reductive Perdurantist. For example, consider a malleable clay statue of Goliath (the Philistine giant who was slain by King David in I Samuel). The statue consists of a certain lump of clay, which we can name (somewhat unimaginatively) "Lump." Suppose that the statue is squashed and rolled into a clay ball. The statue does not persist through the squashing, but the lump of clay does. Given Leibniz's law, which ensures that two identical things have all the same properties at all times, we can conclude that Goliath (the statue) is not identical to Lump (the lump), even before the squashing. But when they both exist, they have all the same material parts – they are each composed of exactly the same clay molecules. Hence, we seem to have two distinct but coincident objects before the squashing.

Nonetheless, many philosophers have resisted the very idea of coincident objects. In the case of Goliath and Lump, we could deny that there is anything that persists through the act of squashing, except for the constituent atoms. We could say (with Peter van Inwagen) that there never is such a thing as Lump, or we could suppose (with Michael Burke 1994) that Lump is brought into existence only when Goliath is destroyed. One might even say that Goliath survives the squashing, just not as a statue (that is, that Goliath and Lump are really identical, although it would be misleading to call Lump "Goliath" after the squashing).

Another puzzle that threatens to introduce coincident objects is that of Tib and Tibbles (Geach 1962: 215–216). The puzzle is based on an ancient one (Deon and Theon) constructed by the Stoic logician Chrysippus. In Geach's version, we have a cat named "Tibbles." Consider all of the cat except its tail, and call this thing "Tib." Clearly, Tib and Tibbles are different things, since one includes a tail and the other doesn't. Suppose that Tibbles loses its tale. At that point, the distinction between Tib and Tibbles vanishes, and the two seem to be identical. However, they can't be identical, since Tibbles has just lost a tail and Tib never had a tail to lose. Thus, we seem to have two coincident objects after the removal of Tibbles' tail.

Those who object to coincident objects have several possible solutions to the Tib/Tibbles puzzle. Van Inwagen's solution would be to deny that there was such a thing as Tib before the amputation. The only composite thing is a cat, with a tail before and without one after. Alternatively, they could suppose that no composite things are not mereologically constant – that Tibbles did not really *lose* its tail-parts at all, even if they've become detached.

There are three principal objections to coincident objects: (i) the objection to the multiplication of material objects, (ii) the grounding objection, and (iii) the threat of exotic objects.

9.6.4 The Multiplication Problem

Suppose there are two distinct but coincident people before fission (or after fusion). Each has two hands and a heart and each weighs 150 pounds. Ordinarily, that would mean that we would have four hands, two hearts, and at least 300 pounds of weight altogether, and yet these inferences clearly fail in this case.

The defenders of coincidence could respond that these cases are just extreme versions of Siamese twins. Just as two Siamese twins can share a certain amount of skin and flesh, and even an entire limb, so two coincident human beings can share all of their material parts and all of their mass.

But what about mental acts and passions? Suppose the coincident people experience a red sensation, form a mathematical thought, or freely choose between two options. Do we have two sensations, two thoughts, and two acts of choice, or just one of each? Sensations, thoughts, and choices do not seem to be the sort of thing that could be shared by distinct persons.

9.6.5   The Grounding Objection

The grounding objection focuses on this question: what grounds the distinctness of the coincident entities during their coincidence? The two people before fission share all of their present or occurrent parts and properties: they are made up of exactly the same things, in exactly the same arrangement, sharing the very same powers and location. And yet one of these persons can survive the loss of her right side but not her left, while the other can survive the loss of the left side and not the right. What grounds this difference?

In the case of the longevity paradoxes, Methusaleh-500A has existed for thousands of years and will be destroyed by the next transformation, while M-500B has just come into existence and will persist through the next 500 changes (until M-1000). What grounds this difference in age and in robustness? During the five-hundredth stage, the two persons share all the same intrinsic characteristics.

This is an especially acute problem for the Supervenient i-Endurantists, who hold that all non-instantaneous facts (except for the facts about persistence) are non-fundamental. They must believe in bare, metaphysically ungrounded distinctness in these cases.

Reductive Perdurantists, in contrast, do have a solution. They can identify the coincident entities with four-dimensional spacetime "worms." A *spacetime worm* is a whole composed of instantaneous objects that lie together along a smooth or continuous path through space and time. It is appropriate to call them "worms" because they look like extended strings or worms in a diagram in which the dimension of time is represented by a spatial dimension, as in the following:

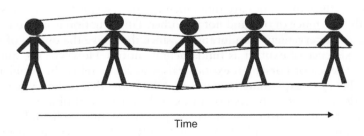

Time

Figure 9.1

Coincident objects correspond to two or more distinct spacetime worms that overlap, exactly coinciding in space for some limited interval of time. The distinctness of the two worms is grounded in their divergence in the future (or the past).

There is, however, a version of the grounding objection that applies to the spacetime worm proposal. Consider cases of *merely potential* fission. Suppose that some person *A* will not in fact ever undergo the process of fission, but suppose that it is metaphysically possible that *A* should do so: no impossibility would be involved in supposing *A* to be so divided. In order to explain the potentiality for fission, it seems that we must posit coincident objects even in cases of merely potential fission. There must be two coincident persons in this case as well: person *A-L* who could survive the loss of his right side, and *A-R* who could survive the loss of his left side. Since no fission will in fact occur, the spacetime worms corresponding to *A-L* and *A-R* are exactly the same. Once again, we have no grounds for their actual distinctness.

9.6.6   The Threat of Hirschian Exotic Objects

Once we have opened the door to coincident objects in recherché cases like fission or extreme longevity, there is a danger that we will have to acknowledge the coincident existence of a vast number, perhaps an infinity, of exotic objects in everyday situations. Consider, for example, Eli Hirsch's conception of an *incar* (Hirsch 1992, 1993). An incar is an automobile or largest part of an automobile that is located inside a garage or other structure. When an ordinary car is inside a garage, it is coincident with an incar. As the car is driven outside the garage, the incar gradually shrinks as more and more of the car passes the garage boundary and until finally it ceases to exist altogether once the car is entirely outside. Once the car is driven back into a garage, a new coincident incar is brought into existence. The basic recipe for such Hirschian exotic objects is clear: take any familiar object and impose upon it some strange set of persistence and non-persistence conditions.

Since, for the Reductive Perdurantist, neither the ordinary persistent objects nor the exotic ones are fundamental, there seems to be no reason to affirm the existence of one and not the other. This situation is not so clear in the case of Supervenient i-Endurantists, since they have the option of denying the existence of exotica as fundamental entities. However, the question of the existence of Hirschian exotica raises in sharp relief the problem for the SIE theory of explaining how it is that we know that ordinary persistent objects do and exotic objects do not exist. Neither set of objects make any difference to the distribution of causal powers or the predictable flow of events, considered qualitatively. See Michael Rea (2004) for more details on this epistemological problem.

Reductive Perdurantists might seek to appeal to common sense or a kind of epistemic or ideological conservatism as justifying belief in ordinary objects and disbelief in Hirschian exotica. However, such an appeal is a two-edged sword, since common sense is no fan of coincident objects of any kind, including the ones required by Reductive Perdurantists in response to the paradoxes of intransitivity.

Once we see that Reductive Perdurantists must accept the existence of an infinite variety of exotic persistent objects, this trivializes their commitment to persistence, since any logically possible set of persistence conditions is realized by some persistent entity. Each of us is really an infinite number of distinct, persistent entities, each with a different set of persistence conditions. None of them is the *real me* – they are all equally self-conscious thinkers, and so there is no reason to take the ordinary human being to be the unique reference of the first personal pronoun "I." This is the problem of the many with a vengeance. (For an example of such a view, see Bennett 2004.)

9.6.7 Process-Based Endurantism

How does a process-based, Anti-Instantist Endurantism handle the various puzzles of intransitivity? We will assume that p-Endurantists also embrace the thesis of Compositional Pluralism (from Chapter 6). That is, they should reject both mereological Nihilism (Atomism) and Universalism, as well as Cosmic Monism. In some but not all cases, material things compose something. Where composite things exist, there will be emergent qualities and causal powers.

When p-Endurantism is combined with such Compositional Pluralism, we should expect to find some causal explanation for the initial emergence and for the persistence of fundamental composite things. In particular, wherever there is a fundamental composite object, there will be at least one underlying process that is responsible for its persistence. In some cases, the participants of this process will include only the parts of the emergent whole, and in other cases the emergent whole will itself be a participant in the process responsible for its own persistence. For example, living organisms enter into certain fundamental processes (such as sensory perception or self-guided behavior) with their own organs and sub-systems, processes which together constitute their lives and which sustain the organism in existence over time.

First, let's return to the Chisholmian paradoxes of longevity. The processes that sustain real or emergent composition are typically homeostatic in character: that is, they tend to repair and restore the organism to something like its earlier state. If the changes are slow and gentle enough, these homeostatic tendencies will ensure that the organism never reaches a state incompatible with persistence. M-1000 will still resemble M-0 in its essential features. If, in contrast, the changes are rapid and intrusive enough to overwhelm these homeostatic tendencies, they will instantaneously interrupt the biological processes underlying persistence, providing grounds for a sharp dividing line between successive entities.

Second, the cases of fission and fusion. Suppose that a person is divided along the left–right midplane. Intervalists, who deny that there are any fundamental instantaneous states, will simply look for continuous processes that bridge the moment of division. If there are such processes, they must go either to the left or to the right. If no process bridges the moment of division, then the division must have killed the original person. For defenders of Brentano's theory, in which both processes and instants are fundamental, there are three possibilities concerning the instantaneous state at the moment of division. Either (i) it is internal to a process continuing to the left, (ii) it is internal to a process continuing to the right, or (iii) it is a terminal state of the underlying life process. Only the third case is truly symmetrical, and in that case the original organism dies, and so persistence occurs. An exactly similar explanation (*mutatis mutandis*) applies to the case of fusion.

However, it is not at all clear that these process-based solutions can be extended beyond the case of living organisms. Artifacts, for instance, are also subject to the paradoxes of intransitivity. Imagine a bottle opener that is gradually changed into a wrench, or a fork that is changed into a spoon. There are no homeostatic processes at work in such tools to resist the gradual transformation. Imagine a key that is divided laterally into two slimmer versions of the same key-shape. It seems that a key can survive being shaved into a much thinner version of itself, and it is implausible to suppose that there is some set of intrinsic processes whose continuity or discontinuity can decide whether a given key has survived fission, and if so whether as the left or right fragment. Coincidence also seems implausible in such cases, so it may be that a thoroughgoing Anti-Realism about artifacts is justified. And, the situation with respect to natural formations like rivers and mountains is even less promising for the Realist.

9.7 Extreme Perdurantism: Who Needs Persistence?

The last two sections provide good grounds for rejecting the combination of Instantism with Persistence Supervenience. These arguments count against Reductive Perdurantism, but they leave Extreme or Eliminative Perdurantism as an option for Instantists.

Extreme Perdurantists treat the persistence of material things as a useful fiction, or as only "quasi-true" (to use Sider's terminology; Sider 1999: 9–10). A quasi-true statement is one that is false but successfully describes how the world would be if certain false metaphysical presuppositions were true. For example, suppose that one says:

(1) That is the same book you gave me yesterday.

According to Extreme Perdurantists, a statement like (1) is false, since nothing really persists. However, we can use (1) to convey information about the four-dimensional mosaic – in particular, it can tell the audience that there is a continuous, book-shaped spacetime worm that joins the book-stage existing now with a similar book-stage that was part of a giving event yesterday. If Endurantism were true, statement (1) would be true, given that array of instantaneous facts.

Alternatively, the Extreme Perdurantists can provide a semantic account of ordinary discourse that counts a great deal of it as true, using the method of *temporal counterparts*. (The reader may find it helpful to revisit the discussion of modal counterparts in Chapter 7; the ideas are closely connected.) Although, strictly speaking, no material objects endure, we could paraphrase (1) by means of (2):

(2) This book-stage stands in the same-book relation to the book-stage you gave me yesterday.

Of course, we would also have to paraphrase away the reference to persisting people, which results in the somewhat complicated (3):

(3) This book-stage stands in the same-book relation to the book-stage that a person-stage that stands in the same-person relation to you gave to a person-stage that stands in the same-person stage to me. (Where "you" and "me" designate the instantaneous person-stages of the speaker and the addressee.)

The same-book and same-person relations are not forms of identity. They stand between distinct instantaneous objects that are connected in appropriate ways by spacetime worms. Since they are not forms of identity, they need not be transitive. So, Methusaleh-0 can stand in the same-person relation to M-500, and M-500 can stand in that relation to M-1000, even though M-0 does not stand in the relation to M-1000. Similarly, in the case of fission, both Lefty and Righty can stand in the same-person relation to the stages of the original person without standing in the same-person relation to each other.

How do Extreme Perdurantists deal with Hawthorne's collapse problem? They must say that all motion is merely apparent, since to move a material thing must persist through time. For Extreme Perdurantists, the perception of motion is a kind of pervasive illusion, of the sort we experience while watching a cinematic movie. (This is not to deny that they can give an account according to which sentences ascribing "motion" to things are literally true (thanks to temporal counterparts): it is simply to point out that there are no real entities at different locations at different times, according to Extreme Perdurantism. The world as it appears in perception does not correspond to the metaphysical facts, on this view.) This provides a strong piece of evidence in favor of Endurantism.

In addition, Extreme Perdurantists must treat all diachronic experience of the passage of time as an illusion, since there is no single entity (the experiencing person) that is really the subject of two or more successive moments.

Finally, Extreme Perdurantism conflicts with many of our ethical and legal practices. We commonly take personal persistence to be a real phenomenon with profound ethical and legal consequences. Such concepts as legal liability for past actions, guilt, gratitude, loyalty (to friends, family, community), and the ownership of property all presuppose that persons really persist. John Rawls, in his influential *A Theory of Justice* (1999), argues for the existence of a deep connection between persistent personal identity and justice. Rawls criticized utilitarianism for failing to take seriously the real distinctness of people. Harm to one person cannot be compensated for by benefits to another: instead, political theory must start with a conception of fairness to each.

Derek Parfit's work confirms the reality of this tension between Extreme Perdurantism and the ethics of common sense. Parfit argues (1984), on Perdurantist grounds, that real personal identity is an illusion. Consequently, all that we should care about is that we are survived by some suitably related person-stage. Given our common humanity and sentience, this thesis undermines the rationality of the privileging of self-interest or the interests of our family, friends, or local communities. It also undermines all duties other than that of benevolence. If we resist Parfit's ethical conclusions, we must also reject the metaphysical theory upon which it rests.

You may notice the similarity between this objection and Kripke's Humphrey Objection to modal counterpart theory at the end of Chapter 7. The Counterpart Theorist can insist that it is true that one human-being stage at one time is *the same person as* a human-being stage at another time, even if there is no real entity existing at both times. So, the crucial question becomes: do our ethical and legal practices simply presuppose the truth of certain sentences in English and other natural languages, or do they presuppose the metaphysical theory that seems (*prima facie*) to be expressed by those sentences, namely, the real persistence of human beings?

Should ethical knowledge (or what we take to be ethical knowledge) be treated as data for metaphysical theorizing? Why not? Many ethical truths are as certain as any observable truths. Is it really doubtful that we owe special duties to those who have graciously benefited us in the past, or that we should respect the property rights of others? Surely these are less controversial than most metaphysical questions.

9.8   Conclusion: Two Metaphysical Packages

At this point, we would like to look back, not just over the contents of this chapter, but also over the contents of this book as a whole. As we have surveyed the various central issues in metaphysics, we have typically found two major contenders for the truth of the matter. We find, even more strikingly, that these plausible answers group themselves naturally into two packages, one following the model of Aristotle's philosophy and the other mirroring the work of David K. Lewis. This isn't, however, a matter simply of the ancients versus the moderns: Aristotle has many contemporary defenders, and Lewis's work has ancient and early modern precedents, including especially the ancient materialists like Empedocles and Lucretius and David Hume.

Here is a table that summarizes the two packages, in the order of the issues as we have taken them up:

	Aristotelian	*Ludovician*
Truthmakers	Atomic Truthmakers	Truth Supervenes on Being
Dispositions	Powerism	Neo-Humeism
Properties	Realism	Resemblance Nominalism
Particulars	Constituent Ontology	Extreme Nominalism
Composition	Emergent Pluralism	Universalism
Modality	Abstractionism	Concretism
Passage of time	A Theory	B Theory
Time's structure	Brentano's theory	Instantism
Persistence	Process-based Endurantism	Extreme Perdurantism

A number of logical connections help to bind the two packages together. Powerism and some form of Realism are a natural combination, since Powerists believe that it is of the very essence of properties that they confer certain powers on their bearers, requiring some commitment to the reality of properties. The Ludovician package, in contrast, is founded on the Neo-Humeist mosaic of intrinsically inert qualities spread out in four dimensions. Commitment to this mosaic, in turn, requires the B Theory of time and a Concretist conception of possibility, since the only fundamental relations are the spatial and B-theoretic temporal ones. Possible worlds must be self-contained four-dimensional mosaics, just like the actual world, and both temporal and modal modifiers are treated uniformly as indexicals.

In a similar way, the commitment to the priority of powers on the part of Aristotelians leads naturally to the A Theory and a process-based conception of the structure of time and the persistence of material objects. On the matter of composition, the question of which objects are the bearers of fundamental properties and powers rules out any sort of "ontological free lunch" with respect to composite entities. Aristotelians take seriously the reality of human consciousness and agency, as well as our material composition as living organisms, and so a form of emergent pluralism naturally follows.

Both sets of theorists take seriously respect for Ockham's Razor, since each aims at an economical explanation of the facts. There is some significant difference as to what should count as the data for metaphysical theorizing. Ludovicians have a strong bias toward privileging fundamental theoretical physics, while Aristotelians draw equally from the special and experimental sciences and from that knowledge rooted in ordinary, everyday action and experience.

There are at least two alternatives to these standard packages. First, there is the group of Australian philosophers, led by David M. Armstrong, whose views we could label "Fortibracchian" ("fortibracchus" is Latin for "Armstrong"). Like Aristotelians, the Fortibracchians embrace Realism about properties and a strong version of Truthmaker Theory (either Maximal or Atomic). However, they reject Powerism in favor of Nomism, which is itself a kind of hybrid of Powerism and Neo-Humeism. Timothy O'Connor and H. Y. Wong (O'Connor and Wong 2005) labeled it "second-order Humeanism." On composition, the Fortibracchians are *de facto* Nihilists or Atomists, although they are often officially mereologically Universalists, treating composite objects as ontological free lunches. Like Neo-Humeists, they are B Theorists as a rule (with significant exceptions, such as Michael Tooley), although they also tend to side with the Aristotelians in favor of Endurantism. On modality, they prefer a mathematical or combinatorial version of Abstractionism.

The final alternative is that of the Anti-Truthmaker camp, including W. V. O. Quine, Alvin Plantinga, Peter van Inwagen, and Trenton Merricks. They are often skeptical about the very notion of fundamentality, so we might justly call them "the Flatlanders." Flatlanders are implicitly what we have called "Ostrich" Nominalists and "Extreme" Nominalists, rejecting both tropes and universals except, perhaps, in the form of human or divine concepts. They would certainly deny that universals *ground* similarity, which places them in the "Nominalist" category, as we have defined it.[4] They eschew the search for explanatory metaphysical theories and place little or no reliance on Ockham's Razor. Many, following Plantinga, are unapologetic Hypotheticalists about dispositions. They typically side with common sense on composition and time (although Quine was an important exception), endorsing the A Theory, Endurantism, and Compositional Pluralism without the need for any emergence. They are Abstractionists about modality, differing from the Aristotelians only their failing to see any need to anchor mere possibilities in actual powers or dispositions.

While these packages are not the only logically consistent ones, and while one rarely finds philosophers who embrace every item in one of the packages, they are marked by a mutual affinity among the views that compose them. This is especially true of the Aristotelian and Ludovician packages, and makes them all the more formidable. At any rate, noting these packages can help those who are new to metaphysics sense systemic connections among seemingly disparate discussions.

Notes

1 At least, modern science did so until recently. Some work in quantum theory suggests that time may be discrete (not dense).
2 There is a complication here. It is possible for a Perdurantist to embrace Intervalism and the fundamentality of processes, so long as they hold that the only persisting things that participate in such processes are points or regions of space (and not persisting material objects). For simplicity's sake, we shall ignore this possibility.
3 See also Section 2.2.2, on Atomic Truthmaker Theory.
4 Some of these theorists would resist the categorization.

10

Concluding Unmetaphysical Postscript

We have now completed a survey of contemporary work in metaphysics. In this final chapter, we want to reflect upon the meaning and significance of the subject. Is there any reason to think that we are closer to *the truth* about these questions than we were at the beginning? Is there any reason to believe that there is such a thing as *the truth*, or any kind of truth at all, concerning metaphysical issues?

We'll turn first, in Section 10.1, to the question of defining what "truth" in metaphysics might mean. One who believes in truth in a given field is usually described (within philosophy at least) as a "realist" about that field. Thus, "realist" has for us now a specialized meaning. It doesn't mean, as it might in everyday life, one who takes a brutally "realistic," almost cynical view, of the facts (like a disillusioned detective in a *film noir*). Instead, a philosophical realist about a subject X is one who believes that there are real X-facts to be explored. A theological realist, for example, thinks that there is a fact about whether or not God exists, a fact that is in principle independent of our beliefs and practices. Similarly, a metaphysical realist believes that there are genuine metaphysical facts. (A "realist" in Chapter 4 was defined as one who believes in character-grounding universals. This is just one kind of realist, as we are using the term in this chapter.)

Next, we move on (in 10.2) to certain questions about metaphysical language. Does metaphysics involve a kind of abuse of language? Does it commit what are called "category mistakes," misplacing questions that are appropriate in one context into a different context? Are metaphysical questions simply nonsensical? In addition, we will consider questions of ambiguity and disagreement. Are defenders of different metaphysical systems really disagreeing with each other,

Metaphysics: The Fundamentals, First Edition. Robert C. Koons and Timothy H. Pickavance.
© 2015 Robert C. Koons and Timothy H. Pickavance.
Published 2015 by John Wiley & Sons, Ltd.

or are all metaphysical disputes merely verbal? Are metaphysicians just talking past each other, thinking that they are disagreeing about substantive issues when they are in fact just following different linguistic conventions?

In Section 10.3, we will take up questions of metaphysical knowledge. Even granting that there are genuine metaphysical disputes and that one side or the other is objectively right, are we ever in a position to know who is right? Should we be global skeptics about metaphysics, denying the very possibility of metaphysical knowledge? If metaphysical knowledge is possible, how is it possible? Why do we find so much less agreement and convergence of opinions in metaphysics as compared with science or history?

In Section 10.4, we will consider a further anti-realist possibility: that all metaphysical theories and models are really mere fictions. Such a fictionalist theory is compatible with both metaphysical truth and metaphysical knowledge. For instance, it is true (in a sense) that Sherlock Holmes lived on Baker Street, and it is relatively easy to know this: one must simply become familiar with Arthur Conan Doyle's celebrated stories. Are metaphysical truths similarly fictional? Did Plato, for example, make it true that there are universals: true in the sense that in Plato's metaphysical fiction, universals exist (just as Holmes exists in Conan Doyle's stories)? If metaphysics were fictional, what would its point be?

Finally, in Section 10.5, we will ask whether metaphysics is avoidable. Is it really possible to avoid engagement with metaphysical questions? If not, how should we cope with them when they arise?

10.1   Metaphysical Truth: Anti-Realism

David Chalmers (Chalmers 2009: 80–85) has argued that we must make a distinction between ordinary and metaphysical assertions. For example, consider proposition (1):

(1) There are infinitely many prime numbers.

If made within the context of the practice of mathematics, (1) is an ordinary assertion, and it poses no metaphysical questions. All metaphysicians should accept it as *correct*, even those who believe that there are no numbers at all. However, there is another way of asserting (1), a way that involves making a *metaphysical assertion*. Metaphysical Realists insist that when statements are asserted metaphysically, they are sometimes true, even when they would be false if asserted in an ordinary way. A Metaphysical Realist who believed that there really are no numbers would assert (2) metaphysically, even while asserting (1) in the ordinary way:

(2) Numbers do not (really) exist.

The apparent conflict between (1) and (2) disappears once we distinguish the two modes of assertion.

Metaphysical Realism: Some metaphysical assertions are true.

A Metaphysical *Anti-Realist*, in contrast, could be defined as someone who thinks that all metaphysical assertions are simply false. For the Metaphysical Anti-Realist, the metaphysical mode of assertion is one that simply leads one away from the realities grasped in the ordinary way.

Metaphysical Anti-Realism: No metaphysical assertions are true.

How could such Metaphysical Anti-Realism be right? Consider, for example, proposition (3):

(3) There (really) are numbers.

It would seem that it is impossible for both (2) and (3) to be false. The logical principle of the Law of Excluded Middle dictates that, for every proposition p, it is a logical truth that (p or not-p). From this, it seems plausible to infer that either p or not-p must be true. Since (2) is simply the negation of (3), one or the other must be true.

In response, the Metaphysical Anti-Realist must suppose that metaphysical assertions fail to express genuine propositions. Consider a nonsensical statement, like the following one from Lewis Carroll's "Jabberwocky":

(4) It was brillig.

There is in fact no word in English (or any other language, as far as we know) as "brillig." Hence, an assertion of (4) fails to say anything. It certainly cannot be true. At the same time, the denial of (4) is equally meaningless:

(5) It was not brillig.

Since neither (4) nor (5) express genuine propositions, neither assertion can be true, despite the fact that one appears to be the negation of the other. The Metaphysical Anti-Realist could claim that all metaphysical assertions are like (4) and (5), including (2) and (3). Of course, Anti-Realists owe us some explanation for thinking so. Unlike (4) and (5), metaphysical assertions like (2) and (3) contain nothing but ordinary, meaningful English words. When meaningful words are put together in a meaningful order, how can the result be nonsensical? We will take up the most plausible answer (the theory of *category mistakes*) in the next section.

Chalmers makes a further distinction: between "Lightweight" and "Heavyweight" Metaphysical Realism (Chalmers 2009: 94–99). The Lightweight Metaphysical Realist thinks that there are metaphysical truths, but they are all trivial or *analytic*. An *analytic* truth is one that can be known by anyone who understands the meanings of the terms involved. A Heavyweight Metaphysical Realist, in contrast, thinks that there are substantive metaphysical truths.

> Lightweight Metaphysical Realism: All metaphysical truths are trivial or analytic.
> Heavyweight Metaphysical Realism: Some metaphysical truths are substantive (neither trivial nor analytic).

To return to Chalmers's example of the numbers, Lightweight Metaphysical Realists would probably claim that it is trivially true that there are really numbers, even when this is intended as a metaphysical assertion, and not as an ordinary mathematical one. If we understand what we mean by "numbers" and "exists," we shall see that it simply must be the case that numbers do exist. A Heavyweight Metaphysical Realist, in contrast, thinks that whether or not there are numbers is a hard metaphysical question, one to be settled by formulating and comparing competing metaphysical theories.

Let's return to the question of metaphysical versus ordinary assertions. As we saw in Chapter 6 (on material composition), some metaphysicians disagree about whether artifacts really exist. If we were to ask those who deny the existence of artifacts whether they thought that there are things like forks and chairs, they would presumably want to distinguish a "loose and popular" way of speaking from the kind of strict and philosophical mode of speaking that is appropriate to metaphysical disputes. Hence, we would need something like Chalmers's distinction between two modes of assertion.

However, some metaphysicians might insist that metaphysical disputes do not require any such distinction. For example, two metaphysicians might agree that artifacts exist but disagree about whether they are among the world's fundamental entities. Talk about "fundamental" entities makes the dispute metaphysical, without the need to distinguish two modes of assertion. As we have seen, the distinction between fundamental and derived entities can be made in one of two ways: we could draw the distinction in terms of Truthmaker Theory (Chapter 2), or we could suppose that there is some intuitively primitive relation of grounding that holds between some things and other things. When one thing is grounded in another thing or things, the former exists by virtue of the existence of the latter.

Metaphysical Anti-Realists must claim that there is no such relation of fundamentality. They must deny that some things ever exist by virtue of the existence of other things, a denial that seems implausible. In addition, if there is such a thing as a metaphysical mode of assertion, they must insist that everything that is claimed in that mode is false. It is hard to see how such denials could be supported without relying on some sort of metaphysical foundation, like nihilism.

A more promising route for those with doubts about the metaphysical enterprise is to embrace Chalmers's Lightweight Metaphysical Realism. We can say true things in metaphysics, but they are all trivial and hence unimportant. There is no room for argumentation or evidence in metaphysics. All one has to do is to pay close attention to the logical forms of the propositions and the definitions of the terms they contain.

The great problem for the Lightweight Realists is to explain the fact of over 2000 years of apparent metaphysical disagreement and argumentation. Lightweight Realists must suppose that all of this is a product of some kind of confusion or self-deception. Perhaps the explanation lies in the realm of language. Perhaps there is something about natural languages (like Greek, Sanskrit, Latin, German, and English) that leads their users astray, confusing trivial truths with substantive claims. We will turn to this possibility in the next section.

10.2   Metaphysical Language: Nonsense and Verbal Disagreement

There are two ways in which language might be responsible for the illusion that Heavyweight Metaphysical Realism is possible. First, it might be that everything we say in metaphysics is mere nonsense, but nonsense artfully disguised as meaningful statements. Second, it may be that everything we say in metaphysics is trivially true or false, so there is never any real disagreement, but confusion over the meaning of our words makes us think that we are disagreeing.

10.2.1   Is Metaphysics Nonsense?

William Alston (1958) argued that all metaphysical claims are guilty of *category mistakes*. It is obvious that there are possibilities, but metaphysicians insist on asking questions about possibilities that make no sense. For example, are possibilities simple or complex? Do we interact with possibilities? Are possibilities located in space or time? It is similarly nonsensical to ask such questions about facts, properties, propositions, and so on.

Presumably, Alston would have classified many of the issues we've discussed as category mistakes. Perhaps asking whether or not space consists of an infinite number of actual parts is to ask a question with no real meaning. We can ask how many actual parts there are in a physical object;

for example, we can ask how many moving parts there are in a washing machine. However, an Anti-Realist could argue, there is no sense in arguing about how many *parts* there are in a cubic meter of empty space.

The notion of "category mistake" that Alston made use of in 1958 was introduced by Oxford philosopher Gilbert Ryle in his influential *The Concept of Mind* (1949). Ryle gives several examples of category mistakes, such as thinking of the "Average Taxpayer as if he were a fellow-citizen - an elusive insubstantial man, a ghost who is everywhere yet nowhere" (18). Ryle argued that there is a similar mistake involved in supposing that "mental processes are causes and effects but different sorts of causes and effects from bodily movements" (19). He also contended that many debates about whether mental events or processes are observable also involve the ignoring of the difference between two grammatical categories:

> The reason I cannot catch myself seeing or deducing is that these verbs are of the wrong type to complete the phrase "catch myself." (1949: 152)

Ryleans could argue that many of the theses and anti-theses debated in this book are based on such category mistakes. Consider the following pairs of statements:

(6) My rocking chair is composed entirely of wood.
(6′) Space is composed entirely of points.
(7) The edges of the building coincide spatially with the edges of the company's property.
(7′) There are two internal edges of material bodies that coincide spatially.
(8) There are infinitely many prime numbers.
(8′) There are infinitely many actual things (other than sets, numbers).
(9) My life had a beginning.
(9′) Time had a beginning.

Anti-Realists argue that (6)–(9) are meaningful, but (6′)–(9′) are meaningless, applying to one kind of thing concepts that make sense only when applied to another kind of thing.

The problem with these charges of "nonsense" and "category mistakes" is that they must deny the universality of certain principles of classical logic. If "F" and "G" both name meaningful predicates, then we know that it must be true either that something is both F and G, or nothing is both F and G. So, for example, if "is a possibility" and "has proper parts" are both meaningful predicates, we can ask whether any possibility has proper parts or not. One answer or the other must be right. In order to deny this, the believer in category mistakes must deny the linguistic principle known as Compositionality, the principle that the meaning of a whole sentence is a function of the meanings of the parts.

Are there convincing counter-examples to Compositionality? Consider the following questions:

(10) Is it noon on the Sun?
(11) Is the king of France bald?
(12) Is the largest natural number even or odd?

Neither a "yes" nor a "no" answer to these questions would seem to be correct, and yet both answers are made up of entirely meaningful words put together in apparently grammatical way. Isn't the fact that it is nonsensical to say that it is or that it isn't noon on the Sun proof that CPM sometimes fails?

Such statements seem to involve what linguists call "presuppositions," such as: that there are time zones on the Sun, there is a king of France, or a largest natural number. When these presuppositions are false, the resulting statement is meaningful but lacks a *truth-value* (that is, it is neither true nor false). Such statements are apparent counter-examples to the Law of Excluded Middle:

> Law of Excluded Middle: If "S" is a meaningful assertion and "$\sim S$" is the negation of "S," then: S or $\sim S$.

However, what presupposition is there in asserting that spatial regions have infinitely many actual parts? Do we presuppose that regions are the sort of things that could have parts? If this presupposition is false, then so is the original assertion. If regions can't have parts, then it is simply false (and not nonsensical) that every region has infinitely many parts. The failures of the presuppositions in question are themselves straightforward metaphysical questions. It is up to metaphysics to sort things into the correct categories. Hence, the Category Mistake or Presupposition Failure Theories cannot be used to condemn all of metaphysics as meaningless.

10.2.2   Are Metaphysical Disputes Merely Verbal?

As we've said, there is a problem with Lightweight Metaphysical Realism. If all metaphysical propositions are trivially true or false, why do so many metaphysicians disagree about so many propositions? How can large numbers of metaphysicians remain ignorant of trivial truths? It seems an indisputable fact of history that many metaphysical truths have been the subject of active and persistent disagreement.

The Lightweight Realists must respond that there has not in fact been any significant disagreement about the actual metaphysical truths. Instead, metaphysicians merely think that they are disagreeing with each other, because they are (without fully realizing it) using the same words in different senses. There are systematic possible ambiguities in the sort of language we use in framing metaphysical debates, and these ambiguities result in many merely *verbal* disagreements over facts that all really agree about. Consequently, Lightweight Metaphysical Realism entails that the expression of any metaphysical truth involves some potential ambiguity or semantic indeterminacy.

The principal argument for semantic indeterminacy:

1   Metaphysical concepts (like *real, existent, one entity*, and *cause*) cannot be operationalized empirically. That is, the actual use of metaphysical terms in observable contexts is never sufficient to determine a unique meaning.
2   The only way in which meaning can be determined is by actual use in observable contexts.

Therefore, metaphysical terms are inherently indeterminate in meaning.

However, premise 2 is far from obvious. If premise 2 were true, there would be good reason to think that none of our terms (including the terms of everyday English and of our scientific vocabularies) are determinate in meaning. The attempt (in the early twentieth century) to reduce all meaning to *verification procedures* was one of the most significant failures in the history of philosophy. As a result of that failure, it is now widely accepted that meaning transcends use.

David K. Lewis (1983) has offered a more sophisticated proposal about the nature of meaning: meaning is determined jointly by use and *eligibility*. That is, the meaning of a term T is the most *eligible* extension or intension that is a close match to our actual practice. An eligible class is one that corresponds to the instantiation of some natural property. The interpretation of meaning is a matter of finding the *best* combination of eligibility and closeness of fit to our practice. A Metaphysical Realist could reasonably claim that each metaphysical concept is close in practice to some uniquely eligible property or feature: existence, unity, causation, and so on.

Some metaphysical claims can be expressed in purely logical vocabulary. For example, the denial of monism and nihilism can be expressed by stating simply: there exist at least two things. The only vocabulary needed to express this truth is the existential quantifier ("there exists"), negation, and numerical identity.

(13) $(\exists x)(\exists y) \sim (x = y)$. Informally: there exists an x and a y that are not identical to one another.

As Ted Sider (2009) has pointed out, there doesn't seem to be any room for ambiguity in any of these elements. They aren't plausibly vague in the way that "bald" or "heap" are vague. Something either exists or it doesn't, and two things are either identical or distinct. There are no borderline cases of existence or identity.

These claims could certainly be disputed. One might think that the existential quantifier is vague, because it is possible for us to associate different sets of entities (the domain or range of the quantifier) to the sentences. This sort of tacit restriction of the quantifier is a commonplace occurrence. For example, consider the following sentence:

(14) There is no beer.

We can imagine someone using (14) to express the truth that there is no beer within a salient environment, like a party or a pub. It needn't be taken as expressing the obvious falsehood that no beer exists anywhere in the universe.

However, the Heavyweight Realist (like Sider) can respond that the very claim that metaphysical claims are ambiguous or indeterminate presupposes that there is a universal, God's-eye viewpoint, from which we can say that there exist multiple interpretations of "existence" or "entity." That is, one must assume a relatively "plenitudinous" metaphysics in order to have available a plurality of possible interpretations of the quantifier or the identity sign.

Is language like "more fundamental," "grounded in," "made true by" subject to the same kind of indeterminacy? Could one plausibly suppose, for example, that Powerists and Nomists really agree? When Powerists say that powers are more fundamental than laws, do they really mean the same thing as when Nomists say that laws are more fundamental than powers? It's hard to believe that this could be so. Surely the concepts of fundamentality, grounding and truthmaking are connected with a variety of logical, inferential, and explanatory concepts that are shared by those in different metaphysical camps, in such a way as to guarantee that they mean essentially the same thing when they deploy these concepts.

10.3   Metaphysical Skepticism

Even if there are non-trivial truths about metaphysical matters, the practice of metaphysics is not necessarily vindicated. For example, what if there are metaphysical truths but we can never discover them, no matter how hard we try? This is the challenge of the metaphysical skeptic: even if there are metaphysical truths, they are unknowable, at least by us.

Metaphysical skepticism is itself a philosophical thesis (a thesis about epistemology, the theory of knowledge). Like any other philosopher, the metaphysical skeptic owes us some reason for thinking that he is right. Here are some of the most popular arguments for skepticism about metaphysics:

1   Pessimistic induction. Metaphysicians don't agree with one another, and there is no tendency of convergence toward a consensus. Most metaphysicians are therefore wrong most of the time, supporting the conclusion that metaphysics is an inherently unreliable enterprise.

2   Metaphysics is unscientific. Metaphysical theories are not empirically testable: they cannot be verified, falsified, confirmed, or disconfirmed by observation or experiment. Metaphysical conclusions do not follow from our best theories in science: scientific theories are typically compatible with a wide variety of metaphysical frameworks. Since all of our knowledge is scientific in nature, and metaphysics is unscientific, we lack metaphysical knowledge.

3   Methodological worries. There is no possible explanation for the reliability of metaphysical methods. Metaphysical realities are causally inert. Consequently, it is impossible for there to be any causal explanation of our reliability in doing metaphysics, even assuming that we are in fact reliable. No other form of explanation has been offered, so the lack of causal grounding for our reliability gives us good reason to doubt that we are in fact reliable in metaphysics, which in turn provides us with a defeater for any claim to metaphysical knowledge.

4   Pragmatism. Metaphysics assumes that we can pursue *explanations* without any concrete, practical context. All explanation is pragmatic in character – we seek to explain things in order to be more effective in our actions, to be more adept at controlling circumstances. Different modes of explanation are appropriate in solving different kinds of practical problems. There is no "God's eye point of view," abstracted from all practical exigencies.

Some responses on behalf of the possibility of metaphysical knowledge:

1   Contra the pessimistic induction. There is in fact some consensus in metaphysics, as well as some evidence of progress and convergence in metaphysical theories. The great majority of metaphysicians have rejected monism, nihilism, and most forms of idealism. Although there is no single metaphysical theory that commands conviction among the majority, there is some significant winnowing down of acceptable theories over time, as discussions in earlier chapters evince.

2   Metaphysics is scientific, or, at least, methodologically continuous with science. All theories, including well-accepted theories in natural science, suffer from the problem of the under-determination of theory by data.

If we were to require that observation and experiment alone pick out a unique theory, we would have to discount all scientific knowledge.

3   Methodological worries are ubiquitous. It is equally difficult to explain why our preference for simple and elegant theories in science should be a guide to the truth. It also difficult, if not impossible, to explain how *a priori* knowledge of logic and arithmetic is possible, since it doesn't seem that we can literally perceive or interact with logical or mathematical facts.

4   Contra pragmatism. As G. K. Chesterton (1908) put it, pragmatism is supposed to insist on relating everything to real human needs, but one of our real human needs is the need to be more than pragmatic. We do have a disinterested love for truth itself, apart from the "cash value" of any particular truth. As Aristotle put it, philosophy begins with a state of "wonder," of pure, impractical curiosity about reality. In addition, the pragmatist's rejection of metaphysics is self-defeating, since the doctrine of pragmatism is itself an impractical, metaphysical thesis.

5   There is no way to rule out the possibility that we have *a priori*, nonempirical knowledge of many truths in metaphysics, analogous to our *a priori* knowledge of the truths of logic or arithmetic.

6   Metaphysical skepticism is self-defeating, since any epistemology must presuppose the truth of some metaphysical principles, for example, that there are truths and minds. If we have no knowledge of metaphysics, then we must similarly have no knowledge of epistemology. Without epistemological knowledge, it is impossible to claim to know that we have no metaphysical knowledge.

7   Even if it is impossible to secure knowledge or certainty in metaphysics, we might still be able to distinguish between more and less reasonable conjectures.

10.4   Metaphysical Fictions

Even if metaphysical theses are meaningful and true, and even if they can be known to be true, there is still one last strategy for the Anti-Realist: Fictionalism. Fictionalism about a subject (like mathematics, science, religion, or metaphysics) is the theory that the subject consists of a body of knowledge, not about reality, but about a fictional world. For example, it is possible to discover the truth and acquire knowledge about J. R. R. Tolkien's Middle-Earth. In that fiction, for example, it is true that dragons are highly intelligent and avaricious. One can become an expert in the geography, languages, or ethnology of Middle-Earth, even though there really is no such place.

Some philosophers take a similar view about various fields of knowledge. For example, Hartry Field (1980) argues that the world of mathematics, including numbers, sets, and functions, is an entirely fictional world. There are in fact no numbers in reality, but numbers do exist in the mythical world of mathematics, and the study of this mythical world can bear important dividends in reasoning about complicated physical theories.

It is possible to take a similar view about metaphysics. One paradigm of this is the Fictionalist interpretation of Lewis's possible-worlds realism, such as that of John Divers (2002). Divers contends that there are in reality no possible worlds but the actual world. Nonetheless, there are worlds in the world devised by David K. Lewis in his theory of modality (which we discussed in Chapter 7). Although Lewis believed that he was describing reality, it is possible for us to treat Lewis's theory as a philosophically useful fiction.

A second case: we could treat abstractions (including universals or spatiotemporal boundaries) as fictions. In his second commentary on Porphyry's *Isagoge*, the late Roman philosopher Boethius argued that through abstraction we separate in our minds what is united in reality (see Spade 1994). We could understand this as supposing that universals (properties or essences that are really distinct from their instances) are merely fictional. Two physical circles are not related to any real universal of circularity, but we can imagine a fictional circle itself that is instantiated by them.

There are two main difficulties with Fictionalism, if we understand it to imply that all of metaphysics is fictional. First, it seems that fictions cannot be used to offer valid explanations of real things. In metaphysics, we are attempting to explain such things as the laws of similarity, geometry, and causation. Second, Fictionalism either is itself a metaphysical theory or presupposes some metaphysical theory as a background. This can be seen once we ask what a *fiction* is supposed to be. It would seem that a fiction is either a set of propositions or a set of possible (or even impossible) states of affairs. Thus, it would be inconsistent to suppose that propositions and states of affairs are themselves fictional.

10.5   Conclusion: The Inevitability of Metaphysics

Aristotle claimed that to deny metaphysics is to do metaphysics. We have seen some reason for agreeing with Aristotle. The arguments against metaphysics, whether Anti-Realist, Lightweight Realist, Skeptical, or Fictionalist, are all based on certain conceptions about truth, meaning, knowledge, and explanation that inevitably raise metaphysical questions.

If metaphysics is inevitable, then our aim must be to do it as well as we possibly can. Skepticism can be helpful as an aid to humility, and humility can in turn be a propellent for open-mindedness and new discoveries. We have tried to demonstrate, in these ten short chapters, that a new age of metaphysical discovery is indeed under way.

References

Adams, Robert M. (1974) "Theories of Actuality." *Noûs* 8: 211–232.
Adams, Robert M. (1979) "Primitive Thisness and Primitive Identity." *Journal of Philosophy* 76: 5–26.
Adams, Robert M. (1981) "Actualism and Thisness." *Synthese* 49: 3–41.
Alston, William P. (1958) "Ontological Commitments." *Philosophical Studies* 9: 8–17.
Anscombe, G. E. M. (1975) "Causality and Determination." In E. Sosa (ed.), *Causation and Conditionals*. Oxford: Oxford University Press, pp. 63–81.
Aristotle (1984) *Complete Works of Aristotle*, ed. Jonathan Barnes. Princeton, NJ: Princeton University Press.
Armstrong, David M. (1968) *A Materialist Theory of Mind*. London: Routledge.
Armstrong, David M. (1978) *Universals and Scientific Realism*. Cambridge: Cambridge University Press.
Armstrong, David M. (1980) "Identity through Time." In Peter van Inwagen (ed.), *Time and Cause: Essays Presented to Richard Taylor*. Dordrecht: D. Reidel, pp. 67–78.
Armstrong, David M. (1983) *What Is a Law of Nature?* Cambridge: Cambridge University Press.
Armstrong, David M. (1997) *A World of States of Affairs*. Cambridge: Cambridge University Press.
Armstrong, David M. (2004) *Truth and Truthmakers*. Cambridge: Cambridge University Press.
Augustine (1991) *Confessions*, trans. Henry Chadwick. Oxford: Oxford University Press. Orig. pub. 398.
Baxter, Donald (1988) "Identity in the Loose and Popular Sense." *Mind* 97: 575–582.

Metaphysics: The Fundamentals, First Edition. Robert C. Koons and Timothy H. Pickavance.
© 2015 Robert C. Koons and Timothy H. Pickavance.
Published 2015 by John Wiley & Sons, Ltd.

Benardete, José A. (1964) *Infinity: An Essay in Metaphysics*. Oxford: Oxford University Press.

Bennett, Karen (2004) "Spatio-Temporal Coincidence and the Grounding Problem." *Philosophical Studies* 118: 339–371.

Bennett, Karen (2011) "Truthmaking and Case-Making." *Philosophy and Phenomenological Research* 83: 187–195.

Berkeley, George (2009) *Principles of Human Knowledge and Three Dialogues*. New York: Oxford University Press. Orig. pub. 1710.

Bigelow, John (1996) "Presentism and Properties." *Philosophical Perspectives* 10 (Metaphysics): 35–52.

Bird, Alexander (1998) "Dispositions and Antidotes." *The Philosophical Quarterly* 48: 227–234.

Bird, Alexander (2010) *Nature's Metaphysics: Laws and Properties*. New York: Oxford University Press.

Bishop, Robert (2005) "Patching Physics and Chemistry Together." *Philosophy of Science* 72: 710–722.

Black, Max (1952) "The Identity of Indiscernibles." *Mind* 61: 153–164.

Boolos, George (1984) "To Be Is to Be the Value of a Variable (or to Be Some Values of Some Variables)." *Journal of Philosophy* 81: 430–449.

Bradley, F. H. (1930) *Appearance and Reality*. Oxford: Clarendon Press. Orig. pub. 1893.

Brentano, Franz (1973) *Psychology from an Empirical Standpoint*, ed. Ted Honderich. London: Routledge and Kegan Paul. Orig. pub. 1876.

Brentano, Franz (1988) *Philosophical Investigations on Space, Time and the Continuum*, ed. Stephen Körner and Roderick M. Chisholm, trans. Barry Smith. London: Croom Helm.

Broad, C. D. (1925) *Mind and Its Place in Nature*. London: Routledge & Kegan Paul.

Burke, Michael (1994) "Preserving the Principle of One Object to a Place: A Novel Account of the Relations Among Objects, Sorts, Sortals, and Persistence Conditions." *Philosophy and Phenomenological Research* 54: 591–624.

Cartwright, Nancy (1983) *How the Laws of Physics Lie*. Oxford: Oxford University Press.

Cartwright, Nancy (1994) *Nature's Capacities and Their Measurement*. Oxford: Oxford University Press.

Chalmers, David J. (1996) *The Conscious Mind: In Search of a Fundamental Theory*. Oxford: Oxford University Press.

Chalmers, David J. (2009) "Ontological Anti-Realism." In David J. Chalmers, David Manley, and Ryan Wasserman (eds.), *Metametaphysics: New Essays on the Foundations of Ontology*. Oxford: Clarendon Press, pp. 77–129.

Chesterton, G. K. (1908) *Orthodoxy*. Garden City, NY: Garden City Publishing Company.

Chisholm, Roderick (1967) "Identity through Possible Worlds: Some Questions." *Noûs* 1: 1–8.

Chisholm, Roderick (1976) *Person and Object: A Metaphysical Study*. La Salle, IL: Open Court.

Chisholm, Roderick (1989) *On Metaphysics*. Minneapolis: University of Minnesota Press.

Davis, Richard Lawton (2014) "A Theory of Insession," manuscript.

Descartes, René (1993) *Meditations on First Philosophy*, 3rd ed., trans. Donald Cress. Indianapolis: Hackett. Orig. pub. 1647.

Devitt, Michael (1980) "'Ostrich Nominalism' or 'Mirage Realism'?" *Pacific Philosophical Quarterly* 61: 433–439. Reprinted in D. H. Mellor and Alex Oliver (eds.), *Properties*. Oxford: Oxford University Press (1997) pp. 93–100.

Divers, John (2002) *Possible Worlds*. New York: Routledge.

Donnellan, Keith S. (1966) "Reference and Definite Descriptions." *The Philosophical Review* 75(3): 281–304.

Dowe, Phil (2000) *Physical Causation*. Cambridge: Cambridge University Press.

Dretske, Fred (1977) "Laws of Nature." *Philosophy of Science* 44: 248–268.

Dretske, Fred (1995) *Naturalizing the Mind*. Cambridge, MA: MIT Press.

Evans, Gareth (1982) *The Varieties of Reference*, ed. John McDowell. Oxford: Oxford University Press.

Field, Hartry (1980) *Science without Numbers*. Oxford: Blackwell.

Fine, Kit (1994) "Ontological Dependence." *Proceedings of the Aristotelian Society* 95: 269–290.

Fine, Kit (2001) "The Question of Realism." *Philosophers' Imprint* 1(2): 1–30.

Forrest, Peter (1999) "Supertasks and Material Objects." *Logique & Analyse* 167–168: 441–446.

Frege, Gottlob (1950) *The Foundations of Arithmetic*, trans. J. L. Austin. Evanston, IL: Northwestern University Press. Orig. pub. 1884.

Garcia, Robert (2010) "Moderate Nominalism: Tropes vs. Tropers." Unpublished manuscript.

Geach, Peter (1962) *Reference and Generality: An Examination of Some Medieval and Modern Theories*. Ithaca, NY: Cornell University Press.

Gettier, Edmund L. (1963) "Is Justified True Belief Knowledge?" *Analysis* 23: 121–123.

Goodman, Nelson (1951) *The Structure of Appearance*. Cambridge, MA: Harvard University Press.

Goodman, Nelson (1954) *Fact, Fiction, and Forecast*. Cambridge, MA: Harvard University Press.

Grover, Dorothy (1992) *A Prosentential Theory of Truth*. Princeton, NJ: Princeton University Press.

Grünbaum, Adolf (1967) *Modern Science and Zeno's Paradoxes*. Middletown, CT: Wesleyan University Press, pp. 78–135.

Haldane, John (2007) "Privative Causality." *Analysis* 67: 180–186.

Hasker, William (2001) *The Emergent Self*. Ithaca, NY: Cornell University Press.

Hawthorne, John (2000) "Before-Effect and Zeno Causality." *Noûs* 34: 622–633.

Hawthorne, John (2001) "Causal Structuralism." *Philosophical Perspectives* 15: 361–378.

Hawthorne, John (2006) *Metaphysical Essays*. Oxford: Oxford University Press.

Hawthorne, John, and Brian Weatherson (2004) "Chopping up Gunk." *Monist* 87: 339–350.

Hendry, Robin Findlay (2006) "Is There Downward Causation in Chemistry?" In D. Baird, L. McIntyre, and E. R. Scerri (eds.), *Philosophy of Chemistry: Synthesis of a New Discipline*. Dordrecht: Springer, pp. 173–189.

Hendry, Robin Findlay (2010) "Emergence vs. Reduction in Chemistry." In Cynthia MacDonald and Graham MacDonald (eds.), *Emergence in Mind*. Oxford: Oxford University Press, pp. 205–221.

Hirsch, Eli (1992) *The Concept of Identity*. Oxford: Oxford University Press.

Hirsch, Eli (1993) *Dividing Reality*. Oxford: Oxford University Press.

Hochberg, Herbert (1999) *Complexes and Consciousness*. Stockholm: Thales.

Horwich, Paul (1998) *Truth*. Oxford: Blackwell. 1st ed. 1990.

Hume, David (1777) *An Enquiry Concerning Human Understanding*, edited by L. A. Selby-Bigge, 3rd ed. Revised by P. H. Nidditch. Oxford: Clarendon Press, 1975.

Humphreys, Paul (1997) "How Properties Emerge." *Philosophy of Science* 64: 1–17.

James, William (1893) *Principles of Psychology*. New York: H. Holt and Company.

Johnston, Mark (1992) "How to Speak of the Colors." *Philosophical Studies* 68: 221–263.

Jozsa, Richard (1986) "An Approach to the Modelling of the Physical Continua." *British Journal of the Philosophy of Science* 37: 395–405.

Kaplan, David (1989) "Demonstratives: An Essay on the Semantics, Logic, Metaphysics, and Epistemology of Demonstratives and Other Indexicals." In Joseph Almog, John Perry, and Howard Wettstein (eds.), *Themes from Kaplan*. Oxford: Oxford University Press, 481–563.

Kenny, Anthony (1963) *Action, Emotion and Will*. London: Routledge Kegan & Paul.

Kim, Jaegwon (1993) "'Strong' and 'Global' Supervenience Revisited." In *Supervenience and Mind: Selected Philosophical Essays*. Cambridge: Cambridge University Press, pp. 79–91. Orig. pub. 1987.

Kim, Jaegwon (2007) *Physicalism, or Something Near Enough*. Princeton, NJ: Princeton University Press.

Koons, Robert C., and George Bealer (2010) *The Waning of Materialism: New Essays in the Philosophy of Mind*. Oxford: Oxford University Press.

Koons, Robert C., and Timothy H. Pickavance (forthcoming) *Surveying the World: A Compendium of Metaphysics*.

Koslicki, Kathrin (2008) *The Structure of Objects*. Oxford: Oxford University Press.

Kripke, Saul A. (1980) *Naming and Necessity*. Cambridge, MA: Harvard University Press.

Leonard, H. S., and Nelson Goodman (1940) "The Calculus of Individuals and Its Uses." *Journal of Symbolic Logic* 5: 45–55.

Lewis, David K. (1973) *Counterfactuals*. Malden, MA: Blackwell.

Lewis, David K. (1976) "The Paradoxes of Time Travel." *American Philosophical Quarterly* 13: 145–152.

Lewis, David K. (1979) "Counterfactual Dependence and Time's Arrow." *Noûs* 13: 455–476.

Lewis, David K. (1980) "A Subjectivist's Guide to Objective Chance." In Richard C. Jeffrey (ed.), *Studies in Inductive Logic and Probability*, Volume II. Berkeley: University of California Press, pp. 263–293.

Lewis, David K. (1983) "New Work for a Theory of Universals." *Australasian Journal of Philosophy* 61: 343–377.

Lewis, David K. (1986) *On the Plurality of Worlds*. Oxford: Blackwell.

Lewis, David K. (1991) *Parts of Classes*. Oxford: Blackwell.

Lewis, David K. (1993) "Many, but Almost One." In John Bacon (ed.), *Ontology, Causality and Mind: Essays in Honour of D. M. Armstrong*. New York: Cambridge University Press.

Lewis, David K. (1994) "Humean Supervenience Debugged." *Mind* 103: 473–390.

Lewis, David K. (1997) "Finkish Dispositions." *Philosophical Quarterly* 47: 143–158.

Lewis, David K. (2001) "Truthmaking and Difference-Making." *Noûs* 35: 602–615.

Loux, Michael (1978) *Substance and Attribute*. Dordrecht: D. Reidel Publishing Company.

Loux, Michael (2006) "Aristotle's Constituent Ontology." In Dean Zimmerman (ed.) *Oxford Studies in Metaphysics*, Volume 2. Oxford: Clarendon Press, pp. 207–250.

Lowe, E. J. (2010) "How Not to Think of Powers: A Deconstruction of the 'Dispositions and Conditionals' Debate." *Monist* 94: 19–33.

Manley, David (2002) "Properties and Resemblance Classes." *Noûs* 36: 75–96.

Mantegani, Nicholas (2010) *Toward a Quinean Realism*. Doctoral dissertation, University of Texas at Austin.

Markosian, Ned (1993) "How Fast Does Time Pass?" *Philosophy and Phenomenological Studies* 53: 829–844.

Markosian, Ned (1998) "Brutal Composition." *Philosophical Studies* 92: 211–249.

Martin, C. B. (1994) "Dispositions and Conditionals." *Philosophical Quarterly* 44: 1–8.

McCall, Storrs (1976) "Objective Time Flow." *Philosophy of Science* 43: 337–362.

McCall, Storrs (1984) "A Dynamic Model of Temporal Becoming." *Analysis* 44: 172–176.

McCall, Storrs (1994) *A Model of the Universe*. Oxford: Clarendon Press.

McDaniel, Kris (2010) "Composition as Identity Does Not Entail Universalism." *Erkenntnis* 73: 97–100.

McLaughlin, Brian (1997) "Supervenience, Vagueness, and Determination." *Philosophical Perspectives*, 11: 209–230.

McTaggart, J. M. E. (1908) "The Unreality of Time." *Mind* 18: 457–484.

McTaggart, J. M. E. (1927) *The Nature of Existence*. 2 vols. Cambridge: Cambridge University Press.

Meehl, Paul, and Wilfrid Sellars (1956) "The Concept of Emergence." In Michael Scriven and Herbert Feigl (eds.), *Minnesota Studies in the Philosophy of Science* 1: 239–252.

Merricks, Trenton (2003) *Objects and Persons*. Oxford: Clarendon Press.

Merricks, Trenton (2007) *Truth and Ontology*. Oxford: Clarendon Press.

Millikan, Ruth Garrett (1984) *Language Thought and Other Biological Categories*. Cambridge, MA: MIT Press.

Molnar, George (2003) *Powers: A Study in Metaphysics*. Oxford: Oxford University Press.

Moore, G. E. (1922) *Philosophical Studies*. London: Routledge & Kegan Paul.

Mourelatos, A. P. D. (1978) "Events, Processes, and States." *Linguistics and Philosophy* 2: 415–434.

Neander, Karen L. (2011) "Teleological Accounts of Mental Content." *Stanford Encyclopedia of Philosophy*. plato.stanford.edu. Accessed July 3, 2014.

O'Connor, Timothy, and H. Y. Wong (2005) "The Metaphysics of Emergence." *Noûs* 39: 659–679.

Parfit, Derek (1984) *Reasons and Persons*. Oxford: Clarendon Press.

Paul, L. A. (2002) "Logical Parts." *Noûs* 36: 578–596.

Paul, L. A. (2006) "Coincidence as Overlap." *Noûs* 40: 633–659.

Paul, L. A. (2010) "Temporal Experience." *Journal of Philosophy* 107: 579–590.

Paul, L. A. (2012) "Building the World from Its Fundamental Constituents." *Philosophical Studies* 158: 221–256.

Pearl, Judea (2009) *Causality: Models, Reasoning and Inference*. Cambridge: Cambridge University Press.

Pickavance, Timothy H. (2009) "In Defence of 'Partially Clad' Bare Particulars." *Australasian Journal of Philosophy* 87: 155–158.

Pickavance, Timothy H. (2014) "Bare Particulars and Exemplification." *American Philosophical Quarterly* 51: 95–108.

Pickavance, Timothy H. (forthcoming) "The Natural View of Properties of Identity." In Robert Garcia (ed.), *Substance*. Munich: Philosophia Verlag.

Pickel, Bryan (2010) *Reduction, Ontology and the Limits of Convention*. Doctoral dissertation, University of Texas at Austin.

Pickel, Bryan, and Nicholas Mantegani (2012) "A Quinean Critique of Ostrich Nominalism." *Philosophers' Imprint* 12: 1–21.

Plantinga, Alvin (1974) *The Nature of Necessity*. Oxford: Clarendon Press.

Price, Huw (1996) *Time's Arrow and Archimedes' Point*. Oxford: Oxford University Press.

Prior, A. N. (1959) "Thank Goodness That's Over." *Philosophy* 34: 12–17.

Pruss, Alexander R. (2003) "David Lewis's Counterfactual Arrow of Time." *Noûs* 37: 606–637.

Pruss, Alexander R. (2011) *Actuality, Possibility, and Worlds*. New York: Continuum.

Ramsey, Frank (1927) "Facts and Propositions." *Proceedings of the Aristotelian Society* 7 (Supplementary): 153–170.

Ramsey, Frank (1978) *Foundations*. London: Routledge & Kegan Paul. Orig. pub. 1928.

Rawls, John (1999) *A Theory of Justice*. Cambridge, MA: Harvard University Press. Orig. pub. 1971.

Rea, Michael (2004) *World without Design: The Ontological Consequences of Naturalism*. New York: Oxford University Press.

Reichenbach, Hans (1958) *The Philosophy of Space and Time*. New York: Dover.

Rosen, Gideon (2010) "Metaphysical Dependence: Grounding and Reduction." In Bob Hale and Aviv Hoffman (eds.), *Modality: Metaphysics, Logic and Epistemology*. New York: Oxford University Press, pp. 109–136.

Russell, Bertrand (1959) "The World of Universals." In *The Problems of Philosophy*. New York: Oxford University Press, pp. 91–100. Orig. pub. 1912.

Russell, Bertrand (1913) "On the Notion of Cause." *Proceedings of the Aristotelian Society* 13: 1–26.

Russell, Bertrand (1936) "On Order in Time." *Proceedings of the Cambridge Philosophical Society* 32: 216–228.

Russell, Bertrand (1956) *Logic and Knowledge*, ed. Robert Marsh. New York: Routledge.

Ryle, Gilbert (1949) *The Concept of Mind*. New York: Barnes and Noble.

Salmon, Wesley (1984) *Scientific Explanation and the Causal Structure of the World*, Princeton, NJ: Princeton University Press.

Schaffer, Jonathan (2004) "Causes Need not Be Connected to Their Effects: The Case for Negative Causation." In Christopher Read Hitchcock (ed.), *Contemporary Debates in the Philosophy of Science*. London: Blackwell, pp. 197–216.

Schaffer, Jonathan (2009) "On What Grounds What." In David Manley, David J. Chalmers, and Ryan Wasserman (eds.), *Metametaphysics: New Essays on the Foundations of Ontology*. Oxford: Oxford University Press, pp. 347–384.

Schaffer, Jonathan (2010) "Monism: The Priority of the Whole." *Philosophical Review* 119: 31–76.

Searle, John (1992) *The Rediscovery of Mind*. Cambridge, MA: Bradford Books.

Sellars, Wilfrid (1963) *Science, Perception and Reality*. London: Routledge & Kegan Paul.

Shoemaker, Sydney (1980) "Causality and Properties." In Peter van Inwagen (ed.), *Time and Cause: Essays Presented to Richard Taylor*. Dordrecht: D. Reidel Publishing, pp. 109–135.

Shoemaker, Sydney (1998) "Causal and Metaphysical Necessity." *Pacific Philosophical Quarterly* 79: 59–77.

Sider, Theodore (1999) "Presentism and Ontological Commitment." *Journal of Philosophy* 96: 325–347.

Sider, Theodore (2001) *Four Dimensionalism: An Ontology of Persistence and Time*. Oxford: Clarendon Press.

Sider, Theodore (2009) "Ontological Realism." In David J. Chalmers, David Manley, and Ryan Wasserman (eds.), *Metametaphysics: New Essays on the Foundations of Ontology*. Oxford: Clarendon Press, pp. 384–423.

Sider, Theodore (2012) *Writing the Book of the World*. New York: Oxford University Press.

Simons, Peter (1994) "Particulars in Particular Clothing: Three Trope Theories of Substance." *Philosophy and Phenomenological Research* 54: 553–575.

Smart, J .J. C. (1949) "The River of Time." *Mind* 58: 483–494.

Spade, Paul V. (trans.) (1994) *Five Texts on the Mediaeval Problem of Universals: Porphyry, Boethius, Abelard, Duns Scotus, Ockham*. Indianapolis, IN, and Cambridge, MA: Hackett.

Strawson, Peter F. (1959) *Individuals*. London: Methuen.

Thompson, James F. (1954) "Tasks and Super-Tasks." *Analysis* 15: 1–13.

Tooley, Michael (1977) "The Nature of Laws." *Canadian Journal of Philosophy* 7: 667–698.

Tooley, Michael (1987) *Causation: A Realist Approach*. Oxford: Clarendon Press.

van Fraassen, Bas (1989) *Laws and Symmetry*. Oxford: Clarendon Press.

van Inwagen, Peter (1990) *Material Beings*. Ithaca, NY: Cornell University Press.

van Inwagen, Peter (1994) "Composition as Identity." *Philosophical Perspectives* 8: 207–220.

van Inwagen, Peter (2011) "Relational vs. Constituent Ontologies." *Philosophical Perspectives: Metaphysics* 25: 389–405.

Vendler, Zeno (1957) "Verbs and Times." *Philosophical Review* 60: 143–160.

Whitehead, Alfred North (1919) *An Enquiry into the Principles of Natural Knowledge*. Cambridge: Cambridge University Press.

Wilson, Jessica (2010) "What Is Hume's Dictum, and Why Should We Believe It?" *Philosophy and Phenomenological Research* 80: 595–637.

Wilson, Jessica (2012) "Fundamental Determinables." *Philosophers' Imprint* 12: 1–17.

Wolterstorff, Nicholas (1970) "Bergmann's Constituent Ontology." *Noûs* 4: 109–134.

Zimmerman, Dean (1999) "One Really Big Liquid Sphere: A Reply to Lewis." *Australasian Journal of Philosophy* 77: 213–215.

Index

Metaphysics: The Fundamentals, First Edition. Robert C. Koons and Timothy H. Pickavance.
© 2015 Robert C. Koons and Timothy H. Pickavance.
Published 2015 by John Wiley & Sons, Ltd.

Printed and bound by CPI Group (UK) Ltd, Croydon, CR0 4YY

25/03/2025

14647324-0005